ĞL

THE
WORK
OF
CHRIST

ROBERT LETHAM

CONTOURS *of*

CHRISTIAN

THEOLOGY

GERALD BRAY
General Editor

INTERVARSITY PRESS
DOWNERS GROVE, ILLINOIS 60515

© 1993 by Robert Letham

Published in the United States of America by InterVarsity Press, Downers Grove, Illinois, with permission from Universities and Colleges Christian Fellowship, Leicester, England.

InterVarsity Press® is the book-publishing division of InterVarsity Christian Fellowship®, a student movement active on campus at hundreds of universities, colleges and schools of nursing in the United States of America, and a member movement of the International Fellowship of Evangelical Students. For information about local and regional activities, write Public Relations Dept., InterVarsity Christian Fellowship, 6400 Schroeder Rd., P.O. Box 7895, Madison, WI 53707-7895.

Unless otherwise stated, quotations from the Bible are taken from the British edition of the Holy Bible: New International Version, copyright © 1973, 1978 and 1984 by the International Bible Society. Published by Hodder and Stoughton Ltd.

ISBN 0-8308-1532-5

Printed in the United States of America ∞

Library of Congress Cataloging-in-Publication Data

Letham, Robert.
     The work of Christ/Robert Letham.
          p.   cm.—(Contours of Christian theology)
     Includes bibliographical references and indexes.
     ISBN 0-8308-1532-5
     1. Jesus Christ—Person and offices.   I. Title.   II. Series.
     BT250.L47   1993
     232'.8—dc20   93-19207
                                                                         CIP

17   16   15   14   13   12   11   10   9   8   7   6
07   06   05

For my father, Andrew Letham (1906–)
In memory of my uncle, Donald Letham (1907–86)

Contents

Series Preface

Contours of Christian Theology covers the main themes of Christian doctrine. The series offers a systematic presentation of most of the major doctrines in a way which complements the traditional textbooks but does not copy them. Top priority has been given to contemporary issues, some of which may not be dealt with elsewhere from an evangelical point of view. The series aims, however, not merely to answer current objections to evangelical Christianity, but also to rework the orthodox evangelical position in a fresh and compelling way. The overall thrust is therefore positive and evangelistic in the best sense.

The series is intended to be of value to theological students at all levels, whether at a Bible college, a seminary or a secular university. It should also appeal to ministers and to educated lay-people. As far as possible, efforts have been made to make technical vocabulary accessible to the non-specialist reader, and the presentation has avoided the extremes of academic style. Occasionally this has meant that particular issues have been presented without a thorough argument, taking into account different positions, but when this has happened, authors have been encouraged to refer the reader to other works which take the discussion further. For this purpose adequate but not exhaustive notes have been provided.

The doctrines covered in the series are not exhaustive, but have been chosen in response to contemporary concerns. The title and general presentation of each volume are at the discretion of the author, but final editorial decisions have been taken by the General Editor of the series in consultation with IVP.

In offering this series to the public, the authors and the publishers hope that it will meet the needs of theological students in this generation, and bring honour and glory to God the Father, and to his Son, Jesus Christ, in whose service the work has been undertaken from the beginning.

Gerald Bray
General Editor

Acknowledgments

I am grateful for the assistance of a number of people. The Rev. David P. Kingdon of IVP has made many useful comments throughout the development of the book, from the time when he first asked me to contribute to the series. My former colleague, Tony Lane, commented helpfully on several of the draft chapters. Others have also contributed as the book developed. Of course, any shortcomings the reader may find are entirely my own. I worked on the manuscript until late 1990. With a few special exceptions I was unable to consider literature published after that time.

My thanks are also due to Mrs Ruth Michell, of Free Church College, Edinburgh for invaluable help with the transfer of electronic data. Last but not least, I am profoundly thankful to my wife, Joan and children, Elizabeth, Caroline and Adam for their patience and kindness during the course of this project.

Robert Letham

Abbreviations

ARG	*Archiv für Reformationsgeschichte*
CCSL	*Corpus Christianorum: Series Latina* (Turnhout, Belgium: Brepols, 1953–)
CD	Karl Barth, *Church Dogmatics*, ed. G. W. Bromiley and T. F. Torrance (Edinburgh: T. and T. Clark, 1956–77)
CSEL	*Corpus Scriptorum Ecclesiasticorum Latinorum* (Vienna: 1866–)
CTJ	*Calvin Theological Journal*
EQ	*Evangelical Quarterly*
ExpT	*Expository Times*
GCS	*Die Griechischen Christlichen Schriftsteller der ersten drei jahrhunderte* (Berlin: 1897–)
Institutes	J. T. McNeill (ed.) and F. L. Battles (trans.), *Calvin: Institutes of the Christian Religion*, Library of Christian Classics, 20–21 (London: SCM Press, 1960).
JTS	*Journal of Theological Studies*
LW	*Luther's Works*, 55 vols. (St Louis: Concordia, 1955–).
MPG	J. P. Migne *et al.* (eds.), *Patrologia Graeca* (Paris, 1857–1866)

MPL	J. P. Migne *et al.* (eds.), *Patrologia Latina* (Paris, 1878–1890)
NAK	Nederlands Archief voor Kerkegeschiedenis
NPNF	P. Schaff and H. Wace (eds.), *Nicene and Post-Nicene Fathers of the Christian Church* (Edinburgh: T. & T. Clark, 1886–1900)
NovT	*Novum Testamentum*
NTS	*New Testament Studies*
SBET	*Scottish Bulletin of Evangelical Theology*
SCJ	*Sixteenth Century Journal*
SJT	*Scottish Journal of Theology*
TDNT	G. Kittel and G. Friedrich (eds.), *Theological Dictionary of the New Testament*, 10 vols. (Grand Rapids: Eerdmans, 1964–1976)
WTJ	*Westminster Theological Journal*

Part One

FOUNDATIONS

1

CHRIST'S WORK
IN CONTEXT

The phrase 'the work of Christ' seems a dry, ponderous expression to use of the heart of the Christian faith. Christ's death on the cross, his glorious resurrection, his startling message of the kingdom of God are all realities with dynamic power. Lives, nations, whole civilizations have been changed and reshaped by the risen Christ. In the twentieth century, the crushing weight of militant, totalitarian atheism has failed to halt the impact of Jesus Christ. His weak, beleaguered followers in the former Soviet Union and Eastern Europe, after decades of oppression, have not merely survived. Christianity has prospered, while atheistic communism has collapsed! This is no new story. It will surely be repeated again in the future.

'The work of Christ', limp as the phrase sounds, actually stands for the most significant realities we can ever face. How can we know God? How can we have a right relationship with God? How can we be forgiven? Can we know what lies beyond the grave? How can the death of a man 2,000 years ago help us today? How does our salvation intersect with the environmental crisis, with poverty and oppression and a host of problems in politics and business? And what does Jesus Christ have to do with it all? These are not questions on the periphery of life. They affect our destiny and that of the planet.

In the pages that follow we will investigate some of these issues, and others besides. We will discuss the teaching of Scripture in some detail. When out for a walk in the country it is helpful at times to have binoculars at hand. An interesting bird, a high-flying aircraft or a panoramic view can be seen at closer quarters and in far greater detail. A biblical understanding of 'the work of Christ' can function for the Christian as, so to speak, theological binoculars. From the vantage point of what Christ has done we can view the vast horizon of world, national, family and personal events with new vision, in sharper focus.

Occasionally, we will refer to what others in the Christian church of the past have said about what Christ has done. What possible relevance can their thoughts have for us? We should keep two factors in mind.

Firstly, we are deluded if we think we can read the Bible alone by ourselves. All interpretation of Scripture is built upon what has gone on before us. In the nineteenth century a small group in the United States decided to have done with the historic teaching of the church and study Scripture for themselves from scratch. They published a journal recording the results of their Bible study called *Studies in the Scriptures*. And so the sect known as the Jehovah's Witnesses was born. Bible study torn asunder from the teaching of the historic Christian church is a recipe for deviation. As it transpired, the Jehovah's Witnesses did nothing really new; they merely reproduced the fourth-century heresy of Arianism.

Secondly, if we belittle the past struggles of the church are we not full of pride? Is it not perhaps a case of our being so caught up with what the Holy Spirit may be showing us now that we pay little attention to what he has shown to others? Part of the reason why today's technology has gone so far is because it has had a long-term basis behind it. It has not tried to re-invent the wheel!

What do we mean by 'the work of Christ'? In short, we refer to all that Christ did when he came to this earth 'for us

18

and our salvation', all that he continues to do now that he is risen from the dead and at God's right hand, and all that he will do when he returns in glory at the end of the age. This is a vast area! In a book of this size we can only skate over the surface. It would be good to discuss in detail every biblical passage that is cited, but then this book would be enormous and the reader would be bankrupted paying for it! My recommendation is for the reader to follow up the biblical references given and work out how far their context supports the claims I make. After all, the best thing we can do as we grapple with the great themes before us will be to give further consideration to all that Christ has done and to appropriate it (and him) for ourselves.

The structure adopted in the book

In this book I have chosen to shape our discussion around Christ's threefold office of prophet, priest and king. This has the merit of following the three great offices or functions in Old Testament Israel. Since Jesus was a Jew and Christianity has definitely Jewish roots, this is a very appropriate way of looking at what he did for us. In order to see what he has to say to us today it is more than helpful to know how he fits into the original framework God had worked out through his struggles with Israel.

According to Wolfhart Pannenberg (1928–), there is no clear-cut evidence that Jesus ever claimed any of these recognized offices for himself. There is certainly ambiguity over exactly how far the New Testament as a whole relates them to him. On the one hand, there is evidence that it did just that. The Letter to the Hebrews regards Jesus as a high priest after the order of Melchizedek (Heb. 5:6–10; 6:20 – 10:18). The risen Christ reigns over his mediatorial kingdom (1 Cor. 15:12–28; Eph. 1:19–23; 1 Pet. 3:18–22; Rev. 1:5, 17–18). The Son is regarded as the final word spoken by God to man, surpassing and superseding that spoken by the prophets of the Old Testament (Heb. 1:1–3). Yet, on the other hand, Jesus clearly could not be a priest in Israel, for he was of the tribe of Judah and the true priestly line belonged to Levi. Moreover, he typically distanced himself from those who

19

regarded him as a prophet, accepting an apparently distinct
identity (Mt. 16:13–16). While he spoke of his kingdom, he
pointed out that it was of a different order from the kingdoms of the world (Jn. 18:36–37). He refused to subscribe to
the wishes of those who wanted to proclaim him king (Jn.
6:15–16). On the surface, it seems that to speak of Christ in
terms of these offices is a serious mistake. Pannenberg argues
that way when he suggests that 'only one of the three offices,
namely the "prophetic office", to some extent properly
characterizes the earthly work of Jesus'.[1] To some extent,
Pannenberg is correct. Jesus never claimed any of these
offices for himself. At first sight, therefore, this model seems
highly problematic.

There are very good reasons, however, why this is a
fruitful, and eminently biblical, way of understanding the
work of Christ. First of all, it is virtually impossible to
understand what Christ did if we abstract him from the
background history of Yahweh's struggles with his covenant
people, Israel. The Jews in the time of Christ were heirs to a
long process in which God had made himself known to them
as a special people who belonged particularly and exclusively
to him. Their national structures were the consequence of his
self-revelation. Israel itself owed its existence to Yahweh's call
to Abraham and to Yahweh's rescuing them from captivity in
Egypt. Israel was the sphere of his special revelation, the
locus of redemption. Christ was himself a first-century Jew.
He was born into a context bearing the marks of the painful
process of God's saving actions. The structures of Israel were
themselves God-given and revelatory. The priesthood and
the sacrificial ritual, prophetism and the word of the Lord,
the kingdom and the theocracy were, or had been, integral to
the life and experience of Israel. This, as T. F. Torrance
indicates,[2] was not only the context of Christ's coming but
also the key to understanding why he came and also the
effect of his coming.

Secondly, while Jesus may not have claimed explicitly any
of the three major offices in Israel, and while there may be
discussion over the extent to which the New Testament
writers applied them to him, nevertheless there is strong
evidence that both he and they understood him to have

performed the functions associated with these offices. In short, the work Christ came to do was seen as the fulfilment of everything that the prophets had foretold, of all that the priesthood and cultus had foreshadowed and of all that the kingdom had imperfectly portrayed.

Much of the evidence will follow in succeeding chapters. At present, we will simply indicate something of the larger picture. The main task of the prophet was to act as the mouthpiece of Yahweh. He confronted his contemporaries with Yahweh's just claims upon them, calling them to be faithful to the covenant (Lk. 4:18–21; Jn. 14:5–11; 15:15). Jesus did just that . . . and more. The major difference was that he claimed to be uniquely identified with God. He set his own word as the standard of authority. On the other hand, the prophets always claimed to be speaking in the name of a higher source than themselves. Moreover, Jesus claimed his own teaching to be of greater weight than the Pharisees' (Mt. 5:17–20, 21–22, 27–28, 31–34, 38–39, 43–44). His message was the same as the Father's (Jn. 5:17–27, 36–40, 43; 6:44–51; 8:54–56; 14:5–11; 15:15; 17:1–8, 14–17; Mt. 11:20–27). Behind all this was the expectation from the Pentateuch of the eschatological prophet whose word was to be binding in Israel (Dt. 18:15f.). The Samaritans shared this expectation, identifying the prophetic figure as a Taheb, a type of teacher and lawgiver. Jesus accepted this description for himself (Jn. 4:25–26). The Letter to the Hebrews sees Jesus as the last prophet who spoke 'in these last days', after the line of God's revelation through the prophets of Israel. He is also greater than they, however, since God's word through the Son is his final word that surpasses and supersedes theirs (Heb. 1:1–3).

Also in Hebrews, Christ's death on the cross and his intercession at God's right hand is seen in priestly terms (Heb. 1:3; 2:14–18; 4:14 – 5:10; 6:19 – 10:18).[3] According to these passages, Jesus' life (and especially his death) cannot be appreciated apart from the Old Testament priestly ritual. He was our substitute, representing us on the cross. Behind all this was the substitutionary function of the Levitical sacrifices and the representative nature of the high priest in Israel.[4]

Finally, while Jesus' teaching centred on the theme of the kingdom of God and while he refused to accept the attempts of the crowds to proclaim him king, we must see this in its historical context. Expectations abounded in Israel. Hidden agendas were rife. Many in Israel wanted a king who would help to overthrow Roman rule. Jesus refused to comply with these wishes. His path was to lead to the cross, not to violent insurrection. Such a route was unacceptable to the masses for the curse of the law lay on anyone who died on a tree (Dt. 21:22–23). Hence, Jesus refused to follow the current clamour. Yet he acknowledged to Pilate that he was indeed a king, but of a different sort (Jn. 18:36–37). After his resurrection, his kingship and mediatorial kingdom is proclaimed (1 Cor. 15:20–28; Eph. 1:18–23; Rev. 1:5, 17–18). The theme of the kingdom of God disappears. The kingship of God's Son comes into view. So much is accepted by Pannenberg when he agrees that 'the title of king . . . thus designates the position that is due to Jesus because of his resurrection'.[5]

In short, the threefold office of Christ as prophet, priest and king highlights his role in (1) speaking and teaching the word of God which ultimately focused on himself; (2) offering himself as a vicarious sacrifice to God; and (3) reigning over his church and the world as risen Lord. The crisis in the doctrine in recent years is largely due to the modern predilection for a christology from below. On such assumptions, the man Jesus is the primary subject. The synoptic gospels are consequently the main source, interpreted as the record of the activity of a man. The man in question appears to disclaim such prominence for himself. Colin Gunton has shown the inherent weakness of christologies from below.[6] They tend to portray Christ as a kind of superman, with extra qualities that set him apart from the rest of us. At the same time, his deity is held in suspense. In other words, they end up with a Christ who is not quite God and not quite human. If, however, the God/man Jesus Christ is seen as the bearer of office, justice can be done both to the hidden nature of the revelation of Christ during his earthly ministry (when, as John the Baptist put it, 'among you stands one you do not know'), as well as (in the period after the resurrection) to the finality of his atoning work and to his exaltation to the right hand of God. Consequently, we can affirm a true revelation of God and at the same time a revelation of God as man.[7]

22

There are ways, however, of looking at the work of Christ other than through the model of the three offices. A prominent theme in the synoptic gospels is that of the kingdom of God. This fits indirectly into the framework of the threefold office, since Christ was to be raised to supreme authority as king at his resurrection. Yet the kingdom of God is an important topic in its own right. Again, the idea of union with Christ is to the fore in the writings of Paul. In fact, some scholars (such as Geerhardus Vos and H. M. Ridderbos) have claimed that, when seen in relation to Christ's death and resurrection, this is at the centre of Paul's theology. Again, there was a strong interest not so long ago among New Testament scholars in investigating the meaning of the various titles used of Jesus in the New Testament, and using them to learn the writers' view of Christ's task. These examples are enough to show that no one approach to the work of Christ will ever command universal support. Moreover, any one model inevitably has its own limitations. Gödel's theorem proved mathematically that no single system can be both comprehensive and consistent. Nevertheless, some such organization is necessary if we are to understand. We simply wish to point out the strengths and also the limitations of the framework we are using. Therefore, while we have selected the prophet/priest/king structure as very suitable to help us understand what Christ has achieved for us, we will introduce other relevant features along the way.

Thus, in chapter 2 we will see how Christ relates to the important biblical categories of covenant and election. In chapter 3 we will ask what the theme of the kingdom of God has to say about Christ's work. In chapter 4 we will focus on union with Christ and the various ways it is expressed in Scripture. Then in chapter 5, we will turn to the three-office framework as we discuss Christ as prophet, in his proclaiming and being the Word of God. In chapter 6 we will look at the much neglected matter of Christ's human priesthood. His priestly work will continue to receive attention in chapter 7 (the nature of the atonement) and in chapter 8 (where we discuss the major ways in which the church has viewed the cross). The relationship between Christ's priestly act of atonement and the doctrine of justification will be the subject of chapter 9. The much debated question of the extent (or intent) of the atonement is treated in an appendix. Finally, in chapters 10 and 11 we will discuss the mediatorial kingship of Christ in its cosmic and personal dimensions.

When talking of Christ exercising a threefold office we must beware of separating the various functions. Together they cohere in the one work of Christ. Hence Christ's prophetic office at once reveals him as both priest and king. His priestly sacrifice reveals the love, grace and justice of God and so it is also prophetic. His kingship provides the authority undergirding all he does in prophetic and priestly terms. In short, Christ is prophet, priest and king simultaneously and continuously. During his earthly ministry he did not simply perform a prophetic role in revealing God and his purposes, then switch to a priestly mode for his sacrifice on the cross and finally become king at his resurrection, each function being jettisoned when the next one took over. There is a progression, for which our structure allows, but it is an historical and soteriological progression, not a separation of functions by chronological order. There is some justice in focusing on the prophetic during the earthly ministry, on Christ's priestly function in the sacrifice of the cross and on the kingly function in the exaltation, but this is simply to provide a focus and to highlight the progression. It is valid only within the context of the one work of Christ 'for us and for our salvation', a work that can no more be divided than can his person.

The unity of the person and work of Christ

What Christ has done is directly related to who he is. It is the uniqueness of his person that determines the efficacy of his work. As John Calvin (1509–64), for one, argued (*Institutes*, II,12,3), only he who was simultaneously true God and true man could obey God on our behalf:

> Accordingly, our Lord came forth as true man and took the person and name of Adam in order to take Adam's place in obeying the Father, to present our

24

flesh as the price of satisfaction to God's righteous judgment, and, in the same flesh, to pay the penalty that we had deserved. In short, since neither as God alone could he feel death, nor as man alone could he overcome it, he coupled human nature with divine that to atone for sin he might submit the weakness of the one to death; and that, wrestling with death by the power of the other nature, he might win victory for us.

Calvin attributes the value of Christ's atoning sacrifice to his being both divine and human. His obedience and atoning death are both dependent on who he is. Calvin was not, of course, alone. The Heidelberg Catechism (1563) argued along the same lines in its questions 15 to 17. In asking what nature the mediator should have, it replied that he must be true and sinless man and yet at the same time true God. The justice of God requires that a man 'in the same human nature that sinned' should make satisfaction for sin but yet he should be without sin himself. Moreover, the power of Godhead was required to support the manhood in the endurance of God's wrath against sin. Such claims have echoed down the church from the early centuries, when Apollinarianism, in its claim that the divine Logos took the place of a human soul in Jesus, was opposed by the counter-assertion of the orthodox that 'what is not assumed cannot be healed'.[8] A less than human Christ could no more be the saviour of human beings than a less than divine Christ could be the true revelation of God. Who Christ is determines what he can do.

In our own century this axiom has been reasserted with vigour. Karl Barth (1886–1968) constantly stressed the unity of the being and acts of God. In terms of the mediation of Christ, 'It is in the particular fact and the particular way that Jesus Christ is very God, very man, and very God-man that He works, and He works in the fact and only in the fact that He is this One and not another.'[9] G. C. Berkouwer (1903–) too warns strongly against any separation between person and work, since, he argues, any such separation will cause us to go astray with respect to both. An isolated consideration of Christ's person is impossible since he can be known only in connection with his holy work. The two constitute but one message. 'To mention Christ's name is to point to his work, and to mention the blessing of his work is . . . to deal with the work of him of whom the Church in adoration confesses: *vere Deus, vere homo*.'[10] From another perspective Pannenberg argues that 'Jesus possesses significance "for us" only to the extent that this significance is inherent in himself'.[11]

This, however, has not always been fully appreciated. The focus of the first few centuries of the church was on Christ's person, on the eternal relation of Christ to God (the problem of the Trinity) and then on the relation of the divinity of Christ to his humanity (the problem of the incarnation). The work of Christ received little direct attention. In part we can understand why. The Hellenistic world was preoccupied with timeless reality, with the eternal, with the question of being. These were the areas in which the doctrinal and philosophical issues arose for the Fathers. They would have failed their own age (and ours) if they had not addressed the gospel to the concerns of their own world. Even as they did so they were well aware of the integral connection between who Christ was in himself and the needs of our salvation. We have already mentioned the church's vehement rejection of the views of Apollinaris in 381. Apollinaris taught that the divine Logos took the place of a human soul in the incarnate Christ. Therefore Christ was not fully human. He had a human body but a divine soul, not a human one. The orthodox rejection of this idea was grounded on the premiss that 'what is not assumed cannot be healed'. If Christ was not fully human he could not save us nor offer a true sacrifice of atonement on our behalf, nor could he empathize with us in our own weakness and temptation. He must be man to represent us just as he must be God to make God known to us. The Fathers' focus was not so much due to a retreat from history, still less a lack of concern for the work of salvation, but rather a deliberate projection of the gospel into the thought world of the day. Moreover, the very concept of the incarnation was itself a frontal challenge to the dualistic character of Greek philosophy and religion. According to much Greek thought, the idea that the material world had an intrinsic worth was anathema. By their stress on the incarnation the Fathers were pointing to the inherent value and worth of the creation and so of history.[12] These are pressing reasons that account for the particular focus of the early church, but nevertheless we cannot deny that what Christ actually did was not a topic of prolonged study.

In our own day, the pendulum has swung to the opposite extreme. Under the impact of a philosophical dualism stemming from Kant, the Western intellectual world has eclipsed eternity and absolutized time. If the historical was neglected in the Hellenistic world it is absolutized in the modern era. For Kant, true scientific knowledge exists only in the realm of the phenomenal, that which can be observed and measured by the senses. Religion and morality are not capable of empirical observation and so do not possess the status of scientific knowledge. They belong in the realm of the noumenal, that which cannot be observed in the above sense. As a result, the post-Kantian world has put a large question mark beside the supernatural. The question of God has become highly problematic. In christology this is seen in the insistence in many quarters on a christology 'from below', starting with and controlled by the historical record of the man Jesus of Nazareth. If deity enters the picture at all, it comes as a deduction from a purely immanentistic portrait drawn by the synoptic gospels or from the very human theologizing by the primitive church. It is seen in Oscar Cullmann's claim, later qualified, that for the New Testament a functional christology is the only kind that exists.[13] It is evident also in Pannenberg's approach to christology via the methods of historical science, in much contemporary writing on early christology from the perspective of New Testament studies and in the work of liberation theologians such as Jon Sobrino.[14] What this trend exhibits is the notion that we must first ask what Jesus actually did and only then can we begin to grapple with the question of who he was. Indeed, at times the distinct impression is given that this latter question is one that ought not to be asked.

Colin Gunton has, as we have already noted, drawn attention to some of the serious weaknesses of this approach. It tends to leave us with a Christ who is little different from a superman, whose human qualities are so elevated that they

are beyond our attainment and who is therefore hardly able
to sympathize with us in our weaknesses. We are left with
little of the New Testament stress on incarnation, that 'God
was in Christ'.[15] Some have spared no pains to explain that
the church has been mistaken in assuming that the New
Testament even teaches such a thing. The result is a Christ
who is not quite God and not quite human as we are. Still
further, such approaches betray an underlying dualism
between time and eternity, function and ontology that has
long since been abandoned in the natural sciences as untrue
to nature. Such dualism is also alien to the biblical doctrines
of creation, providence and resurrection which maintain that
God is the creator of both tangible and non-tangible reality,
that he who is eternal has brought the time/space field into
existence and continues to exercise sovereign authority over
the entire universe. Therefore, a thoroughgoing functional
christology, focusing on the work of Christ to the exclusion of
his person, has grave weaknesses.

The concern to preserve the unity of Christ's person and
work is evident in some of the classic discussions of christology. Irenaeus (c. 130 – c. 200) in his major work *Against
Heresies*, Book V, developed, in his recapitulation theory, the
Pauline idea of Christ as the second Adam. Thus Christ
retraces all the stages of Adam, obeying God where Adam
has disobeyed. He passed through all the stages of human
life, sanctifying each in turn. As Adam was the head of the
race which was now subject to death, so Christ instituted a
new redeemed humanity. The disobedience of Adam enacted on a tree was remedied by Christ's obedience on the tree.
The incarnation underlies it all. Christ became what we are so
as to make us what he is. His incarnation is in order to bring
about our redemption. At the same time, our redemption
could not have taken place had not the Word become truly
human. Incarnation and atonement are both necessary and
mutually defining.

The great work of Anselm (1033–1109), *Why did God become
Man?*, is strikingly similar in its thrust. Anselm argues that
the purpose of the incarnation was that Christ should atone
for our sins. Christ was and is who he was and is in order to
save us. No incarnation without atonement! No atonement

without incarnation! John Calvin also points to Christ having taken the nature and name of Adam so that in Adam's place he might offer our flesh to God to satisfy his judgment. Karl Barth develops this even further when he considers the atonement as covenant, finding expression in the union of deity and humanity in Christ. In line with his stress on the unity of God's being and acts, Barth argues that the act of atonement is to be found in the being of Christ. The union of deity and humanity in Christ is the pivotal point from which the whole of salvation (indeed, the whole of theology) is to be viewed (*CD*, IV/1, pp. 67–78, 123–128). For Barth the incarnation has a controlling influence over the atonement as covenant, and thereby over the whole outworking of salvation. Everything is governed by it. His is an exaggerated focus on Christ. The distinctiveness of the parts tends to be blurred. Yet the connection between incarnation and atonement, person and work of Christ is there.

As a corollary, just as there can be no incarnation without atonement so also there can be no atonement without incarnation. In other words, as Christ became man specifically to die for our sins and to rise for our justification so also his death for sin required his being human. He became incarnate for a particular task. He completed his task successfully because of who he was. If he was not God he could not have revealed the Father. If he was not human he could not represent us, nor could he have rendered human obedience to God, nor suffered the penalty of divine justice for the sins of the human race. If he were not God he would not have the strength to save us. If he were not human he would not have the human experience to save us. If he were not one integrated person but instead some kind of schizoid, God could in no sense be said to have identified himself with us in our suffering. We would instead be left with a hollow Saviour and a God aloof and detached from us at the point of our greatest need.

Incarnation and atonement, however, are not only indispensable the one to the other; they are also mutually definitive. They are part of the one great movement of God's grace to humanity in Jesus Christ. It is not enough that we affirm the truth of the incarnation and then move on to affirm the truth of the atonement as two factors in isolation. They are integral parts of a great whole. The historical appearance of the incarnate God in Christ was to atone for our sins. The atoning sufferings and death of Christ for our sins were those of the incarnate God himself.

This intimate and unbreakable connection has always been part of the church's collective subconscious. Yet undoubted imbalances have developed, due as often as not to historical and cultural factors. For instance, the Western church has been profoundly influenced by legal and forensic categories. Ever since the time of the lawyer Tertullian (c. 160–220), its thinking has owed much to Roman law. Perhaps this was inevitable for, after all, the Roman Empire had its greatest strength in administration and jurisprudence and so bequeathed a legacy to the Latin church which has been faithfully handed down the centuries to today. The development of canon law and the hierarchical cast of the Roman church are obvious consequences. Other results include the strong concentration on the atonement and on justification that developed in the mediaeval period. The legal side of the gospel was developed at length. In the broadest of terms the focus of the Western church was very much on certain elements of Pauline theology, rather than on, say, more ontological and mystical emphases present in John, or even on the dynamic and redemptive-historical aspects of Paul himself.

The Eastern church, on the other hand, was different. Overshadowing all else was the sudden emergence of Islam in the seventh century. The Greek church saw its territory overrun. Before that time, the East had demonstrated acute theological skill. It had been at the forefront in exploring the mysteries of the Trinity and the incarnation. With the hegemony of Islam, the church was pushed on to the defensive. It no longer had freedom to explore the gospel or to proselytize. Its task was simply preservative, to hold on to the dogmas of the great ecumenical councils. This it did through the long centuries that followed. As a consequence, for both historical and theological reasons its focus is very different from that of the West. Historically, the debates on atonement and justification in the West passed the East by for a long time. When theologians in the East were forced to face these issues, they found them as somewhat strange questions to which they were forced to react. Centuries of linguistic and cultural isolation had produced something of a siege mentality. As a small, beleaguered minority in an isolated and alien world, they spoke a language that was for a long time all but unknown in the West, while in turn, Latin became very much an alien tongue for them. Theologically, acting to preserve the dogmas of the past, the church in the East maintained the ontological orientation of those dogmas, rather than the legal concerns of the West. The person of Christ was central. Loosely speaking, the theology was of John rather than Paul. Little insight is needed to see that ideally both should be present together. We need John and we need Paul. We need the person of Christ and we need his work too.[16]

The nineteenth century saw one particularly notable attempt to understand the work of Christ via his person. John McLeod Campbell (1800–72), for his pains, was then deposed from the ministry of the Church of Scotland. We shall discuss his views of the atonement in chapter 8 so we can give only brief consideration to them at this point. The basic premiss of Campbell's theology was that God is love. In Jesus Christ there is a twofold movement. There is a movement of God towards humanity in which his love and forgiveness are revealed together with his judgment on sin. Simultaneously, there is also a responding movement towards God whereby Christ in our humanity offers a perfect vicarious response to the love and judgment of God. We respond personally to this twofold movement through the Holy Spirit, who enables us to participate in Christ's own response made on our behalf. Christ's work is of no avail for us apart from participation in his person. Hence, in the incarnation Christ unites himself with us by taking our humanity into union with himself. In our humanity he repented, believed and died for us all. By the Spirit we are united to him to participate in his vicarious response which, in turn, is a response offered in our humanity.[17]

Campbell has a strong universalist tendency. Since Christ in his incarnation assumes the nature common to us all, when the incarnation controls the atonement the latter is then seen to include in its scope all who share the nature assumed in the incarnation. If Christ unites himself with all people in the incarnation then he also dies for them all on the cross. If his death effectively achieves what he intended then all people are saved. One has yet to find anything in Campbell (or in Barth and T. F. Torrance who also adopt an incarnational approach, while formally rejecting universalism) that satisfactorily avoids that conclusion. Incarnational universalism is not taught in the Bible. As we shall discuss in chapter 4, union with Christ always comes to be expressed on our side by faith in the incarnate, risen Christ (see Jn. 1:12). However, where the incarnation, although held to be true, is nonetheless not given adequate theological weight, the link between Christ and humanity is eroded. Catholic thought developed in this direction after the ecumenical councils of the first six centuries (such as those of Nicea in AD 325, Constantinople in AD 381 and Chalcedon in AD 451), insofar as Christ was viewed in his supreme deity and his common nature with humanity was neglected. Consequently, the need arose for some additional form of human mediation between us and the exalted Christ. The Virgin Mary was the approved solution.

A survey of discussion on the work of Christ

Several broad themes keep recurring in the church's understanding of what Christ did. Firstly, Christ as teacher and example was a prominent focus in the early centuries. Shortly after the death of the apostles a legalistic outlook developed. Christ was viewed as an example to follow and the gospel began to be defined as a new law. At the same time, the church was forced to defend itself against heresy. It also had to unfold the faith in contrast to Judaism. Consequently, Christ was seen as teacher. Yet, secondly, the church did recognize the centrality of the cross. Irenaeus, in his theory of recapitulation, spoke of Christ repairing Adam's disobedience by his own obedience on the tree, so overcoming what had undone us. Christ's death was a sacrifice. The cross was not entirely eclipsed. The tree of Adam's disobedience was repaired by the tree of Christ's obedience.[18] Thirdly, in the early church Christ's death was often understood as the payment of a ransom price to the devil. He was released from the devil's power by his resurrection, so ensuring the complete deliverance of his people. Hence, salvation was secured by Christ's resurrection and exaltation.[19] Such ideas were dominant for a millennium. Fourthly, in the East the even more basic theme of deification (*theōsis*) underlay all this. According to Irenaeus, the reason the Son of God became what we are was that we in turn might share in his perfection (*Against Heresies* V, preface: *MPG*, 7/2, 1120). For Athanasius, the goal God set for humanity in creation was participation in the divine Logos. The redemptive work of Christ re-established this goal (*On the Incarnation* I, 3, 14; *MPG*, 25, 96–97, 100–101, 120–121).

The three models most common in the early church (the focus on the life of Christ, his teaching and example; on his death as a sacrifice for sin; and on his resurrection as a triumphant conquest over sin, death and Satan) all figure in various guises at later times. (The theme of deification has largely been confined to the East.) First of all, the triumphant victory of the resurrection has continued to provide a basis for an understanding of Christ's work. For instance, in his book, *Christus Victor*, the Swedish theologian Gustav Aulén (1879–1977) drew attention to what he called the classic doctrine of the work of Christ. He saw this as Christ's conquest over Satan and the evil powers and as the reconciliation of the world to himself. This view, he claimed, dominated during the first thousand years, was eclipsed by Anselm, revived by Luther but neglected thereafter. His case was exaggerated. We shall see why later. Yet the theme was present. Reflection today on the resurrection as a promise of hope in the midst of suffering in some ways shares this slant.[20] Secondly, Anselm forced debate on the work of Christ to focus on his sufferings and death. With the penitential system of the Roman Catholic Church and the social fabric of mediaeval feudalism as cultural reinforcements, Anselm's theory of the death of Christ as a satisfaction of God's honour was not only influential in its own right but it also directed concentration to the cross as the fulcrum of

Christ's work. Thirdly, the life of Christ received most attention in the nineteenth century. In keeping with the strongly immanentistic spirit of the times, New Testament scholars were busy searching for the historical Jesus. A new historical awareness was emerging. The infant disciplines of psychology and anthropology appeared on the scene. For nineteenth-century liberalism, what the man Jesus of Nazareth did was the decisive thing for the Christian faith. F. D. E. Schleiermacher (1768–1834) saw Jesus as exhibiting the highest form of God-consciousness, unimpaired and unique. Consequently, he was the supreme form of a universal human trait of absolute dependence, a trait that comes to expression in piety and religious activity but which is obscured to a greater or lesser extent in us all. Only in Jesus Christ was this total dependence on God undiluted. Consequently, human beings are now redeemed by participating in the community Jesus founded. For Schleiermacher, Jesus' impact on his followers, while inherently religious, occurs through normal human social processes. The work of Christ, however (while religious), was at the same time exemplary.

Much of liberal theology followed in the same vein. True, not everything was reduced to the imitation of Christ. Due to a concentration on the life of Jesus, however, a dominant stress fell on his ethics and teachings. With Jesus seen in purely human terms as one who preached and taught about God the Father and the kingdom of God, the church tended to be seen as a community assimilated to the vision of Jesus. Thus, for A. Ritschl (1822–89), no direct link between Jesus and God existed. Jesus was an historical figure. The supernatural was excluded from consideration. Jesus was simply a man, his significance to be explained in purely human terms. His historical uniqueness lay in his founding the church, in establishing the kingdom of God. As such, he could not be rivalled.[21] Again, A. Harnack (1851–1930), while not reducing Christ to his teaching or ethics as such, nevertheless followed in the line of liberalism in detaching the essence of the Christian faith from the person of Jesus. For him, Christianity transcended all forms of its historical promulgation, including that of Jesus himself. As Jesus proclaimed it, the gospel related to the Father alone and not to the Son.

When Paul appeared on the scene, the focus turned to Jesus.[22] For Harnack, while Jesus' teaching was of huge importance, it was merely in a similar category to all other historical understandings of Christianity. Christianity essentially involved humanity's relationship to God the Father. Its link to Jesus is historical not theological. He is simply the first to proclaim that relationship.

A prior position on the person of Christ has often influenced conclusions about the work of Christ and his significance for the church. If Jesus is exclusively human, it follows that he points towards something other than himself, something greater than himself, to which both he and us are to commit ourselves. Primarily, Jesus is an example, whether his ethics are to be followed or whether, instead, he merely has an historical priority as the first Christian or as the church's founder.

In today's terms, liberation theology has similarities with nineteenth-century liberalism. In his major work, *Christology at the Crossroads*, Jon Sobrino (1938–) concentrates on the history of Jesus in the synoptic gospels. Jesus' teaching focuses not on himself but on the kingdom of God. Using the tools of Marxist social analysis, Sobrino claims that the kingdom of God was seen by Jesus as a struggle for justice in society, as an attack on poverty and its causes. Jesus located sin mainly in oppressive political and social structures. Jesus identified with the poor and oppressed in their struggle. He offered an ethic of love and commitment to the kingdom of God. His death demonstrated God's own identification with the poor and oppressed in their suffering. His resurrection is promise, offering hope for the future of the struggle. For Jesus, doing came before knowing, orthopraxis (right conduct) had priority over orthodoxy (right belief). So also Jesus' ethics require us to follow him as disciples. This discipleship is a full commitment to a struggle against oppression through solidarity with the poor in their suffering. Clearly, for Sobrino Jesus is an ethical exemplar. He is a catalyst for us in a discipleship committed to social, political and economic change on Marxist lines. Similar themes occur in the writings of other liberation theologians who have addressed issues of christology in some depth, such as Juan Luís Segundo (1925–) in *The Historical Jesus of the Synoptics*.

From Schleiermacher to Sobrino, in all these 'Jesuologies' we see a bias towards the synoptic gospels. This rests on the idea that the life of Jesus has a priority over the proclamation of the risen Christ by the church. Is it not true, however, that the portrait of the earthly Jesus painted for us in the synoptics is in fact a work of the early church itself? The gospels are themselves samples of the apostolic or apostolically supported proclamation of the church. It is simply not possible to disentangle the teaching and ethics of the earthly Jesus from the preaching of the risen Christ *in such a way* as to use the former as a separate and prior textbook claiming historical and therefore theological primacy over the latter. The history of Jesus in the synoptic gospels is also itself interpretation. The gospels are theological documents. That makes the gospels no less historical. Certainly, the gospel writers did not attribute their own teaching to Jesus. On the contrary, all the evidence points the other way. Their teaching was based on the deeds and teaching of Jesus. The old, yet still current, claim that the recorded words and deeds of Jesus are simply projections of later ecclesiastical or theological reflection is a misunderstanding of the evidence. We should be cautious, however, about the kind of naivety shown by nineteenth-century liberalism and to some extent shared by contemporary liberation theologians in their major focus on the ethics of the earthly Jesus. It is obvious that the life of Jesus is vital to an understanding of what he did and that the gospels are the sources from which to learn this. Yet these should be read as part of the whole apostolic teaching.

In recent years attention has once again been directed towards the cross, but in strikingly new ways. Taking up a theme in Luther, that of the *theologia crucis* (theology of the cross), the German theologians Jürgen Moltmann (1926–) and Eberhard Jüngel (1934–) have developed the theme of 'the crucified God'. At the cross, the claim goes, God himself participated in the suffering and desolation of the world by enduring the curse of abandonment which only the outcast and deprived could undergo. In fact, Moltmann sees the cross in trinitarian terms. Jesus' cry of dereliction signifies his abandonment by the Father, while the Father in turn suffers the Son to be delivered up. The Spirit who justifies the godless proceeds from this event. This breathtaking insight runs counter to the traditional doctrine of the divine impassibility (that God cannot be involved in suffering), an idea borrowed from Greek philosophy and of great impact in patristic times but which leaves God aloof and remote from human need. Yet despite both Moltmann and Jüngel making a close connection between the cross and the resurrection of Christ, how far have they done justice to the totality of biblical testimony about Christ's work? While the crucifixion is unquestionably the centre of God's revelation and also the heart of salvation, more is involved than simply that.[23] The New Testament abounds in joyous reflection from the vantage point of Christ's resurrection. A new world has begun and the old is passing away. We shall attempt to grapple with these great themes in the chapters which follow.

2

CHRIST AND THE PLAN OF SALVATION

The concept of covenant is highly important for an understanding of Scripture. As one recent scholar has indicated, 'Virtually every school of biblical interpretation today has come to appreciate the significance of the covenants for the understanding of the distinctive message of the Scriptures.'[1] Old and New Testaments are simply another way of saying old and new covenants. How the work of Christ fits into the theme of God's covenant is a crucial question.

How does the Bible understand covenant? One option it avoids is to see it as an agreement made by two co-equal parties, much as a commercial business contract. For instance, the translators of the Septuagint declined to translate the Hebrew word *bᵉrît* by *synthēkē*, which normally meant a mutual pact or agreement. Instead they used the word *diathēkē*, denoting a sovereign imposition by one party on another. In their view, the covenants God made were one-sided. Human beings were not God's equals. The covenants were thus impositions by a sovereign God. In this sense, both John Murray (1895–1975) and O. Palmer Robertson (1937–) stress that, throughout biblical history, covenant-making is an act of God's sovereignty.[2] In fact, the form of the Mosaic covenant is very similar to the Hittite suzerainty treaties that were a feature of the period. These treaties were imposed on defeated vassal nations. They were not pacts between equals. Rather, they contained promises of benefits the suzerain was to grant and listed the obligations to which the vassal was bound.[3]

During the course of the Reformation period, the covenant became a theme of great importance. It was used in defence of infant baptism and, later, in the political realm as a means of regulating (and so limiting) the powers of kings. At this time, under the influence of Roman law, many came to see the covenant as a contract. This was a departure from the biblical teaching,[4] at the heart of which is the idea of fellowship, seen especially in the promise 'I will be your God, you shall be my people'. A covenant meal attends both the institution of the Mosaic covenant (Ex. 24:8–11) and the new covenant (Mt. 26:20–29 and parallels). Abraham's meal with his theophanic visitors may have had a similar function (Gn. 18:1f.). A meal of fellowship points to a far closer relationship between the parties than in a contract. It goes beyond a purely legal relation. The marriage relationship is a more accurate picture of the deep reconciliation and friendship of the biblical covenant. This is the way the Bible frequently describes it (*e.g.* Ezk. 16:1f.; Je. 2:1f.; Eph. 5:22–23).

Is promise or law paramount in God's covenant? For Murray, the covenant is 'a sovereign administration of grace and of promise'.[5] For Kline, however, law has priority because God is by nature just, whereas his grace is dependent on his will.[6] These differences are more than incidental. They affect the way we view the whole gospel and thus impinge on the work of Christ.

From an examination of Paul's discussion of the relationship between the promise of the Abrahamic covenant and the law of the Mosaic covenant, it is hard to see the two as competitors. They coexisted. The law did not set aside the promise. It was added. It did not supplant, but served the promise:

> What I mean is this: The law, introduced 430 years later, does not set aside the covenant previously

established by God and thus do away with the promise. For if the inheritance depends on the law, then it no longer depends on a promise; but God in his grace gave it to Abraham through a promise.

What, then, was the purpose of the law? It was added because of transgressions until the Seed to whom the promise referred had come . . . .

Is the law, therefore, opposed to the promises of God? Absolutely not! . . . (Gal. 3:17–22).

The covenant is certainly a sovereign administration of grace by God to man. We are not only mere creatures but also sinners who have lost all rights. Yet law also has a regulative role. Sin and righteousness have content. They can be and are defined. Paul, in attacking the legalism of the Judaizers, does not set aside the law itself (Rom. 3:31; 7:7, 12, 14, where he calls the law 'spiritual' and thus according to his customary usage 'originating from the Holy Spirit'). In this sense, grace is constitutive of the covenant relation, while law is regulative. It is by pure grace that God establishes his covenant. It is by grace that we are brought into such a relation with him. It is the law, however, that defines both what sin is and also in what obedience consists. It maps out the path we are to follow in fulfilling our covenantal obligations. Jesus, in the Sermon on the Mount, endorses the Decalogue and intensifies its scope by relating it not only to external actions but also to the thoughts, motives and attitudes of the heart. As David Hill comments on Matthew 5:18, 'the validity of the Law is emphasised', and again '. . . in none of these passages is there an intention to annul the demands of the Law, but only to carry them to their ultimate meaning, to intensify them, or to reinterpret them in a higher key. This is the time of the fulfilment of the Law, not its destruction.'[7]

The biblical covenants form a unity

Despite the historic division into Old Testament and New Testament we have one Bible. Although Scripture records a number of covenants, such as the Noahic, the Abrahamic, the Mosaic, the Davidic and the new covenant, all of which differ in context and content, yet it also sees them in harmony. When we talk here of the covenant of grace we are not setting up some abstraction that ignores the historical truth that there are a series of biblical covenants. God's covenants, made in such specific historical contexts, cannot be viewed rightly if the historical dimension is lost. At the same time, the important point to grasp is that these progressive covenants are not disconnected or discontinuous.

Firstly, covenant unity exists in terms of God's purpose. God has one purpose of grace, one decision in election, one mediator, one salvation. This purpose Zachariah, referring to the entire process of redemptive history in the Old Testament, indicates as fulfilled in Jesus. The promise of Yahweh to David, to Abraham and to the holy prophets he calls *diathēkēs hagias autou* ('his holy covenant', Lk. 1:72), one integrated whole, one organic unity.

Moreover, secondly, God's covenants are not arbitrary. There is a unity in the variety of historical manifestations of God's redemptive grace. It is to this congruity that the term covenant (singular) testifies. For example, each successive covenant builds on what has gone before. The Mosaic covenant is based on the Abrahamic. When up Mount Sinai with Yahweh, while Israel under Aaron was worshipping the golden calf, Moses pleads for mercy to God on the basis of the promises of the Abrahamic covenant (Ex. 32:13–14). Entry to Canaan is seen as fulfilling God's promise to Abraham (Jos. 1:3; Ex. 23:31; *cf.* Gn. 15:18), yet this event took place long after the Mosaic covenant was instituted. In turn, the Davidic covenant was introduced against the backcloth of the Mosaic covenant, which remained the constant theme of the prophets as they denounced Israel and Judah for their unfaithfulness to the terms Yahweh had laid down at Sinai. The exile was interpreted as punishment for persistent failure to obey the Mosaic covenant. The new covenant is anticipated long before its time (Je. 31:31–34; Ezk. 34:24; 37:21–28). The central covenant promise, 'I will be your God, you shall be my people', is repeated at each covenantal administration (Gn. 17:7–8; Je. 11:4 with respect to the Mosaic covenant; Je. 24:7 with the return from the Exile in view; Je. 30:22; 31:33; 32:28 with reference to the new covenant; Rev. 21:3). More specifically, this promise can be seen as a loving promise by God to sinners of forgiveness and fellowship.

Thirdly, there is also unity with the people of God at all stages of covenant administration. Because of the principle of corporate solidarity,[8] God is seen as making his covenant not only with those alive or physically present at the time but also with an endless succession of generations thereafter, regarded as present by virtue of their incorporation into the community of God. The promise of the Abrahamic covenant was not merely to Abraham himself but also to his seed throughout their generations for an everlasting covenant (Gn. 17:7–8; *cf.* 15:18). The same principle held true in the Mosaic and Davidic covenants (Ex. 20:5–6; 2 Sa. 7:12–16). Thus, Moses regards his hearers as present forty years earlier at Sinai when he addresses them prior to entry into Canaan (Dt. 5:2–3) and he also indicates that this covenant was made with generations yet unborn (Dt. 29:14). The Abrahamic covenant extended to a thousand generations (Ps. 105:8–10), effectively for ever, and is seen in this psalm as continuing in force after the covenant at Sinai was enacted. Nor was it a purely national covenant, for the gift of the Holy Spirit was an integral part of what it promised (see Gal. 3:14; *cf.* Is. 59:21) and it opened out to all nations, should they turn to Yahweh.

So much is clear when we examine those New Testament contexts which reflect on the older covenants. Firstly, as we have seen (pp. 40–41 above), Paul in Galatians 3:15–22 undercuts the Judaizers' attempt to impose circumcision on Gentile converts by arguing from the continuity of the Abrahamic covenant with the contemporary scene. Since even a human covenant cannot be set aside by later transactions (verse 15), the covenant made by God with Abraham cannot be abrogated by something which occurred 430 years later (verse 17). The Mosaic did not and could not set aside the Abrahamic. The inheritance promised Abraham was by grace, through the promise. The law, given through Moses, was not therefore inconsistent with the promise to Abraham. It was added (verse 19). It was a regulator, not an alternative. The two co-existed thereafter, the law promoting the purposes already operative through the promise. The Mosaic covenant was added for a set reason – until Christ came, the seed to whom the promise had been made (verse 19). The Abrahamic covenant promised the coming of Christ to fulfil the promise; it is therefore fulfilled in the new covenant. The Mosaic covenant was added as a custodian for Israel in its minority (verses 24–26; 4:1f.). It served a protective function for the people of the Abrahamic covenant until that covenant was fully realized. The two covenants were not successive but overlapping. Their functions were not competitive but complementary. Grace was constitutive, law regulative. The Judaizers had misunderstood the purely regulative role of the law.

Traditional Protestant exegesis held that the Judaizers were looking to the law to save them from sin, which it could never do. Recently, the work of E. P. Sanders has brought about a revolution in Pauline studies. He has shown that no known section of first-century Judaism had this attitude.[9] Jewish thought was unanimous in holding to entry to God's covenant by grace alone. Justification by faith was accepted as axiomatic. The real stumbling block was Jesus. James D. G. Dunn, while accepting this new perspective, has indicated that the Jews so prized the law that they defined salvation in specifically Jewish terms, based on key elements in the law such as circumcision, sabbath observance and food regulations. This became a nationalistic badge of covenant membership to which Gentile converts were required to submit. Grace was unwittingly undermined. The Judaizers shared these perspectives. Paul in Galatians redefines the law for the people of God as 'a basic guideline for social living' rather than as 'the law misunderstood in too distinctively Jewish terms'. Dunn describes the older view as 'a gross caricature' which has fed an evil strain of Christian anti-Semitism.[10] No-one can afford to ignore that we are now in what one scholar has termed the 'post-Sanders' era. The idea that Paul would have the church abandon the law just will not do.[11]

Secondly, in Hebrews 8:6–13 it appears that the writer is contrasting the Mosaic with the new covenant. The new is a better covenant, since it is based on better promises than the Mosaic one (verse 6). This is certainly the theme. The section is largely a citation of Jeremiah 31:31–34, so we should be careful not to overexegete the passage. The point, however, is not that one law has been replaced by another or by none, but rather that the law in the Mosaic covenant was purely external and could not of itself bring compliance. The Mosaic economy, viewed in itself, was purely prescriptive. Now, however, by the Holy Spirit obedience is willingly performed to the same laws ('my laws'), which are no longer only external but are internalized, written by God on the hearts of those who know the Lord. As P. E. Hughes put it, '. . . it is the same law that is associated with both old and new covenants . . . the law of God is the standard of holiness required of [the Christian believer]; only now he is enabled to love and obey the commandments of God which before he hated and disobeyed'.[12] In the wider setting of the letter, the author argues that the weakness of the Mosaic covenant lay in its being a shadow, a type, of what was to come, the new covenant being the guiding model on which it was based. Therefore, within the theme of the new covenant super-seding the old, he portrays a basic continuity between the two.

Thirdly, in 2 Corinthians 3:6–11, Paul also focuses on differences between himself and Moses as representatives of the two covenant ministries, again in probable defence of his own apostolic role against Judaizing opponents. The weak-ness of Moses' ministry was that it was an external one. The law was written on stone tablets, while Paul's ministry results in the law being engraved on the heart, effecting a change in the person who receives it. In consequence, Moses' ministry is one of death and condemnation, since all the law was able to do was to define sin and to prescribe its penalty. Paul's ministry, in contrast, brought life and righteousness, since the Spirit effected a transformation of life. His is a permanent and lasting work, whereas Moses' was temporary. Yet, throughout the antitheses and comparisons of the passage the underlying continuity is still evident. Glory was present in Moses' ministry as well as in Paul's. True, the glory of Moses' ministry was fading, while the glory of Paul's ministry was increasing and permanent. Yet in both instances the glory of God was evident. Moreover, the same laws were operative in both. Hughes states, '. . . the law came into being in glory. As coming *from God*, it was necessarily glorious . . .

This, then, is a sufficient contradiction of the calumnies of those adversaries who were suggesting that Paul ... is a despiser of the law'.[13] As Cranfield states, it is simply the effectiveness of the two ministries that is in view.[14] In fact, the goal and purpose of Moses is realized in Paul, who sees himself as a second Moses,[15] an argument designed to win over his detractors rather than to repel them.

Overall, Paul denies that the law has been set aside. It is God's law (Rom. 7:22, 25; 8:7). It is holy (Rom. 7:13) and good (Rom. 7:13, 16). Obedience to the law will bring life (Rom. 7:10). Above all, he insists that the law is 'spiritual' (Rom. 7:14), an expression that Paul uses to denote origination by the Holy Spirit. Indeed, as Cranfield points out, 'For Paul the giving of the Spirit is the establishment of the law'.[16]

Christ is Lord of his covenant

The importance of all this is that, from within an analysis of the covenant, Christ assumes a central and dominant position. In each redemptive covenant there are common features. Each contains certain promises, indicates the need for a mediator between God and his people, and places on the latter obligations which they are required to fulfil as partners of God in the fellowship of his covenant. Ultimately all these features find their realization in Christ.

Christ is the final fulfilment of the promises of God's redemptive covenant. Firstly, the threefold promise of the Abrahamic covenant was not exhausted by what was immediately apparent or accessible. In the case of the promise of the land (Gn. 12:7; 13:14–17; 15:18–21; 17:8), Abraham never enjoyed ownership of anything but a burial plot. He was little more than a temporary squatter. In fact, his major preoccupation was with 'a city which has foundations, whose builder and maker is God' (Heb. 11:10). His expectation was directed to Canaan, but also beyond Canaan to the inheritance which God gives to the church in Christ, a reality to which Canaan was something of a sacramental pointer. The promise of the great nation owing its ancestry to Abraham (Gn. 12:2; 13:16; 17:4–6; 22:15–18), while being realized in Israel, was hardly thereby exhausted. All Yahweh's dealings with Israel at every twist and turn were preparatory to the coming of Christ. Moreover, the seed of Abraham in whom all the nations of the earth were to be blessed (Gn. 12:3; 22:18) was to find full expression only in the one who was to be the occasion for the extension of redemption to the Gentiles (Gal. 3:16). However little he knew it, when Yahweh made his covenant with him, Abraham stood before Christ.

Secondly, the Mosaic covenant also displayed the promise of Christ to Israel. The sacrificial ritual of Leviticus included a series of pronouncements about the status of the one offering sacrifice. Regarding a whole range of offences Yahweh declared the verdict 'he is guilty'. Then, the required offering having been made according to the law of the covenant, there came the verdict 'he is forgiven' (Lv. 5:1ff.). As such, the covenant law defined sin and made known the guilt of humanity each time these sacrifices were made. Yet it also taught the forgiveness of sins to Israel and made it clear that this came through the shedding of sacrificial blood. Of course, as the writer of Hebrews says, animal blood cannot atone for the sins of human beings. Nor could the repetitive sacrifices of the Mosaic covenant deal definitively with sin. No, their constant use emphasized that sin remained an unresolved problem. Some other, superior sacrifice was needed 'of nobler name, and richer blood than they' (Isaac Watts). The promise of forgiveness of sins was therefore only prospective, dependent on the eventual atoning sacrifice of Christ on the cross.

Thirdly, in the Davidic covenant the promise that David was to have a son who would reign over his house for ever (2 Sa. 7:12–16) was obviously unrealized in any of the kings of Israel or Judah. In the first instance, Solomon was clearly in view since he was David's immediate successor and built a house for Yahweh. Yet the terms of this promise were not fulfilled in him. In fact, the kingdom was soon divided during the reign of Rehoboam, and eventually it came to an end with the exile. Only with 'great David's greater son', Jesus Christ (Mt. 1:1) was there one who, by his resurrection, was given the throne of David for ever. Hence, the constant focus of the biblical covenants was to disclose God's one great promise and gift, Jesus Christ his Son.

Moreover, at each stage Christ is the one and only mediator of God's covenant. Because of sin, human beings were estranged from God, expelled from fellowship with him and condemned to death. They were unable to effect any change. Only God, by himself providing mediation, could restore them to friendship and life. As the God/man, Jesus Christ has in his incarnation united our humanity to God, and by his death and resurrection has atoned for our sin, united us to himself, and raised us with him to the presence of God. All this was foreshadowed in the history of God's covenant. In the first place, the Abrahamic covenant had mediatorial elements. As Abraham, acting under orders, was about to offer the promised son of the covenant as a burnt offering, a ram was suddenly provided as a sacrifice in Isaac's place (Gn. 22:9–15). The principle of substitutionary sacrifice was already presaged. Again, Yahweh took on himself a self-maledictory oath as he himself passed between the pieces of the divided birds, calling on himself the curses of the covenant should he prove unfaithful to his promises, effectively guaranteeing to Abraham his faithfulness to his covenantal word (Gn. 15:1–21). It was Yahweh himself who underwrote the covenant. He himself was the pledge and guarantor of fellowship. Secondly, the elaborate ritual of the Mosaic covenant directed attention to atoning sacrifice as the means of forgiveness and reconciliation between God and his human creatures. The Letter to the Hebrews is a large-scale discussion of all that that involves. As we have observed, it was only in Christ that the blood of atonement was definitively offered. At the same time, this was the only basis for covenant fellowship as a reality.

In terms of what God requires of us, do we not, on our part, have to do something either to ratify or complete the covenant ourselves? In each case, faith and obedience is required. Abraham was accounted righteous because he believed God (Gn. 15:6). He was obliged to walk before God and to be perfect (Gn. 17:1), to circumcise the male persons in his household (Gn. 17:9–14) and to offer Isaac as a burnt offering (Gn. 22:1f.). The need for obedience was obvious in the Mosaic covenant, and when it was lacking the prophets waxed eloquent in denouncing Israel (cf. Mi. 6:6–8). Yet at the same time God's covenant is sovereignly made. There is a great disparity between God and humanity, the creator and his creatures. We are not on the same level as he. He is our maker. He is to be feared. Any fellowship we have with him is due to his condescension. Consequently, anything we may do in response to his goodness does not in any way bring the covenant into effect. Rather, it is simply a display of gratitude on our part for what he has done for us. Faith and obedience are our obligation to him, nothing more. They are never adequate. They are themselves dependent on his grace, the result of the Holy Spirit's work within us and the work of the ascended Christ for us. They are from him. More than that, our faith and obedience have value precisely due to Christ's faithful obedience on our behalf. As man, he trusted his heavenly Father. His worship of God was pure and sinless. He obeyed God's law totally, fulfilling its precepts and suffering its sanctions on our behalf. All that he did is on our behalf, throughout his life as well as on the cross. He himself was and is the active, human, bodily expression of God's faithfulness, of 'God with us' (Mt. 1:23). But as man, he was and is active human faithfulness, the second Adam whose obedience has overthrown the first Adam's disobedience. In this sense, our faith and obedience have value because of the faithful obedience of the Saviour on our behalf. It is his response, not ours, which fulfils the covenant. Our faith involves abandoning reliance on our own works and instead entrusting ourselves to the faithfulness of someone else.[17]

Therefore, from all points the covenant directs us to Christ. He is the Lord of the covenant. The covenant exists to make him known. He is its constant theme, at first hidden and obscure but then with increasing clarity disclosed as the new covenant is introduced. All God's promises are realized in Christ and are utterly trustworthy. He is the one mediator of the covenant, who has restored fellowship between God and humanity, and so also among human beings. His is the faith and obedience accepted by God, ours having value because of his. That is why Christ himself (seen as the suffering servant in Isaiah) is described as God's covenant with his people (Is. 42:6).

The development of covenant theology

Historically, the covenant began to receive detailed theological attention in the sixteenth century. The initial impetus came from the challenge to infant baptism posed by the anabaptists. The anabaptists' hermeneutic stressed a large element of discontinuity between the Old Testament and the New. Theological focus was directed to the New Testament. In the absence of explicit New Testament command to baptize infants the anabaptists drew the conclusion that the practice was unwarranted.[18] Another implication of this hermeneutic concerned army service, for the anabaptists maintained that the New Testament gave no sanction for the use of military force.[19] The Reformers saw these ideas as threatening the stability of civil government and so as a potential threat to the Reformation, heavily dependent as it was on the patronage of the civil authorities. Moreover, the rejection of infant baptism was seen as an assault on the express institution of God.

How was a proper defence to be made? The solution was found in the covenant. Here was a theological tool to maintain the unity of Old and New Testaments. As a result, infant baptism could be defended on the grounds of an analogy with the Old Testament practice of circumcision. Since Abraham and his male seed were required to be circumcised in the Old Testament, so believers and their seed are required to be baptized in the New Testament. The underlying presupposition was the unity of the Testaments. Because of this unity the bearing of arms could also be defended as a legitimate occupation for the Christian.

The theme of the unity of the covenant was central in the first flowering of covenant thought begun by Zwingli[20] and carried on by his successor at Zürich, Bullinger,[21] by Oecolampadius at Basel,[22] and by Bucer[23] and Capito[24] at Strassburg. Zwingli himself introduced a strongly salvation-historical emphasis in his *Commentary on True and False Religion* (1525), arguing that the New Testament projects itself back into the Old Testament in the form of promise, while in his *Reply to Hubmaier* (1526) he expressly used covenant unity to defend infant baptism, as was also the case in his

Refutation of Anabaptist Tricks (1527).[25] Covenant unity for Zwingli rested in the historical work of Christ, the focus of the history of salvation. The new covenant is essentially one with the covenants made with Adam after the fall, with Noah, Abraham and David. The Mosaic covenant was distinguished and somewhat set apart as a temporary and conditional mode of administration. On the other hand, the new covenant was seen in unbroken continuity with the Abrahamic and as sovereignly imposed by God, unilateral and gratuitous in its essential nature.[26]

In Zwingli's thought the sovereignty of God and the centrality of Christ were both maintained together. Others were to follow in preserving this vital point.[27] Zwingli's successor at Zürich, Heinrich Bullinger, however, gave covenant theology a somewhat different slant, one which was to lead to unforeseen developments later on. In his *De Testamento seu Foedere Dei Unico & Aeterno Brevis Expositio* (*Concerning the One Eternal Testament or Covenant of God*, Zürich 1534)), the first treatise devoted specifically to the covenant theme, Bullinger followed Zwingli's use of covenant unity to defend infant baptism, but his definition of covenant was quite different. He saw it as a pact, a conditional, mutual, bilateral agreement.[28] Conditions affected both parties, God and humanity. The ten commandments were a paraphrase of the covenant conditions to which human beings are bound. Since infant baptism was one such condition, the anabaptists' neglect of it meant they could not expect the blessings of God's promises. Only if we obey the conditions can we receive the promise. The promise is therefore conditional, dependent on the fulfilment of the stipulated conditions on our part. Certainly, Christ has fulfilled the covenant but God's promise to us in Christ is a conditional promise, made effective only by our meeting the required terms. Later, in his *Decades* (a series of sermons preached from 1549 to 1551) the covenant was treated as part of the law, focusing again on our obligations.[29]

Bullinger's view of covenant had an extensive impact. Perhaps the most influential Reformed leader of the sixteenth century,[30] his views travelled far and wide, to England, to

Heidelberg via his disciple Ursinus and thence into German and Dutch Reformed theology, into the Scottish universities and church and even into the framework devised by Arminius.[31] The focus was no longer so much on what God had done in Christ in fulfilling the covenant for us, but on what we ourselves were required to do in fulfilling it on our part. Hence, the development between Ursinus' *Compendium of Theology* (1561) and Robert Rollock's *Treatise on Effectual Calling* (1597) of the description of the pre-fall situation as a covenant of works is understandable as representing a pre-occupation with human beings and their task, rather than with God and his grace.[32] The influence of the philosophy and methodology of Peter Ramus (1514–72) is possible at this point. Pierre de la Ramée was a French humanist who espoused the Protestant cause, eventually to die in the St Bartholomew's Day massacre. He devised a system of usually dichotomous subdivision whereby any body of knowledge could be reduced to diagrammatic form for easy comprehension. Ramism's stress on pedagogical utility was allied with Puritanism's interest in piety, the covenant of works gaining rapid acceptance with the aid of the dichotomous subdivision that was a central part of Ramist method.[33] Moreover, instead of the history of salvation (seen in the acts of God in Israel climaxing in the death and resurrection of Christ), attention was directed to the *ordo salutis* (the logical order of salvation in its outworking in the life of the individual). Individual personal piety became a central issue. And so pietism emerged, with its concern for individual Christian experience rather than arid dogma. Christian assurance suffered. Since the promises of God were made only to those who had met the stipulated conditions, a laborious process of self-examination and introspection was needed if one was to be sure of salvation. Exponents of this view, which, although never unanimously held, gained ground from the end of the sixteenth century, lost sight of the crucial point that the covenant of grace centred upon and was fulfilled by Christ on our behalf. It is his covenant. It is not an end in itself but is simply the way through which God leads us to himself in Jesus Christ.

A further, more extreme development, was the notion of

the pre-temporal covenant of redemption, first broached by Cocceius in 1648, in which the Father and the Son were said to have covenanted together to save the human race. The Holy Spirit tended to be left out of such a model and strong elements of subordinationism were introduced in the case of the Son. Tritheistic tendencies have also been noted.[34]

Christ and election

As the biblical doctrine of covenant has its centre in Christ so also does election. Since the covenant is God's covenant, instituted by him and fulfilled in the incarnate Christ, it directs us to the sovereign purpose of God. We are brought face to face with the fact that our salvation is dependent on a decision made by God over which we had absolutely no influence. That is the meaning of Paul's statement that we were chosen in Christ before the foundation of the world (*exelexato hēmas en autō pro katabolēs kosmou*, Eph. 1:4). There is no need here to labour the point that not only Paul but Peter, John and Jesus himself all frequently attest the reality of election.[35] Rather, we are concerned with the role of Christ.

Attention has been focused on this question since Karl Barth made his major criticism of the way election had been handled. His brilliant reconstruction set in motion what has amounted to a Copernican revolution in the treatment of the doctrine. His criticism of traditional dogmatics is well summarized in the words of J. K. S. Reid:

> Christ is merely the exhibitor of a decision already made in an eternity in which He has Himself been, even if existent, at least inoperative. On the other hand, His role is to give effect to a decree, in whose formation He has apparently had no hand.[36]

A glance at standard works of systematic theology, such as those of Charles Hodge and Louis Berkhof, will make that clear. Before Barth's strictures, there was hardly a murmur on the role of Christ in election. How could this be, seeing Paul is so insistent that election is in Christ, in every context where he deals with the topic? Barth's response was to reject the idea of a decree by God-in-himself concerning 'man-in-himself', which he saw as the hallmark of orthodoxy and which bore resemblance to the Islamic notion of fate. In its place, he proposed a solution centring on the incarnate Christ. For us, there can be no God-in-himself, since he is known only in Christ. Again, only in Christ is humanity truly made known. Hence, Christ is both God who elects and man who is elected. There is no election outside Christ. In Christ, humanity is chosen and in Christ God is reprobate for us.[37] While Barth himself denied it to be a necessary implication of his teaching, it is hard to escape the conclusion that there are definite universalistic overtones here.[38] Moreover, as Berkouwer suggests, has not Barth made faith superfluous, since it is in a very objective sense that he held us to be elect in Christ?[39] Again, his vigorous christocentrism is certainly exaggerated, almost to the point of a christomonism. While his overall theology is strongly trinitarian,[40] he hardly did justice to the consistent emphasis of the New Testament that it is God who chose us and that election is particularly a work of the Father (*e.g.* Eph. 1:4). That the Son was involved is undoubtedly true, for Father, Son and Spirit are all active in all God's works. Jesus claimed the right to choose (Jn. 15:16). Yet, since the persons of the Trinity work in harmony, rather than in unison, the Father is as much the author of election as it was the Son who died on the cross or the Holy Spirit who was sent at Pentecost, neither of which latter events occurred to the exclusion of involvement of some sort by the other trinitarian hypostases. A purely christological doctrine of election robs the Father of his glory.

Barth's criticism of Reformed orthodoxy is, however, justified up to a point. Prior to the Arminian controversy of the early seventeenth century, it had been customary for theologians in the Reformed churches to link election and christology. Thus, Calvin could describe Christ as the mirror of election, so that if we wanted to know if we were elect we should look no further than him.[41] Again, John Knox (*c.* 1514–72) in the Scots Confession (1560) refers to election when asking why Christ had to have two natures, and when he discusses election he points to the union of deity and humanity in Christ![42] The Second Helvetic Confession

(1566), Zanchius, Polanus and others also followed in similar vein.[43] The picture changed, however, once Arminius appeared on the scene. Arminius (1560–1609), reacting against the rationalistic supralapsarianism of his teacher, Theodore Beza, recast the doctrine of election along christo-centric lines. God first elects Christ as the foundation of election. Then he decrees to save all who repent and believe, and finally to damn all who are impenitent. In other words, election for Arminius was on the basis of God's foreknow-ledge of our faith.[44] His views, together with those of his followers, were rejected at the Synod of Dort (1618–1619). In short, Arminius saw election not as a sovereign act of God, as God choosing us, but instead as his foreseeing that we would choose him. Additionally, by questioning perseverance, Arminius and his followers were seen as undermining assur-ance of salvation, since they did not rule out the possibility of an elect person falling finally from grace. For these reasons, talk of Christ as the foundation of election was thereafter suspect in the Reformed churches. Arminius had stolen the idea. His construction was itself open to objections, however, for God was seen to elect on the basis of the work of Christ, an idea akin to the false notion that the wrathful Father was appeased by a loving Christ. In both cases a wedge is driven between the Father and the Son, with obvious implications for the doctrine of God. Because of the unhelpful direction of Arminius' notion of Christ as foundation of election, the whole idea had come to be unacceptable for Reformed theo-logy. When Martinius of Bremen unwittingly proposed Christ as foundation of election on the floor of the Synod of Dort, the conservative Gomarus challenged him to a duel![45]

Hence, Barth's criticisms have force from the seventeenth century on but before that time they are wide of the mark. Nevertheless, since his discussion of the question no sensible treatment of election can fail to address the *en Christō* dimen-sion. In Ephesians 1:4, for instance, we should see Paul's comments in the light of his regarding the whole of salvation, as he defines it in verses 3–14 and 2:1–10, existing in Christ (note the constant repetition of the cryptic phrases *en autō, en hō* or *en Christō*). Thus, our entire salvation is received in Christ, election included. Union with Christ is existent at the point of our election in eternity. It is not something separable and so following at a later time, as Charles Hodge and Louis Berkhof argued in their respective volumes of systematic theology. In chapter 4 we will deal with this matter further. We can only hint at the immense pastoral implications of a connection between election and union with Christ. For those troubled by election the solution is not found in a protracted introspection. It lies, as Calvin insisted, in looking to Christ in whom our election consists. Is that why it is never a problem in the Bible? Is that why Paul always discusses it in a context of joyous confidence, and intends it to be a source of comfort?

Summary

Christ is central to the biblical doctrines of both covenant and election. Both are ways of bringing us to him. The entire plan of salvation, from the purpose of God in eternity to its out-working in human history, comes to focus in Jesus of Nazareth. Just as the work of Christ cannot be separated from his person, so what he did and who he is are right at the heart of the biblical message. Christology is the heartbeat of the Christian faith. In thinking of the work of Christ we will be considering the very nature of Christianity. Our whole salvation is bound up with this question. To this vital task we now turn.

3

CHRIST AND THE KINGDOM
OF GOD

A central feature of Jesus' ministry was the kingdom of God. Even a cursory glance at the gospels will demonstrate that. It is so clearly of paramount importance for Jesus' understanding of what he had come to do that it is essential for us to make an attempt to find out what he meant by it and then to set it in the context of his overall work. Today this task is doubly urgent. The topic has been the subject of lively debate. In Latin American liberation theology the theme assumes dominant proportions. Its resulting conclusions pose a serious challenge to the theology and the practice of the church.

Jesus and the kingdom

Right at the start, we note that Matthew's use of 'the kingdom of heaven' is interchangeable with Mark's and Luke's reference to 'the kingdom of God'. The expression 'kingdom of heaven' is peculiar to Matthew but he does also use 'kingdom of God' on a handful of occasions (Mt. 12:28; 19:24; 21:31, 43). A comparison of the usage of the two terms, however, shows no subtle distinctions between them. What Matthew's phrase may demonstrate is that the focus is not on a realm in which rule is exercised but on the reign which God himself has over the world.[1] Secondly, the preponderance of references are to the kingdom belonging to the Father or simply to God. Jesus appears to distance himself from the reign which God exercises. His teaching is therefore focused on something and someone other than himself. Indeed, his first announcement in his ministry, according to Mark, was 'The time has come, ... The kingdom of God is near. Repent and believe the good news!' (Mk. 1:15). Whatever it may mean, the kingdom of God was a very important theme for Jesus. It was the heart of the post-resurrection instruction he gave his apostles (Acts 1:3). Not that this was anything remarkably new. After all, when Jesus began his ministry it was with the simple declaration of the nearness of God's kingdom.

Such a message presupposed an understanding of God's kingdom and what it was. The startling thing about it was that this kingdom was at hand, and this demanded immediate repentance by Israel. This theme was present in some sense in the understanding of Israel in the time of Jesus. Its background most probably lay in the Old Testament itself. We recall Daniel's vision of the overthrow of successive human kingdoms by a stone cut without hands, which in turn became a kingdom that endured for ever (Dn. 2:31–45). Another vision of Daniel is of everlasting dominion being given to the Son of Man (Dn. 7:9–14). Both visions referred to circumstances in the future in relation to Daniel's day. Again, a vibrant expectation developed in the Old Testament that Yahweh himself would come to deliver his people.[2] Jesus was, in fact, telling Israel that this time had actually come.

What did Jesus mean when he said 'the kingdom of God is at hand'? Immense debate has surrounded this question. Did he teach that the reign of God was actually present in its fulness? Or did he simply mean that it was drawing near but had not yet arrived? In other words, was it something completely present or wholly future? A growing consensus has developed in recent years that neither of these alternatives fits the picture. In fact, to be true to the teaching of Jesus we must recognize aspects in which the kingdom of God is already present and other ways in which it is still a reality to be consummated in the future. There is, in short, a tension between the 'already' and the 'not yet'. It will be useful to look briefly at both these elements of Jesus' teaching in turn.[3]

Firstly, there are ways in which Jesus sees the kingdom of God as already present. His comment in Mark 1:15 is prefaced by his declaration that 'the time is fulfilled'. In essence, Jesus claims that the whole period of preparation had now come to fruition. The days of expectation were over. The kingdom was not merely near. It was a present reality. Moreover, Jesus relates the overthrow of demonic powers, seen in the exorcisms he performed, to the presence of the kingdom (Mt. 12:28; Lk. 11:20):

> But if I drive out demons by the Spirit of God, then the kingdom of God has come upon you (Mt. 12:28).

He tells parables which stress the hidden, yet present, dynamic of growth in the kingdom (Mt. 13:1–46). The kingdom is of incalculable value (Mt. 13:44–46; Lk. 17:20–21; 15:4–32), so much so that it is worth selling all to have it. There are signs Jesus performs which point to the kingdom of God. These could hardly refer to something absent (Mt. 11:5–6; Lk. 7:22–23). The prophets and righteous people of the old covenant had longed to see what Jesus' disciples had seen. They looked forward to the fulfilment of the promise. The disciples saw the reality of the kingdom at first hand:

> But blessed are your eyes because they see, and your ears because they hear. For I tell you the truth, many prophets and righteous men longed to see what you see but did not see it, and to hear what you hear but did not hear it (Mt. 13:16–17).

Even John the Baptist is in an inferior position. Those who now live in the age in which God himself has come to deliver his people are thus in a place of greater privilege (Mt. 11:11–13). As such, Jesus is the one on whom the kingdom of God is focused. As Beasley-Murray indicates, he is seen as the initiator, instrument, representative, bearer, revealer and mediator of the kingdom of God.[4]

Secondly, we also notice that the kingdom of God is described in terms which put it in the future. For instance, the disciples are taught to pray 'Your kingdom come'(Mt. 6:10; Lk. 11:2). Jesus talks of the appearance of the kingdom of God in power as a definitely future event (Mk. 9:1; Mt. 16:28; Lk. 9:27). He describes it as a feast at which Abraham, Isaac and Jacob will sit down to eat with many from the far corners of the earth but from which some of those who expected to be present will be excluded (Mt. 8:11–12; Lk. 13:28–29). In the Sermon on the Mount, Jesus says the poor (in spirit) and those who are persecuted for righteousness shall inherit the kingdom of God. In the account in Luke 6:20–26 there is a strong future orientation. The blessings of the kingdom of God are counter to the way things appear in the present. Those who now weep, who are poor and oppressed will (*in the future*) receive the blessing of God:

> Blessed are you who are poor, for yours is the kingdom of God. Blessed are you who hunger now, for you will be satisfied. Blessed are you who weep now, for you will laugh ... But woe to you who are rich, for you have already received your comfort. Woe to you who are well fed now, for you will go hungry. Woe to you who laugh now, for you will mourn and weep (Lk. 6:20–21, 24–25).

Again, many of Jesus' parables tell of the kingdom coming as the result of a long and imperceptible process of growth (Mt. 13:1–9, 24–33, 47–50; Mk. 4:1–9, 26–32; Lk. 13:18–21), or as an event that will take place at the end of the world (Mt. 25:1–30; Lk. 19:11–27).

It appears that Jesus understood the kingdom of God as a powerful demonstration of the rule of God, in line with the Old Testament expectation of his coming to deliver his people. From one perspective, the kingdom was already present with his own coming. In another sense, only the end of the world would finally make clear all that is implied in the reality of the kingdom. This is brought to light in Jesus' dialogue with the disciples of John the Baptist as they relay the anxious questions of their mentor (Mt. 11:1–14). John, in prison, was growing unsure of Jesus. Jesus' response was to point to his miracles of healing, and to his preaching of good news to the poor. He cites Isaiah 35:5–6 and 61:1 in support of his own messianic ministry. He omits, however, all reference to judgment, to 'the day of vengeance of our God'. John's own preaching had focused on the necessity of repentance and the imminence of judgment. Jesus points to his works of grace and mercy to the oppressed. Does he reject judgment? Hardly so, for his teaching is full of it. What is apparent is that John's vision of the kingdom had encapsulated the entire process of grace and judgment. Jesus made clear to him that the judgment lay ahead in the future, that there were elements of the kingdom of God that were not to be realized for a while yet. John was inhibited by his own perspective. He stood outside the kingdom looking in. He belonged to the age of preparation and thus saw everything telescoped together into one, much as an observer may see a mountain and its nearer foothills as one massive prominence. In reality, there were two mountain peaks (grace and judgment) separated by a wide area of intervening land John was unable to see.

The relation of the kingdom to Israel and to the Gentiles is prominent in Jesus' teaching, and it is a noticeable theme in Matthew in particular. We have seen already how the background is the Old Testament hope of deliverance through the coming of Yahweh. It is interesting that Matthew portrays Jesus as the royal Messiah in his opening genealogy. He is the promised Son of David who would rule over the house of Israel for ever and the seed of Abraham through whom all nations are to be blessed (Mt. 1:1–17). As such, all the covenant promises of God are fulfilled in him. It is in this context that the angel announces that Jesus is to save his people from their sins (Mt. 1:21) and that he is 'God with us' (Mt. 1:23). His experience as an infant bears striking resemblance to that of Moses. He is rescued from a decree requiring all male children to be killed and is sent into exile (Mt. 2:13–18); he is a greater Moses leading his people to deliverance. All this is set in the context of God's historical dealings with Israel. Yet the forward focus of the gospel is towards a kingdom of God that expressly includes the Gentiles. Gentile magi come to honour him (Mt. 2:1–12). In fact, many of Israel will be excluded while a whole host will come from east and west, north and south, to sit down and eat with Abraham, Isaac and Jacob (Mt. 8:11–12). There will be unity and continuity with the past yet the future will be more extensive, its sweep embracing the entire world. In line with this, the Roman centurion is singled out as an example of faith (Mt. 8:5–13) as is the Canaanite woman (Mt. 15:21–28). Peter's confession of faith occurs at Caesarea Philippi, at the junction of Israel and the nations (Mt. 16:13–18) . . . and so on. At the end of the gospel, the risen Christ tells his apostles to make disciples of all nations (Mt. 28:19–20), baptizing them into the one covenant name of Father, Son and Holy Spirit, the new covenant inaugurated by Jesus' blood extending through the entire world and not being restricted to Israel alone.

The nature of the kingdom

As we have seen, the kingdom of God is the rule or reign of God, inaugurated with the coming of Jesus Christ but not fully consummated until his return at the end of the world. We have not yet, however, considered of what this kingdom consists. We know that it is the fulfilment of the Old Testament covenant expectations. It is the focus of Jesus' post-resurrection teaching to his apostles, which argues for it being the virtual equivalent of the apostles' own message. It is helpful to consider here the proposals of liberation theology, since these are highly provocative and can assist us in developing a coherent grasp of the question for ourselves.

Latin American liberation theology has agreed that the kingdom of God was inaugurated with the coming of Jesus. It goes on to claim that it consists in a preferential love by God for the poor. The background of this movement lies in the extreme social and economic inequalities in many parts of Latin America. Frequently, significant sections of the population have been deprived of the basic necessities of life while rich and powerful élites are concerned simply with bolstering their own position of privilege. This has been the pastoral context in which the mainly Roman Catholic theologians of liberation theology have worked. The need to frame a relevant, practical Christianity has been glaringly obvious. On the other hand, traditional theology has been seen to bolster social injustice. This is so because of its refusal to address critically social and economic problems. Its bias to theoretical intellectual dogma has discouraged active participation in the struggle against oppression. Silence in the face of such evil has only reinforced the ruling élites. Liberation theologians have often felt forced to look elsewhere for analytical tools with which to combat these problems, and Marxist theory has frequently been used. Its positive attraction is obvious. It is concerned with changing the world in concrete social ways. For liberation theologians, the corollary has been to view sin primarily in terms of social and corporate injustice and to see redemption as liberation from such injustice.

The beatitudes are popular with liberation theologians. There Jesus pronounces blessing on 'the poor in spirit' (Mt. 5:3) and 'the poor' (Lk. 6:20), for 'theirs' (Mt.)/'yours' (Lk.) is the kingdom of God. The difference in wording may be important. Luke's reference to 'the poor' seems to support a bias to the poor by God. Matthew's reference to 'the poor in spirit' appears to focus on the prime need for spiritual poverty, such as humility. Did Matthew spiritualize a Lucan original? Did Jesus use different phrases at different times, like a preacher using the same illustration in differing ways to different congregations? Luke's use of the second person is a departure from the normal use in blessings at this time. Does that point to his sources reflecting the original? If so, may that again give priority to his phrase 'the poor' over Matthew's 'poor in spirit'? In both passages, the pronouns 'theirs' (*autōn*) (Mt.) and 'yours' (*hymetera*) (Lk.) are in a place of emphasis, possibly reflecting that the kingdom belongs to the poor/poor in spirit and to them alone.[5] Luke, however, records the beatitudes being given to Jesus' own disciples (Lk. 6:19). That places the blessing on the poor squarely in the context of discipleship. It is to the disciples who are poor, who are hungry, who weep and who are persecuted because of the Son of Man, that the kingdom of God belongs.[6]

63

The issue of bias to the poor is, however, to be decided on a wider level than the above point of exegesis alone. For liberation theologians such as Gutiérrez, Segundo and Sobrino[7] the case rests on a number of interlocking supports. They all point to Jesus attesting that the kingdom is now a present, albeit incomplete, reality. They maintain that it was not only a matter affecting the inner person but included the restructuring of visible social relationships. Jesus moved in a situation of conflict. His association with the lowly and with sinners attracted the hatred of Israel's ruling class. This élite was organized around rabbinical education and the cultus of the temple. It was a religious élite that had economic and political power concentrated in its hands and had used its privilege to reduce the poor utterly in status, by depriving them of the rabbinical instruction that was the hallmark of acceptance. In the face of this, Jesus identified with the poor. He lived a life of poverty. He attacked injustice and oppression. His onslaught on sin was directed mainly against its corporate form. He aroused the murderous opposition of the élite. Throughout, he was in solidarity with the poor, recognizing that they were more sinned against than sinning. The poor heard him gladly. The rich and powerful, perceiving themselves to be under political threat, did him to death. In turn, the church, if it is to be faithful to the reality of the kingdom, must live in solidarity with the poor and the marginalized, recognizing that God has a preferential love for them. The church has the task, then, of struggling against the structures which cause poverty and injustice. These structures enhance the privilege of the ruling class. For the kingdom of God to be consummated in human history it is necessary that the poor be liberated.

Liberation theology highlights some glaring and woeful inadequacies in the theology of Western Europe and North America. Due to the impact of a dualistic world-view, inherited latterly from Kant, the inner world of the soul has been hermetically sealed from contact with the material framework of creation. Consequently, the church has concentrated on the 'spiritual' at the expense of the 'material'. As a result, the gospel (and the concept of the kingdom of God) has been understood as having primary bearing on personal individual sin and therefore on personal individual piety, to the neglect (and frequently to the exclusion) of the world of politics and everyday life. A sacred/secular dichotomy has ruled. Consequently, the focus of liberation theology on praxis (practice, doing), and thus on the issues of poverty and corporate sin, is to be welcomed. The universe is God's creation and God's rule extends throughout the world. Our personal salvation is part of a redemption that includes the whole person, the whole cosmos and therefore the whole of our social relationships. Therefore, the kingdom of God cannot be restricted arbitrarily to the inner life. It governs our whole life, as individuals and in community. Does not the eighth commandment 'You shall not steal' tell us that economic exploitation is a sin and therefore to be opposed? Is there not a wholistic unity in the Bible between belief and action that has been split apart by the Western intellectual tradition and to which liberation theology would redirect us? Is not that part of the message of Jesus in his preaching of the kingdom?

The claim of Latin American liberation theology is equally truncated, however, although in somewhat different directions. Its message looks to the future in the hope that a struggle against corporate injustice will one day succeed, and it is hard to see in it the New Testament stress on Christ as having already achieved salvation in his death and resurrection. Even if injustice of this kind were to be swept aside, would that of itself eliminate the problem of human sin? Moreover, the risen Christ's instructions to his apostles focused on the kingdom of God (Acts 1:3). The apostles' teaching itself is therefore the unfolding of all that is implied in Jesus' own message about the kingdom. Social and economic issues, however, while present at times explicitly and more often by implication in the teaching of the apostles, do not figure as dominantly as they do in liberation theology and therefore cannot be said to be as overwhelming in Jesus' own teaching about the kingdom as its exponents would have us believe. We agree that they are present, since they are an important part of life and so are to be subject to the reign of God. And as we have noted, liberation theology is voicing necessary concerns. Its message is a vital corrective to the truncated gospel that has too often been evident in the

Western world. What we dispute is the overwhelming pre-dominance it accords to economic and political factors.

What, then, is the kingdom of God? It is nothing less than the reign of God in human affairs. It is inaugurated with the coming of Jesus. His teaching and ministry, his message of the kingdom, all point forward to the climactic event of his death and resurrection. After he rose from the dead he taught his apostles about the kingdom of God. Consequently, their own teaching was an elaboration of the central message of the kingdom as it had been taught by Jesus and as it had been given new and decisive significance by his death and resurrection. Just as for Jesus himself, however, the full manifestation of the kingdom of God lay in the future, at the time of harvest when the Son of Man was to come to judge the nations, so too with the apostles the ultimate fruit of the death and resurrection of Christ still lies ahead in the indefinite future, when he returns. There is still the perspective of the 'already' and the 'not yet'.

This reign of God extends across the whole gamut of human life. The ethics of the kingdom certainly impinge on the inner life of human beings. Jesus applies the decalogue to inner attitudes to God and to other people. Rather than relaxing its demands, he intensifies them. The commandment 'You shall not kill' relates not only to murder but also applies to malicious anger and hatred of one's fellow human beings (Mt. 5:21–22). The reign of God operates over thoughts as well as deeds. At the same time, God's kingdom also has its rightful place over social and corporate life. The scribes and Pharisees are singled out by Jesus for withering condemnation as groups. Their characteristic sins are flood-lighted with ruthless zeal. Despite the general popularity of the Pharisees in Israel (after all, most of them were laymen rather than religious professionals) Jesus does not mince his words. Marital relationships, child care, business ethics, political responsibilities and financial matters are some of the areas he indicates as subject to God's reign. The work of God in our salvation extends to the renewal of society and the cosmos. As such, the kingdom of God as proclaimed by Jesus and elaborated in the teaching of the apostles is as extensive in its claim as the whole of human life.

The healing miracles as signs of the kingdom

According to the Old Testament, the Messiah was to liberate the oppressed, give sight to the blind, hearing to the deaf and mobility to the lame (Is. 35:5f.; 61:1–2). The arrival of the kingdom of God was to be the occasion for deliverance, liberation and fulfilment. Judgment would also take place. In Isaiah 61:2, the anointed one was also to proclaim 'the day of vengeance of our God'. In Malachi 3:1–4, the messenger of the covenant was to purify the Levites. His coming was to be terrible in its justice, purging the covenant community like fire. When John the Baptist sent his disciples to question Jesus concerning his true identity, Jesus replied in terms of this Old Testament expectation. He was indeed the coming one since he was doing the works of the kingdom, healing and giving sight. We saw that the point John needed to hear was that judgment lay ahead in the more distant future and was not to come at once, as he had supposed.

The gospel records are full of accounts of dramatic healings, and so too is Acts. Indeed, Luke describes his gospel as the record 'of all that Jesus began to do and to teach' (Acts 1:1), implying that the teaching and deeds of the apostles were the continuation of Jesus' earthly ministry. That is why Peter and Paul include their own testimony as part of the gospel message. God takes up their witness to Christ's death and resurrection into the gospel message itself. The healing miracles of the apostles should be seen in conjunction with those of Jesus as collectively bearing witness to the coming of the kingdom of God.

It is important to note the overall theological context of the miraculous in the history of revelation. In the Old Testament, miracles are not scattered throughout but occur unevenly. The principal occasions where miraculous activity takes place are during the time between the exodus and the conquest, and also at the start of the prophetic era in the ministries of Elijah and Elisha. Even more significant is the conjunction between miracle and outbursts of eventually inscripturated revelation. The uneven distribution of miracles is not haphazard. Miracles occur at times when fresh revelation is given by God. Moreover, fresh revelation itself is associated

67

with acts of redemptive power by Yahweh. There is a correlation between redemptive deed and revelatory word throughout, attended in turn by miraculous signs. These interventions are consequently not spectacles in their own right. They are pointers to something else, signposts to the redemptive works of the living God of Israel. Along these lines, it is hardly surprising if at the climax of God's works and ways in salvation there should be a fresh, and even more pronounced, occurrence of the miraculous. The coming of God's own Son was his supreme self-revelation. He came to save his people. This was the event to which the whole of Scripture had pointed. The miracles of healing and deliverance which Jesus did, and which the apostles performed in his name, were the apex of the biblical pattern of signs witnessing to the salvation of God.

If this connection between redemptive deed, revelatory word and miraculous sign is valid, there are a number of corollaries. First, Christ (as we shall see later) has achieved a complete salvation. Nothing additional is needed. He left no theological deficit to be made up. All that God continues to do for us now is an outflow of what he achieved in the incarnate Christ. No further redemptive deeds can add to that. Thus also, God's revelatory words are complete too. Holy Scripture is sufficient for our salvation (2 Tim. 3:16–17). Christ's ministry, in person and through his apostles, is complete. Of course, God continues to apply the fruit of his labour to us continually by the Holy Spirit. Nevertheless, if this is valid (which historic Christianity has affirmed that it is) further displays of the miraculous in the above sense are unnecessary and theologically superfluous. It could be said that we now live in 'the age of the Spirit' and so the miraculous is to be expected on an ongoing basis. Of course, God is free to do whatever he chooses. It would be foolish to argue that miracles cannot occur or even that they do not occur. We are, it is emphatically true, in 'the age of the Spirit'. Yet, the Spirit's chief work is to testify of Christ. He does this through the Scriptures he inspired and through the teaching of the apostles whom he empowered and who were appointed by Christ himself to be witnesses of his own resurrection. After Christ there is no theological deficit to be filled in. God's supreme revelation, his unsurpassable action took place in him.

Prominent features of our Lord's healing miracles are as follows. Firstly, we note his sovereignty in healing. He did not heal everyone. He delivered only one of very many at the pool of Bethesda (Jn. 5:1f.) and left the rest disabled. The cripple at the temple healed by Peter and John (Acts 3:1–10) had begged there every day for years. Jesus had been a frequent visitor to the temple. Evidently, Jesus had ignored the crippled beggar despite his pleas. Secondly, there exists a frequent connection between healings and faith. This is not uniform. Of ten lepers healed on one occasion, only one returns to thank Jesus. Sometimes a man is healed in connection with the faith of others. The paralytic lowered through the roof is healed and his sins forgiven because of the faith of his friends (Mt. 9:1–8; Mk. 2:1–12; Lk. 5:17–26)![8] There is also a connection between healing and the forgiveness of sins, as in the above incident. Thirdly, the miracles are primarily signs. Indeed, one of the most frequent words for the miraculous in the New Testament (*sēmeion*), means just that. As such they point us not to themselves but to something else, much as a signpost directs us to a destination other than itself. They are, as Jesus told John the Baptist, signs of the kingdom of God, of his own messianic credentials. They point to the fulfilment of the age of preparation: 'The time has come. The kingdom of God is at hand. Repent and believe the gospel.' This was a unique time. Jesus was a unique person. The events surrounding his ministry and its attestation by the apostles were also unique.[9] Fourthly, while it is interesting to relate the miracles of Jesus to the theology of his person, we need to be careful that we see them more in the redemptive-historical sense I have just described. Donald Baillie's suggestion that these were works of Jesus' human nature deserves further consideration (Mt. 9:8 tends to support it), but it has something of a Nestorian flavour, as if the two natures of Christ can be separated and considered in isolation. Surely, the miracles were works of the person of Christ first and foremost, as the Chalcedonian dogma would tell us?[10] Fifthly and finally, we should note that the miracles as signs of the kingdom of God did not of themselves bring about a great surge of faith. When Jesus died, he died alone. Even after his resurrection, his disciples numbered a paltry 120. Jesus expressly taught that if people did not believe the Old Testament Scriptures, the greatest of all miracles would not persuade them to change (Lk. 16:27–31; *cf.* Jn. 5:45–47). Certainly, there were some who attached themselves to the disciples because they were impressed by Jesus' miraculous power. Jesus did not commit himself to them, however, for he knew about human nature and saw that their allegiance was superficial and untrue (Jn. 2:23–25).

Why does the theme disappear in the rest of the New Testament?

Outside the synoptic gospels there are strikingly few references to the kingdom of God. Whereas Jesus centred his preaching on the kingdom, the apostles draw attention to Jesus Christ. This has sometimes been seen as a major conflict. In short, it has been claimed that Paul and the others distorted the central message of Jesus about the fatherhood of God and the necessity of love, into a religion about Jesus.[11] This claim, however, is based largely on the superficial question of the presence or absence of a particular phrase. We have seen how the eschatological tension in the synoptic presentation of the kingdom is directly related to the relationship between the death and resurrection of Christ on the one hand and his parousia on the other. The kingdom is present, yet awaits fulfilment. It is determined by the decisive event of the cross and resurrection. Yet the full outworking of his death and resurrection will not occur until his return. As a consequence, we are in a situation of existing fulfilment and provisionality simultaneously. In that sense, the focus of the apostle Paul, for instance, can be seen to be on the fuller implications of the crucial event of the death and resurrection of Christ, which from the perspective of Jesus before the resurrection was rather a towering event that lay ahead in the future. The difference is one of perspective.

For Jesus himself, his impending death and resurrection was to be the great turning point of his mission. In Matthew 16:21f., the question comes to light immediately after the account of Peter's confession of faith at Caesarea Philippi. At this decisive point, where recognition has dawned on the disciples concerning Jesus' identity, he begins to explain to them what is going to happen to him in Jerusalem. It is the beginning of a new stage of instruction. Following his rebuke of Peter for his well-meaning attempt to prevent it, Jesus lays down some clear and stringent guidelines for discipleship and points to his imminent appearance in his kingdom. In Mark 9:31 Jesus tells his disciples privately about his forth-coming death and resurrection but they fail to grasp its significance. Evidently, they were filled with foreboding, unwilling or unable to ask further. In Luke 18:31–34, they are seen simply as failing to understand what Jesus' comments were about. The meaning was hidden from them:

> Jesus took the Twelve aside and told them, 'We are going up to Jerusalem, and everything that is writ-ten by the prophets about the Son of Man will be fulfilled. He will be turned over to the Gentiles. They will mock him, insult him, spit on him, flog him and kill him. On the third day he will rise again.' The disciples did not understand any of this. Its meaning was hidden from them, and they did not know what he was talking about.

Again, Jesus has told them privately. It was not something intended for public consumption. Only after the resurrection did they recall what he had said and the picture began to fit together. The angel at the tomb reminded the women of Jesus' predictions (Lk. 24:5–7). At that point his words came back to them and they began to fit them into their overall frame of reference. Before, those words had seemed enig-matic, anomalous. Perhaps, their threatening nature had led the disciples to refuse to believe them, to banish the thoughts from their conscious mind. The risen Christ, however, rebukes the two disciples in Luke 24:20–27 for their failure to grasp what he had told them. In fact, he points them to the Scriptures which had clearly foreshadowed these events. The disciples' obtuseness may have been reason enough why Jesus was not more explicit about the meaning of the cross. His

71

practice was to temper his teaching to the capacity of those taught. Whatever the explanation, for Jesus his death and resurrection mark the decisive stage in his ministry and the point at which the kingdom of God finds its inception in the world.

Support for this is found in the apostles' teaching immediately after the resurrection. The sermons of Peter and Paul in Acts focus centrally on the resurrection of Christ. The essence of the gospel is seen to consist in God having raised Christ from the dead in fulfilment of Scripture (Acts 2:14–36; 3:12–16; 17:2–3). Paul says the same to the Corinthians (1 Cor. 15:3–4) as does Peter again (1 Pet. 1:10–12). They all see a decisive change taking place with the resurrection. It is the centre of world history, marking the start of a new creation (2 Cor. 5:17). Yet at the same time we wait until the parousia for the full outworking of the resurrection. We live in a time of fulfilment, but a fulfilment that is still provisional.

There are few specific references in Paul to 'the kingdom of God'. Those that do occur show the same tension that we have noted. On the one hand, Paul sees the kingdom of God as a present reality. It consists of righteousness, peace and joy in the Holy Spirit (Rom. 14:17). All these realities he considers as existent now. The righteousness of God has been revealed (Rom. 1:16–17). Christ has brought peace with God (Rom 5:1; *cf.* Eph. 2:11–22). The Holy Spirit has been poured into our hearts (Rom. 5:5). God has already transferred us from the kingdom of darkness into the kingdom of his Son (Col. 1:13). On the other hand, Paul also looks to the future for the kingdom of God. Immoral people will be debarred from entry into that kingdom (1 Cor. 6:9–10; Gal. 5:21; Eph. 5:5), which strongly suggests that admission as a subject of the kingdom will occur after one's current lifetime is complete. A second major feature of Paul's treatment of the kingdom is his equating it with the gospel, or more specifically with the gospel in its widest dimension as the entire will of God expressed for our salvation. Thus, in his farewell address to the Ephesian elders Paul can describe his preaching as consisting of 'the kingdom' and also, in the same breath, as 'all the counsel of God' (Acts 20:25, 27). The terms are evidently interchangeable. Therefore, the synoptics' theme of 'the kingdom of God' becomes identified with the sum total of apostolic teaching after the resurrection. This is fully in line with the post-resurrection instruction which Jesus gave his apostles.

In a narrow sense, Paul's focus on the kingdom theme becomes sharper and clearer, despite the fact that the characteristic phraseology of the synoptics is largely absent. The point to note is that, with his resurrection, Christ is raised to the right hand of God and invested with full authority over the entire cosmos (Mt. 28:18). That marks the climax of Matthew's gospel; the kingdom theme, traced throughout, is fully expressed in Jesus' elevation to supreme authority. So, for Paul, Jesus is appointed Son of God with power since the resurrection (Rom. 1:3–4). He is exalted to supremacy (Eph. 1:18–22; Phil. 2:9–11; Col. 1:15–20). The writer of Hebrews agrees that with his resurrection Jesus became 'the heir of all things' (Heb. 1:1–4). Therefore, the image changes. It is no longer simply the kingdom of God that is centre stage. Instead, the mediatorial kingdom of Christ bursts into view. As the new covenant is a revelation of the Trinity of God, so God's kingdom is not seen as rule by an undifferentiated monad but as a trinitarian phenomenon. Nowhere is this more evident than in 1 Corinthians 15:20–28. Paul, in discussing Christ's resurrection and ours indicates that, whereas his has already occurred, ours will take place in the indefinite future, when Christ comes back (verses 20–23). At his return we shall rise, death will finally be abolished and Christ will then hand the kingdom back to the Father (verses 24–28). Hence, Paul considers Christ to be reigning now. Indeed, he cites Psalm 110:1 in reference to his current exaltation (verses 25, 27). His reign is therefore circumscribed temporally. It begins with his resurrection and enthronement. Its terminus is his return. It will then revert to God the Father. The purpose of Christ's mediatorial reign is therefore to subdue his enemies. Death is the last enemy, already dealt the death blow in Christ's resurrection, but to be eliminated finally when he comes back. The apostle envisages a progressive triumph by Christ over all his enemies. His kingdom is the reality in which the church functions here and now.

Although the kingdom of God/Christ includes the church as a central and key component, it is not to be identified with it. The kingdom is extensive over the entire cosmos. Roman Catholic theology has typically tended to merge the two. The answer to that is that the church is not the world. Certainly, its role is crucial. The church is, in one sense, Christ's storm troopers, spearheading the progress of the kingdom. But that reign extends over computer-software manufacturers, governments, golf clubs, local education authorities, hospitals, egg producers and scientific research, besides the banking and insurance industries. Since Christ reigns and rules over the entire cosmos as mediator of creation, no aspect of life, public or private, is outside his rightful authority. On the other hand, dispensationalism radically separated church and kingdom. The kingdom was seen as relating to the nation of Israel, which was entirely separate from the church. Thus, God had one plan for Jews and quite another for Christians. Such a dichotomy represents a serious truncation of the kingdom of God. Its extent is based on the priority and hegemony of one nation. It misses the point that in the New Testament the kingdom extends to the whole world. Moreover, it forces a radical dualism between Israel and the church, based on a nature–grace dualism, whereby Israel receives earthly, material promises, while the church has spiritual blessings. We will be exploring the theme of the relation between church and cosmos more fully in chapter 10. For now, however, we point to Colossians 1:15–20 as highlighting the connection. Christ is the creator and sustainer of all things. He rose from the dead and is head of his church. His reconciling death on the cross has secured our transfer to his kingdom and is the means to the reconciliation of all things, the 'all things' which he created and sustains. Church and kingdom are neither to be confused nor separated. They are like two concentric circles within which Christ reigns supreme.

4

UNION
WITH CHRIST

The theme of union with Christ is vital to an understanding
of what he has done. It is foundational to every aspect of our
salvation. We saw in chapter 2 how it relates to election. In
this chapter we will explore its broadest connections, ranging
over the whole field of the work of Christ and its impact.

Christ's representative and vicarious role

We shall consider in detail in chapter 6 how Christ's priestly
work covered his whole life, from the manger to the cross
and beyond. We have seen already in chapter 2 how he
fulfilled the covenant demands of faithfulness for us. His
being our substitute and representative is basic to all he did.
As Irenaeus saw, the background was what happened in the
beginning with Adam. When Adam sinned, all sinned in him.
When he broke God's commandment, the whole human race
was simultaneously condemned. What he did, he did not as a
private person but for the whole race with him. In Paul's
words: '. . . just as sin entered the world through one man,
and death through sin, and in this way death came to all men,

because all sinned . . .' (Rom. 5:12). And 'the many died by the trespass of the one man' (Rom. 5:15). And again, 'by the trespass of the one man, death reigned through that one man' (Rom. 5:17).

Various attempts have been made to explain the relationship between Adam and the race. None exhaust the possibilities. In the first place, it has been interpreted in realistic terms. Adam, it is thought, possessed a universal generic human nature in which all subsequent people share and thus incur his guilt. On the other hand, John W. Nevin (1803–86) saw it in terms of biological evolution, akin to the development of an oak tree from an acorn. Thus, there was an organic connection between Adam and the race which was at the same time dynamic and progressive. All sinned in Adam because all were present in him as the oak is present in the acorn.[1] From a different perspective, covenant theology saw Adam as the legal covenantal representative of all human beings. It was not a natural or organic relationship but one established by the decree of God. Yet again, some have viewed the matter in the light of the Semitic understanding of corporate personality.

The nature of the connection between Adam and his posterity (the truth may lie in some combination of realistic and federal connections) is strictly speaking outside our present field. Crucial to the work of Christ, however, is his place as second Adam. He came to repair the damage caused by the first Adam.

> Oh, loving wisdom of our God!
>   When all was sin and shame,
> A second Adam to the fight
>   And to the rescue came. (John Henry Newman)

As such, Christ was no mere private person either. As Adam's sin had direst consequences for others, so Christ's obedience has even greater results for others too, as Romans 5:12–21 makes clear. For instance, it is striking how the outset of his public ministry is marked by temptation, not in a beautiful garden like Adam but in a desert. Whereas Adam failed the test, although everything was in his favour, Christ successfully faced it, despite the cards being stacked against him (Mt.

4:1–10). Christ as second Adam is a theme developed more by Paul than anyone else. In Romans 5:12–21 he traces the connection between their respective disobedience and obedience, and its impact on those they represented. In 1 Corinthians 15:12ff. he expounds at length the repercussions of the first and second Adam on questions of death and life. The first Adam brought death. In Christ all shall be made alive.

We will explore these themes in more detail in chapters 6 and 11. For the moment, we note that the vicarious human priesthood of Christ (Christ as man living on our behalf and representing us) has been a neglected topic. We recognize readily that he died for our sins on the cross. We are less quick to see that all his life was lived for us: his baptism, his temptations, his faith and faithfulness and so on. If Adam represented us in the garden, Christ represented us in the desert. If what Adam did was on our behalf and in our place, so also was Christ's whole life of obedient faithfulness to God.

Union with Christ through his incarnation

Our union with Christ is grounded on his union with us. We can be one with him because he made himself one with us. As always, the divine initiative comes first. Christ's union with us took place in his incarnation. The classic words of the prologue to the fourth gospel sum it up:

> In the beginning was the Word, and the Word was with God, and the Word was God. He was with God in the beginning.
> Through him all things were made; without him nothing was made that has been made . . . The Word became flesh and made his dwelling among us . . . (Jn. 1:1–3, 14).

Christ's true humanity is emphasized also in Hebrews, particularly in chapter 2 and in 4:14 – 5:10. He is said to have been tempted in all respects as we are and thus able to sympathize with us in our weakness. He did not assume the nature of angels but our own nature (Heb. 2:14–18).

The humanity of Christ was a major issue in the early

77

centuries. One of the first heresies was docetism, which denied the reality of Christ's human nature. Later, the ideas of Apollinaris had to be tackled (see chapter 1). The outcome of the christological debates was the affirmation by the Council of Chalcedon in AD 451 that Christ was not only of one substance with the Father from eternity but also was of one substance with us in terms of his humanity. The eternal Logos had assumed human nature in a real personal union such that his divine and human natures were 'without division, without separation'. Later, at the second Council of Constantinople in AD 553 the dogma of *enhypostasia* was approved, which stated that the Logos was the personalizing centre of the incarnate Christ, the human nature being assumed into union but not having any prior or independent subsistence apart from the union with the Logos. This was an attempt to testify to the identity of Jesus of Nazareth with the second person of the Trinity.

The sometimes abstruse christological debate served to underline the importance of the reality of the incarnation and its necessity for our salvation. 'What is not assumed cannot be healed', was a common claim. If there had been no genuine incarnation, we could not be saved. Sin, misery and death had ravaged the human race. Because of the revealed nature of God, what was required was for God himself to accomplish our salvation from within our own life and experience. Only a human being could atone for the sins of humanity. Only another Adam could undo the damage the first Adam had done.

The human nature Christ assumed was a particular, specific human nature, not a generic one. He was sanctified by the Holy Spirit. As Mary his mother was told by the angel:

> 'The Holy Spirit will come upon you, and the power of the Most High will overshadow you. So the holy one to be born will be called the Son of God . . .' (Lk. 1:35).

A variety of possible word orders exists for the second sentence quoted above. The thought is present, however, that the conception of Jesus was due to the action of the Holy

Spirit. The language is reminiscent of the creation account in Genesis 1, where the Spirit (or wind) of God hovered over the primeval waters. The birth of Jesus thus marks a new creation, a new beginning, equally due to the creative energies of God. The second sentence directs attention to the result that follows. The child to be born will be the Son of God and he will also be holy, set apart by God. The creative work of the Spirit will result in the sanctification of the child. He will be God's. His was to be a normal human birth, but one that was brought about by a new creative action of the Spirit.

In becoming man, Christ united himself with the human race. This follows from his sharing flesh and blood, experiencing human life from embryo through infancy and childhood to maturity. If he was truly human he was also part of the human race. At the same time, he marked a new beginning for the race. His unique conception by the Holy Spirit set him apart as the inaugurator of a new humanity of which he, as the second Adam, was head.

It is important to grasp the new dimension brought about by the second Adam, begun with his conception by the Spirit. Christ's union with humanity is not such as secures the salvation of each and every individual who ever lived. This can easily be implied when talking of Christ's union with *us*. If he became one with the race by his incarnation it seems to follow that the entire race is therefore united with him and so will be saved. The Bible speaks very clearly, however, of judgment and condemnation. It stresses the utter necessity of repentance and faith for salvation. Many have therefore been shy of talking of union with Christ in these terms for fear of encouraging universalism. Again, the inclusive use of the pronouns 'we' and 'us' has often been viewed with suspicion by evangelicals, for similar reasons. These fears are understandable. The *new* relationship of solidarity introduced by the incarnation, however, avoids such pitfalls and justifies talking of Christ identifying himself with the human race as a whole, even though every single individual will not be saved. After all, Christ is human. The Word became flesh. He was, and is for ever, one of us. In his incarnation he united himself with us, becoming the head of the redeemed human race as the second Adam.

Union with Christ effected by the Holy Spirit through faith

As far as we are concerned, union with Christ begins to be a reality when we trust Christ for salvation. This may, in some cases, be a clearly defined point in our lives, which can even be dated. In many instances, however, this is not so. Many Christians cannot identify any one time when they first trusted Christ. This diversity mirrors the experience of the earliest church. For converts from paganism, they often experienced a clear break with the past when they believed (*cf.* 1 Thes. 1:9–10). For those who were raised by believing parents, this crisis experience was often missing. Timothy, for example, appears to have known no such transition; he knew the Scriptures from infancy (2 Tim. 3:14–15). John the Baptist was sanctified from his mother's womb (Lk. 1:13–15, 41–44). Either way, the reality of union with Christ begins in our experience only at the point where we begin to trust Christ, whether that is early or late in our lives.

Union with Christ is, in fact, the foundation of all the blessings of salvation. Justification, sanctification, adoption and glorification are all received through our being united to Christ. This is the basis of what Paul says in Ephesians 1:3–14 when he outlines salvation from election to heaven. This amazing paragraph is headed by a doxology to God the Father:

> Praise be to the God and Father of our Lord Jesus Christ, who has blessed us in the heavenly realms with every spiritual blessing in Christ (verse 3).

What follows is a list of some of these 'spiritual blessings', blessings put into effect by the Spirit. We were chosen before the foundation of the world (verse 4), an election by God that took place *in him*, in Christ. In love God predestined us to adoption as children *through Jesus Christ* (verse 5). *In him* we have redemption through his blood and our sins are forgiven (verse 7). The mystery of God's will, made known to us, was purposed *in Christ* (verse 9). All things in the universe will be brought together *under the headship of Christ* (verse 10). We were chosen *in him* (verse 11). When we believed we were sealed by the Holy Spirit *in Christ* (verses 13–14), and so on. The picture is the same in 1 Corinthians 1:30–31 where Paul states that our wisdom, righteousness, sanctification and redemption is found *in Christ*. Salvation consists in being made alive with Christ and sitting with him in the heavenly places (Eph. 2:1ff.). Our life is hidden with Christ in God (Col. 3:1–4). The whole process of the application of salvation to us by the Holy Spirit (what has been known as the *ordo salutis* – the order of salvation) fits in here as part of what it means to be united with Jesus Christ.

This is indeed the crucial point as far as we are existentially concerned. As Calvin argued, all that Christ has done is of no avail to us until the Holy Spirit applies it to us personally. This he does through faith, which Calvin goes on to say is the principal work of the Holy Spirit.[2] Thus, union with Christ is brought into effect in our own experience through faith and its inseparable companion repentance. This offsets the idea that Christ's union with us in his incarnation leads to universalism. Where union with Christ surfaces in our experience, repentance and faith are always present. In that sense, without repentance and faith, union with Christ does not exist. The Holy Spirit is the author of faith. Repentance is a gift granted to us by the grace of God (*cf.* Acts 11:18). Union with Christ is brought about in our life experience by the Spirit's work. The Spirit himself is sent by the risen Christ. Consequently, Christ unites us to himself by the Spirit and, in so doing, enables us to entrust ourselves into his hands.

Union with Christ exists in faith but it is also connected in the New Testament with baptism. One reason for this is that baptism marks the start of the Christian life. In the New Testament baptism was administered at the point at which a person was regarded as a Christian. There was no lengthy period of waiting. Nor was baptism seen as an optional extra. It was given to all who professed faith, right on the spot. To those who consider that the children of believers were also baptized, baptism would also have been given to such children in their earliest infancy by virtue of their belonging to the church in the covenant of grace through solidarity with believing parents. Therefore there is a theological connection between faith and baptism. Or, from another perspective, the outset of the Christian life is marked by faith on the one hand and baptism on the other, so that the two are integrally related. Hence, union with Christ is brought into close conjunction with baptism by Paul in passages such as Romans 6:1ff., 1 Corinthians 10:1ff. and Colossians 2:11–13. The connection is summarized very concisely in 1 Corinthians 12:13:

> For we were all baptised by one Spirit into one body
> – whether Jews or Greeks, slave or free – and we
> were all given the one Spirit to drink.

Baptism, the Spirit, membership of the body of Christ and thus union with Christ its head: all are connected by an intimate theological nexus.

This does not mean that baptism conveys grace automatically, as the Roman Catholic Church has taught. The efficacy of baptism is that of the Holy Spirit. Paul makes abundantly clear the vital place of faith. Baptism requires faith. Apart from the Spirit's grace it is merely a ritual. On the other hand, the Spirit works graciously in and through baptism. Again, there is no evidence of a specifically temporal relation between baptism, faith, the Spirit and union with Christ, as if a definitely prescribed order has to take place. The connections are theological rather than temporal. In other words, union with Christ is the source of all the blessings of salvation. This union is effected by the Holy Spirit. The Spirit unites us to Christ by faith. This whole process comes to expression in baptism.

What is the nature of union with Christ as we experience it during the course of our life history? There are a number of different ways in which it is expressed. First of all, Christ as the second Adam is our representative. He obeyed God on our behalf. His obedience therefore is ours. Correspondingly, we are in a relation of solidarity with him. All he did was for us. When he did it we were regarded by God as in him, and thus sharing in all that he achieved. This is a relation of legal and corporate solidarity (Rom. 5:12–21).

Secondly, there is another dimension of a more dynamic kind. In this sense, what Christ did has a powerful effect upon us, changing and reshaping us from within by the power of the Holy Spirit. Thus Paul can speak of our being raised with Christ, of our experiencing the same power of God which was evident in Christ's own resurrection (Rom. 6:1–9; Eph. 1:18–22). Thirdly, this dynamic union is itself grounded on a deep personal intercommunion. Jesus speaks of believers experiencing a mutual indwelling, they living in him and he in them (Jn. 14:20; 17:23). Christ himself comes to live within, in and through his Spirit (*cf*. Col. 1:27). In turn, those who believe in him also live in him, the Spirit being the bond of communion between them and Christ. This in turn is grounded on the ineffable intercommunion of the holy Trinity. Jesus himself draws an analogy between the mutual indwelling of the Father and the Son (in the Spirit) and that between him and his people:

> On that day you will realise that I am in my Father, and you are in me, and I am in you (Jn. 14:20).

> My Father will love him, and we will come to him and make our home with him (Jn. 14:23).

> I pray also for those who will believe on me through their message, that all of them may be one, Father, just as you are in me and I am in you. May they also be in us so that the world may believe that you have sent me . . . that they may be one as we are one: I in them and you in me (Jn. 17:20–23).

It is in this sense, I suggest, that we are to understand the statement of 2 Peter 1:4 that through God's 'very great and precious promises' we may 'participate in the divine nature'. The theme of *theōsis* (deification) was a common one among the Greek Fathers. Athanasius, for one, used the idea frequently. This was not normally taken to mean that we are made divine and cease to be human creatures. Rather, it was a way of affirming that in Christ a real, personal intercommunion takes place. We are introduced in Christ to the fellowship of God himself.[3] Surely this is a most profound mystery. Because of that, it is also a most basic truth.

Unfortunately we cannot develop this latter aspect of union with Christ at length here. There appear, however, to be connections with the sacrament of the Lord's Supper or Eucharist. The Eucharist is, among other things, described as a communion or participation (*koinōnia*) in the body and blood of Christ (1 Cor. 10:16–17). If the bread of life discourse in John 6 is sacramental (while this is disputed, I personally believe it is), then Jesus teaches that in the sacrament we chew[4] his flesh and drink his blood, thus receiving eternal life (Jn. 6:25–59, especially verses 48–58). That certainly fits the classic Reformed sacramental theology, expressed by Calvin, the Thirty-Nine Articles of the Church of England and the Westminster Confession of Faith.[5] Once again, as in the case of baptism, union with Christ is not something that occurs automatically simply by taking the sacrament. It is the result of the Spirit's work within us. It takes place in faith. As we exercise faith in Christ through the Spirit, the Spirit enables us in eating the bread and drinking the wine to grow into union with Christ. We thus share or participate in the body and blood of Christ.

Union with Christ in his death and resurrection

While we experience union with Christ in terms of our faith and the work of the Holy Spirit, that by no means exhausts its meaning. In fact, the Bible portrays our union with Christ as based on the death and resurrection of Jesus Christ. The present existential union we enjoy is grounded on something that happened in the past, in the history of redemption. Indeed, there are reasons to see the past historical dimension as even more crucial than our own personal experience.

Union with Christ in his death and resurrection is a basic theme in Paul. When arguing that the Christian is obliged to turn from sin and follow righteousness (Rom. 6:1–23), he draws attention to our having died to sin and risen to new life in union with Christ himself. Just as he died once for all and rose again, never to die, so we died in him and rose to a new life lived in union with the risen Christ. This reality is based on two prior axioms. First of all, Christ actually died and rose in the course of human history. The death he died ended once and for all his experience of living in a context ravaged by human sin and thus in a state of weakness resulting from it.[6] When he rose it was with new power as man, freed from the corruption and weakness that had hitherto attended him. He was 'appointed Son of God with power' (Rom. 1:3–4, *my translation*), raised in the power of the Spirit, incorruptible, immortal, glorious (1 Cor. 15:35ff.). Secondly, all that Christ did in his death and resurrection was *for us*. When he died on the cross it was in our place. When he rose from the dead it was in our place. 'He was delivered over to death for our sins and was raised to life for our justification' (Rom. 4:25). On the basis of both these realities, union with Christ affirms that when Christ died and rose we died and rose *with him*. Because of the inextricable connection between Christ and his people, his death and resurrection were also ours. This is so in all the senses of union we have described. We died and rose in him because he was our representative. We died and rose in him because his death and resurrection have dynamic power by the Holy Spirit, transforming us and raising us to new life. We died and rose in him because of the intimate personal union that prevails. All that he has done is ours by his grace just as all that was ours (our sins) became his on the cross. As Murray argues on this point:

> This sustained introduction of the once-for-all past historical in a context that clearly [Rom. 6:1–11] deals with what occurs actually and practically in the life history of individuals makes inevitable the interpretation that the past historical conditions the continuously existential, not simply as laying the basis for it and as providing the analogy in the realm of the past historical for what continues to occur in the realm of our experience, but conditions the latter for the reason that something occurred in the past historical which makes necessary what is realized and exemplified in the actual life history of these same persons.[7]

85

Union with Christ from eternity

As we saw in chapter 2, our salvation was planned by God from eternity. In the final analysis, it is dependent on a decision by God over which we had no input. Yet, as Paul defined it, our election was made *in Christ* (Eph. 1:4, 11; 2 Tim. 1:9). Eternal election is, in Ephesians, one of the many blessings of salvation. Indeed, it is the first of all since it antedates all that follows. Every facet of salvation, however, is received in Christ (Eph. 1:3), election included. No part of salvation can be excluded from union with Christ, for this is the foundation and basis of all the gifts God gives us. Hence, to separate election from union with Christ, as both Hodge and Berkhof did in their volumes of systematic theology, is a departure from the perspective of Scripture.[8] Both authors considered union with Christ to be the goal of election. We were chosen in order that we should be united with Christ at a later date. In short, they restricted union with Christ to the existential union effected through faith in our own life histories. This is, of course, crucial but it is not the whole story. The problem for both Hodge and Berkhof stemmed from the loss of a christocentric doctrine of election in Reformed theology, the causes of which we explored in chapter 2. Equally, we have seen how election *in Christ* is both true to the New Testament and also offers a sound pastoral solution to many of the practical problems people have with the doctrine. It also avoids a degeneration towards an Islamic doctrine of fate.

If in some sense, however, we are seen as being in Christ at the point of election before the foundation of the world, how is the decisive place of repentance and faith preserved? The crucial thing to note is that predestination is always balanced from our side by our own human responsibility. Election is not fatalism. God's choice requires an answering response on our part, a response elicited by the Holy Spirit it is true, but a genuine and valid human response for all that. Indeed, election in Christ highlights the reality that God's choice of us envisages the inclusion of that response as an indispensable part of his saving purpose. Primarily, Christ's own human response of faithfulness is contemplated in the electing purpose of God. But a secondary meaning is that our own personal response is included too since it derives its own validity from the prior faithfulness of Christ on our behalf. We are not seen in election as severed from Christ or from the faith necessary to please God.

Union with Christ and the future

As union with Christ has dimensions that reach backwards, so also it opens towards the future. We will explore in chapter 11 how Christ's resurrection in AD 30 is part of one reality with our own resurrection in the indefinite future when he returns. Once again, union with Christ is the underlying ground of this. Paul in Ephesians regards our salvation as our receiving God's kindness in Christ Jesus throughout the coming ages (Eph. 2:6–7). Hence, the entirety of our experience of Christ here and now and also in the future participation in the eternal kingdom of God can be described as a growing realization of the many-sided nature of union with Jesus Christ, the second Adam.

Part Two

CHRIST AS PROPHET

5

CHRIST AND THE WORD OF GOD

Jesus' role as a prophet was a topic in our introductory chapter. As we pointed out, he never specifically claimed the office for himself. Indeed, on occasions he even appeared to distance himself from popular notions that he was one of the prophets (*cf*. Mt. 16:13–17). He never once used the stock formula of the prophets, 'the word of the Lord came to me'. All these factors are significant omissions. They seem to dispel any idea that he was a prophet.

Jesus' prophetic ministry

A closer look, however, will indicate why Jesus may have been reticent to identify himself as a prophet. Theologically, the most crucial factor is his own personal identity. As the incarnate Son of God, he was infinitely greater than any of the prophets of the Old Testament. They were, all of them, sinful men. Isaiah himself had to confess to being a man of unclean lips who needed atonement:

> 'Woe to me!' I cried. 'I am ruined! For I am a man of

unclean lips, and I live among a people of unclean
lips, and my eyes have seen the King, the LORD
Almighty' . . . 'your sin atoned for' (Is. 6:5–7).

The record of Elijah shows vividly that, great and powerful
though he was, he was at root a man of moods, subject to
occasional fits of extreme depression and anxiety. The prophets were men of the people, taken and used by Yahweh as his
spokesmen, declaring his word, reproving Israel for its
unfaithfulness, testifying of the eventual fulfilment of all
God's promises, pointing forward fitfully to the future coming of Yahweh himself to vindicate his people in the midst of
their enemies. Yet they were in essence his servants, no more,
no less. Jesus Christ, on the other hand, while he was *the*
Servant of God, was also the Son of God, equal with the
Father from eternity. As a man he was utterly sinless. In the
face of the strict Jewish monotheism all this had to be broken
gently and slowly. Besides this, his role as prophet was simply
one aspect of what he had come to do. Crucial as it was, it was
not the complete picture of who he was and is. He himself
was Yahweh come to deliver his people. He was the focus of
all the prophets (Lk. 24:25–27, 44–47; Jn. 5:45–47; 1 Pet.
1:10–12). In view of all this, might it not have encouraged
misunderstanding if he had declared himself to be a prophet
pure and simple? At least, he would thereby have reinforced
popular uninformed gossip that one of the old prophets
(such as Elijah) had been brought back to life (*cf.* Mt. 16:14).

Nevertheless, Jesus did teach that he was of greater stature
than the prophets. An inescapable corollary was that his own
teaching was of complete authority. For instance, in response
to questioning from his own disciples, he could say 'I am . . .
the truth' (Jn. 14:6), since he was the true revelation of the
Father to human beings. Since God himself is the measure of
all truth and Jesus was co-equal with God, he himself was the
yardstick by which truth was to be measured and understood.
Thus, he could say that whoever received his word had eternal life and was freed from condemnation, having passed
over from death to life. His teaching had such amazing
power since to believe his word was, at the same time, to
believe God who had sent him. In short, his word was God's

word. Therefore, his word gave life to whoever received it (Jn. 5:24–27). Therefore, whoever committed himself to do the will of God would realize that Jesus' teaching was from God. He claimed to be a man of truth, seeking the honour of the Father who sent him (Jn. 7:16–18). On another occasion, he claimed to be 'the light of the world' and accordingly to grant his disciples 'the light of life' (Jn. 12:8–12). In response to the Pharisees' challenge to this assertion, he maintained that he stood shoulder to shoulder with the Father on the matter. The Father sent him; the Father testified to him.

John made similar claims about Jesus. John regarded his coming into the world as the coming of light into a dark place, light that exposed the dark deeds of human evil, light which was often rejected due to sinful hostility to God (Jn. 3:19–21). John understands Jesus himself to be that light, in utter purity the reflection of God's glory. In his prologue to the gospel, he describes Jesus as the Word become flesh, the Word who created all things and who was in the beginning both distinct from and identical to God (Jn. 1:1–5). Hence, Jesus is co-equal with God. He is unique. He is infinitely greater than any of the prophets. His teaching has an authority of its own. Their authority was only derivative.

Moreover, Jesus regards his own teaching as the criterion God will use for the final judgment. While his purpose in coming into the world was to save rather than to condemn, for those who continue to reject him, his very words will be their judge at the last day (Jn. 12:47–50; *cf.* Lk. 9:26). Underlying this (once again) is that Jesus speaks what the Father tells him.

It comes as no surprise that Jesus places his own teaching on a higher plane than that of the Pharisees! In the Sermon on the Mount, he contrasts his own exposition of the Torah with that of the rabbis and so portrays himself as the messianic radicalizer of the law.[1] He is intensifying the demands of the law, applying it to thoughts and attitudes as well as to overt actions, thus fulfilling its true intention. In doing so, however, Jesus bypasses traditional interpretation, intensifying the application of the commandments and seeking to establish their full theological import. In view of his lack of rabbinical education, he effectively claims

93

superiority for his own teaching as against that of the establishment.

Therefore, Jesus never needed to use the familiar prophetic introductions, such as 'thus says the Lord'. He had no need of a special fanfare to distinguish his inspired prophetic utterance from ordinary speech. Since he was God incarnate, all his words were at the same time human and divine. He himself was greater than the prophets. A prophet spoke God's word only when under the influence of the Spirit of God. Otherwise he was an ordinary fallen man, sinful and weak. Jesus, on the other hand, who is our Lord, the Word made flesh, spoke on his own authority.

On our part, obedience to Jesus' teaching is seen as love for God. Moreover, God himself comes to those who obey Jesus' instruction. The Holy Spirit marks out those who follow his prophetic ministry. Jesus states as much in John 14:21–24. Love for God means obedience to Jesus. Once more, this can be only on the basis that Jesus himself is equal with God and, as such, is also the one true revelation of God to humanity. His identity determines the authority of his teaching. His person is the ground of his work. He reiterates this in his farewell message to the apostles (Mt. 28:18–20). They, and after them the church throughout history, are to teach the nations to obey all that Jesus himself commanded them. Discipleship includes of necessity full submission to Jesus' teaching. It also requires us to spread that teaching throughout the world.

Jesus, while he did not specifically claim to be a prophet, nevertheless affirmed his divine identity and the ultimate authority of his teaching and so placed himself in a unique category. All elements in the office of prophet are present. As we saw in chapter 1, Jesus applied the word of God to current issues, he had the burning social conscience of the prophet in his concern for justice and for the oppressed, and he also looked ahead to the future fulfilment of all God's promises. Jesus transcends prophetism, however, for he himself is the truth to which the prophets bore witness. He is greater than a prophet, for he is the Son of God incarnate 'for us . . . and for our salvation'. That is how the writer of Hebrews sees him. He is the chief prophet, for God who spoke in many different ways in the Old Testament by the prophets has definitively spoken to us by his Son. At the same time, he is also the last prophet beyond whom there can be no other. The whole history of God's revelation to the fathers in the prophets existed so as to lead up to his definitive speech in the Son. He is the culmination of God's speech and the completion of his salvation:

> In the past God spoke to our forefathers through the prophets at many times and in various ways, but in these last days he has spoken to us by his Son, whom he appointed heir of all things, and through whom he made the universe . . . (Heb. 1:1–4).

In the mind of the author of Hebrews Jesus Christ, God's Son, is a prophet, the greatest prophet and the final definitive prophet, since he is superior to prophets, angels, Moses and all other possible competitors.[2]

Christ's continuing prophetic role through the apostles

Jesus made careful provision for the continuation of his prophetic ministry after his departure. For this reason he appointed apostles. This plays a crucial part in his entire work. If there had been no reliable record left behind of who he was and what he had done we could have no secure basis for faith. In the gospels we note how he set twelve men apart for this purpose (Mt. 10:1f.; Mk. 3:13–19; Lk. 6:12–16). He gave them authority to exorcise demons, to heal and to preach the good news of the kingdom of God. Their function was the same as his. So was their authority. Theirs was a derived authority, however, received by a specific act of endowment from the Lord himself ('he gave them authority') (edōken autois exousian). There was a pertinent analogy with the šālîaḥ in Judaism. This figure was a representative, an ambassador, regarded as equivalent to the one who sent him, whatever the errand might be.[3] The twelve would have understood themselves to be the commissioned representatives and ambassadors of Jesus himself. He could say to them, 'he who receives you receives me, and he who receives me receives the one who sent me' (Mt. 10:40; *cf.* Mk. 9:37; Lk. 10:16; Jn. 13:20).

The twelve were therefore a special group of Jesus' disciples. The authority he gave them was distinctive. So much is apparent after one of their number, Judas Iscariot, defected. The need for a replacement suggested itself to the eleven as they now were. After studying Scripture, they decided to act. Peter indicated that Judas' defection and also the appointment of a successor were foretold in Scripture. What qualifications were required? Continuous discipleship from the start of Jesus' public ministry was indispensable (Acts 1:21–22). What was the task? The role was to join the eleven as witnesses of Jesus' resurrection. The nature and function of the apostolate was thereby defined very strictly. Not all the disciples were qualified to be apostles, for some had begun to follow Jesus only in the course of his career. To have joined later was not enough. For that reason, it is obvious that all the eleven were themselves disciples from the outset, from the time when John the Baptist was still at work by the River Jordan. This limited the number of possibilities. In fact, only two candidates emerged (Acts 1:23). The eleven then submitted these two to the sovereignty of God, by prayer and the drawing of lots. When the lot singled out Matthias he was added to the eleven and when further references occur in Acts to 'the apostles' we are to consider him, by definition, included. That the primitive church uniformly held these stringent defining characteristics to mark out the apostolate is evident from some of the difficulties in which Paul found himself. His own authority as an apostle was often challenged. His defence was that he too had seen the Lord in his encounter on the Damascus road. He was 'abnormally born' (1 Cor. 15:8). Such a need to defend his apostolic status could hardly have arisen if this restricted (or, better, *closed*) specification had not prevailed.

In short, there were three prominent characteristics of the apostles. Firstly, they received a definite appointment from Christ himself. Through this appointment the apostles received the authority of Christ and became his ambassadors, representing him in the church and in the world. Henceforth, their teaching was to be Christ's own teaching, no less. In the case of Matthias, this appointment was mediated by the entire college of apostles, acting upon the teaching of the Word of God himself. With Paul, the risen Christ appeared to him and gave him his personal authorization. Secondly, the apostles were associated with the ministry of Jesus from the beginning. Thus, the number was a closed number. In this sense, Paul represents a major exception. It was no wonder that some balked at his assertions of apostolic authority. Paul, however, himself acknowledges the anomalous nature of his own apostleship.[4] Thirdly, they functioned as witnesses of Christ's resurrection. Paul fits in here too, for it was by a special encounter with the risen Christ that he was commissioned as an apostle. Once again, the number of apostles is strictly limited by the nature of their task, and this, in combination with the other factors, meant that they constituted a closed circle.[5]

In view of their qualifications and function, it is hardly surprising that Paul describes the apostles as the foundation of the church. If Christ's teaching is continued in theirs, their teaching provides the bedrock for the life of the church at all times and in all places. For example, we recall how Jesus in the upper room told the twelve that he had many things to say but, due to their current state of understanding, he was not at that time able to convey those things (Jn. 16:12–15). When the Holy Spirit comes, however, he would guide them into all truth since he would pass on what he heard from Christ himself. Thus, the apostles' teaching was to be derived from the Holy Spirit and, in consequence, from Christ himself. In practice, the apostles' teaching was to be what Jesus would have taught in person if they had been able to receive it at the time. Therefore, because no foundation other than Christ is possible for the church of Christ (1 Cor. 3:11), the apostles share in this one foundation since their teaching and authority (indeed, their very existence as such) is derived from and delegated by him.

Peter's famous confession at Caesarea Philippi (Mt. 16:13–20) is of interest here. Roman Catholic interpreters have frequently understood Jesus to have affirmed the authority of Peter as the rock on which the church was to be built, the

97

authority of Peter (so the claim goes) as the first bishop of Rome. Protestantism, in contrast, has tended to argue that the church is built on Peter's confession of Christ. May it not be more apposite to see Jesus as pointing to the authority of Peter *as an apostle*? After all, it is Peter's own ministry that is so prominent in the early chapters of Acts.

We must remember one further point. That the apostles' teaching is so closely connected with that of Jesus is also seen in the fact that we know of no Jesus other than the one presented to us in the gospels. Even if the gospels are not all written by apostles (and they are not) or even if none of them were, they all emerged in an apostolic church that devoted itself to the apostles' teaching (Acts 2:42). The apostles' teaching thereby constitutes the grid through which the varied interpretations of Jesus Christ and his significance were filtered. Indeed, just as a model will define not only what is seen but also what can be seen in the future, so the apostolic teaching has presented to posterity the authentic Christian context for approaching Christ.

We can see this dynamic in action in Acts. In the sermons of both Peter and Paul, the details of the life, ministry, death and resurrection of Jesus Christ are rehearsed, followed by a pointed exhortation to repentance and faith. For a Jewish audience, each claim is backed up by reference to Scripture. The events of the resurrection, however, are always supported by the witness of the apostles (Acts 2:32; 3:15; 5:32; 10:39–42; 13:30–31; *cf.* 22:14–15; 26:15–16). On one occasion Peter recounts how the resurrection witnesses were specially chosen by God:

> They [the Jews] killed him by hanging him on a tree, but God raised him from the dead on the third day and caused him to be seen. He was not seen by all the people, but by witnesses whom God had already chosen – by us who ate and drank with him after he rose from the dead (Acts 10:39–41).

The apostles were selected for that specific purpose. Moreover, their testimony to the risen Christ was taken up by God into the gospel message itself. Alongside the saving events of

Christ's life, death and resurrection, their own ministry is graciously granted an integral place. There can be no dichotomy between Jesus and the apostles. We are offered Christ clothed with the apostolic gospel. That is the way God intended and executed it. No other option is given us.

Following on from this, Paul can describe his own preaching as the word of Christ. In referring to the combination of Jews and Gentiles in the church at Ephesus, he recalls that Christ, having made peace by his cross, 'came and preached peace' (Eph. 2:17). Christ never visited Ephesus, however, let alone preached there. It was, of course, Paul who founded the church in Ephesus and who was the preacher through whom it was established. Thus, Paul is thinking of his own preaching as equivalent to Christ's. In Romans 10:14 Paul is speaking in more general terms of the need for preachers to preach to the Jews, that they may hear the gospel, believe and be saved. 'How can they believe him they have not heard?' (*my translation*), he asks. Cranfield comments that 'the thought is of their hearing Christ speaking in the message of the preachers'.[6] Again, Paul reminds the church at Thessalonica that the message it heard from his lips was in reality 'the word of God, which is [continuously] at work in you who believe' (1 Thes. 2:13). Hence, both the written and oral testimony of the apostles carried Christ's full personal authority.

How, then, can we explain the statements of Paul in 1 Corinthians 7:10, 12, 25, where he appears to distance his own teaching from that of Christ and thereby to set it on a lower level? Here, for much of the time, Paul is not issuing edicts requiring obedience but is giving advice which may or may not be followed to the letter. To marry or not to marry? It depends on the situation. There are arguments for and against but neither course of action is sinful in itself. The probability of persecution and turmoil makes the precise practicalities problematic, Paul is saying. On questions such as these, Paul has no specific or definite command from the Lord. He simply gives some advice, which may or may not be followed (verses 25–26). On the one hand, there are some matters relating to marriage which involve very definite ethical principles, and on these he does have definite commands from the Lord (verse 10). It appears that he is talking about whether Jesus himself left any specific teaching in the form of ethical requirements on particular matters. On some he did, on others he did not. On the other hand, Paul himself is prepared to issue commands, founded on clear directives left by Jesus himself and applying those directives to new situations which have arisen in the life experience of the church at Corinth; thus, his command is on the same level as Christ's. Whether or not the Lord left any instructions behind did not matter! Paul, as an apostle, could supply what was lacking and what he said was to be accorded the same level of recognition. The reason for such equality lay in his apostolic status.

Christ's continuing prophetic role in Scripture

In the light of the above, it is appropriate to regard Scripture itself as an aspect of the prophetic ministry of Christ. A number of related themes support this. In the first place, the risen Jesus Christ has sent the Holy Spirit to his church. The Spirit came at Pentecost to equip the church for its great task in the world. When he finally left his disciples Jesus promised to be with them throughout the age (Mt. 28:20). Since he was leaving them, his presence could not be direct. He promised his presence mediated by the Spirit as 'another Counsellor' (*paraklētos*) (Jn. 14:16); he would be present to empower the church, to keep it from being orphaned (Jn. 14:18). At Pentecost, Peter explained that the outpouring of the Spirit was because of Jesus Christ, now raised from the dead and exalted to the right hand of God (Acts 2:33–36). Jesus had looked forward to that time himself (Jn. 7:37–39). So close is the connection between the Spirit, who is sent, and Christ, who with the Father sends him, that Paul can even speak of an identity between them (2 Cor. 3:17). He can hardly mean an identity of essence. Rather, he implies that there is a close harmony of operation in the history of salvation, particularly since the resurrection. A fusion of purpose is certainly in view. Christ sends the Spirit. The Spirit testifies about Christ. The Spirit indwells the church of Christ and transforms its members into the image of Christ (*cf.* 2 Cor. 3:18; 4:4–6). Thus, the risen Christ is 'the Lord, the Spirit', while the Spirit is 'the Spirit of the Lord'.

Secondly, the Holy Spirit is the original author of Scripture. This underlies the statement of Paul when he refers Timothy to the Scriptures, which he says are 'God-breathed' (*theopneustos*) in 2 Timothy 3:16. The breath of God is reminiscent of God's Spirit. The reference is to the Old Testament, for those were the Scriptures that Timothy had 'known from childhood' (verses 14–15) and therefore those about which Paul was writing. Does this undermine any connection with the New Testament documents and thus between the Spirit's inspiration of Scripture and the risen Christ? Hardly, for the overall pattern of the divine origination of the New Testament cannot fundamentally diverge from that of the Old. This is particularly so when we recall that the Old Testament itself pointed forward throughout to the coming of Christ. The Spirit who inspired the prophets was directing them to speak of realities to be fulfilled only when Christ had come. The unity of God's purpose underlies the unity of Scripture itself.

We note also the analogous comment of Peter in 2 Peter 1:20–21. Peter points to the truly human speech in Scripture having its creative origin in the Holy Spirit. 'Men spoke', he says. However, they spoke 'from God' (*apo theou*). They were 'carried along by the Holy Spirit' (*hypo pneumatos hagiou pheromenoi*). Their speech did not result from their own will. Instead, the decisive originator was the Holy Spirit who swept the human authors off their feet, so to speak; yet it was in such a manner that their own distinctive humanity was not overridden, for the thoughts they expressed were truly their own.

Thirdly, Scripture as the word of God is consequently the word of Christ. The Bible is the word of God in the words of human beings. Its origin is from the Holy Spirit. The Spirit proceeds from the Father and the Son. Thus, the production of Scripture can ultimately be traced back to the triune God. In terms of the economy of salvation and, behind that, the relations between the persons of the Godhead, the Bible is a work in which the Son shares also. In terms of the history of

101

salvation, Scripture throughout witnesses to the Son incarnate 'for us . . . and for our salvation'. It is the incarnate Son
himself who, exalted at God's right hand, has sent the Spirit
to his church, the same Spirit who is the primary author of
Holy Scripture.

Fourthly, if we view the prophetic ministry of Christ as
including the production of Scripture we will be helped
towards a more integrated grasp of the gospel. Sometimes
criticisms are levelled against the doctrine of the inspiration
of Scripture on the grounds that the Bible is thereby elevated
to a position of such prominence that it amounts to something of a 'paper pope'. Is not the Bible then seen as a
competitor to Christ? We trust Christ for salvation but then
we are faced with an additional object of faith. We are told
that we must also believe the Bible. One classic Confession
perhaps gives just such an impression:

> . . . by this [saving] faith, a Christian believeth to be
> true whatsoever is revealed in the Word . . . But the
> principal acts of saving faith are accepting, receiving,
> and resting upon Christ alone for justification, sanc-
> tification, and eternal life . . . .[7]

Resting upon Christ and believing to be true whatever is
revealed in the Word; is there a dual object of faith? Does this
open the door to scholasticism and rationalism? If the prophetic office of Christ encompasses redemptive revelation in
Scripture, there is no dualism. The doctrine of Scripture is an
inherent part of the gospel, not an additional extra tacked on
to supplement the redemptive actions of Christ. The Bible
does not compete with Christ. It is complementary. In
entrusting ourselves to the Saviour, we believe, trust and
obey his word to us, given by the Holy Spirit through the
mouths of prophets and apostles. Christ himself is the great,
chief and final prophet, not only declaring to us the works
and ways of God but also embodying in himself the truth of
God, since he is the truth, the creator and sustainer of all that
is. Thus the word of the Spirit to us, as found in the Old and
New Testaments, is Christ's own word to us.

Part Three

CHRIST AS PRIEST

6

CHRIST'S
HUMAN PRIESTHOOD

We are moving into new territory now to discuss Christ's work as priest. We shall spend the next four chapters on this theme. Whereas the prophets are supremely the mouthpiece of God and bring the word of God to bear on the situation of their contemporaries, priests are those whose main function is to intercede for their fellow human beings in the presence of God. Put crudely, if the prophet is God's representative before humanity, the priest is humanity's representative before God. Even so, there were ways in which these two functions overlapped in Israel. The priest was, at one time, the one who could determine the will of Yahweh on pressing and important practical matters. He also had a teaching role. Both these tasks might be termed prophetic. Yet it remained true that 'every high priest is selected from among men and is appointed to represent them in matters related to God' (Heb. 5:1). That meant offering gifts and sacrifices for sins both for himself as well as the community, interceding for those he represented, teaching the people, and pronouncing the blessing of Yahweh on them. He was appointed to this task by Yahweh himself. He was able to empathize with the people, since he himself was one of them, experiencing the same sufferings and temptations as they did.

Aaron and Melchizedek

If we are to understand how Christ is a priest we need to ask further questions about priesthood in the Old Testament. In Israel the office was reserved for Aaron and his direct descendants. Even other members of the tribe of Levi were excluded from the priestly office (Nu. 3:10). The high priesthood was given to the eldest representative of the family of Aaron's son, Eleazer. Certain physical defects (see Lv. 21:16–23) could disqualify people from office. All priests were consecrated to office by washing with water and anointing with oil. This oil was so special that its unlawful use was punished by exclusion from the covenant community (Ex. 30:31–33; see also Ex. chapter 29; Lv. chapter 8). Special sacrifices were also offered for priests at the time of their consecration.

What functions did the high priest perform? Firstly, he was Israel's representative in the presence of God. The distinctive breastplate he wore contained twelve gems, with the names of the twelve tribes of Israel set on them (Ex. 28:17–21). Each time he went into the presence of Yahweh he would carry these gems with him (Ex. 28:29), indicating that he was there on behalf of the people with whom Yahweh had entered into covenant. Secondly, he had prophetic functions. The urim and the thumim were also kept in the breastplate (Ex. 28:30; Lv. 18:8). With the aid of these, he could declare the will of Yahweh on a given matter.[1] Once the prophets appeared, these objects fell into disuse. Possibly the direct revelation of the will of Yahweh through the prophets made them obsolete. After the exile, however, the national leaders wanted them restored (Ezr. 2:63; Ne. 7:65). These objects are closely related to the priests' teaching role (*cf.* Lv. 10:9–11), indicating a certain overlap between priestly and prophetic functions. Thirdly, the high priest shared with all the priests the pronouncing of benediction on Israel, declaring the covenant blessing of Yahweh (Nu. 6:22–27). Fourthly, while the priesthood in general presided over the offering of daily sacrifices, the high priest alone was involved in the annual

106

ritual of the Day of Atonement (Lv. chapter 16). His was in essence an expiatory and propitiatory function.

Only on the Day of Atonement was access to the Holy of Holies permitted by Yahweh. The high priest alone could enter and only under the precise terms prescribed by Yahweh himself. The Holy of Holies, the innermost part of the tabernacle, was where the ark of the covenant was kept, guarded by two cherubim. It was there that the glory of Yahweh was located. When we recall the powerful effects surrounding the presence of the ark (1 Sa. 4:1 – 7:1; 2 Sa. 6:1–23), we can see something of the deep and awesome significance attached to this ban. Sinful human beings had no right of access to God. Even members of God's own covenant people lacked such access. The high priest was therefore the sole representative of the people who could enter. He was able to do so only once a year, however, and even then he could only enter carrying sacrificial blood on behalf of himself and the people. First, he had to wear special linen garments (Lv. 16:4) and offer a bullock as a sin offering for himself and his house (verses 6, 11f.). Then, after sprinkling its blood seven times over the mercy seat as atonement, he had to leave the Holy of Holies and offer a goat as a sin offering for Israel, re-entering the sanctuary to atone for Israel and the Holy Place (verses 15–16). He then sent a live goat into the desert, to carry away the sins of Israel (verses 20–22), whereupon after washing his flesh, changing into his normal high priestly garments, offering burnt offerings and burning the fat of the sin offering, he would take the carcasses of the bullock and goat outside the camp to be burnt (verses 23–27).

The high priesthood remained in the family of Eleazer until the time of Eli, reverting to the house of Eleazer with the replacement of Abiathar by Zadok (1 Ki. 2:26f.). It continued in that family until the deposition of Onias III by Antiochus Epiphanes around 174 BC. As the Letter to the Hebrews states, however, Jesus could not be a priest in Israel. He was not a member of the tribe of Levi, still less of the family of Aaron. Therefore, he simply was not qualified. Moreover, a specific divine appointment was necessary for the assumption of priesthood, which Aaron had received from Yahweh.

This impasse was overcome for the author of Hebrews by

recourse to the priesthood of Melchizedek. The enigmatic character, Melchizedek, appears briefly in Genesis 14:18–20. On Abram's return after the battle of the kings, Melchizedek blessed him, received tithes from him and refreshed him with bread and wine. Melchizedek's significance is that he was a sacral king, combining kingly and priestly offices in one person.[2] He was king of Salem (an early name for the city later known as Jerusalem) as well as priest of 'El 'elyôn (God most high). No account is given of how Melchizedek became a priest, nor is there any obvious direct connection between 'El 'elyôn and the God of Abram, although verse 22 might suggest that there is. The prime fact is that Abram recognized his priesthood as legitimate,[3] since he paid him the tenth and received his blessing.[4]

Melchizedek is mentioned again in Psalm 110:4. Again, a union of kingly and priestly offices is present (cf. verse 1). It is striking that such a union was forbidden in Israel. Uzziah was later to be struck down for usurping, as king, the priestly function of offering incense (2 Ch. 26:16–21). Here, the king, ruling by decree of Yahweh (verse 1), is victorious over his foes. Probably there are echoes of the covenant promise to set David's son on his throne for ever by an unchangeable oath (2 Sa. 7:16; Pss. 89:3–4, 35–36; 132:11). May David's thoughts on entering Jerusalem as king, remembering Yahweh's covenant promise, have turned to his being the first Israelite to sit on the ancient throne of Melchizedek, then to reflect on the dual office of his illustrious predecessor? The priesthood according to the order of Melchizedek described in verse 4 is instituted not only by a decree but also by an oath of Yahweh. It is therefore permanent and irrevocable, in stark contrast to the high priesthood in Israel at the time David took control of Jerusalem, for the family of Eleazer had been deprived of office due to scandalous abuse of their privileges. David would have realized, though he ruled as king, that he could not atone for people's sins nor could the high priest govern the nation. Here, however, was a king–priest, ruling all his enemies and never abusing or losing his priestly office.

Consequently, we conclude that there were in the Old Testament not one order of priests, but two. In the Aaronic high priesthood there was an explicit separation from the royal office, whereas in the Melchizedek high priesthood there was fusion of powers. The Aaronic high priest was time-bound. His legitimacy depended on being born into the line of Aaron, so there was a built-in provision for succession, based on heredity. He was subject to death, and the deaths of the various incumbents were meticulously recorded. In contrast, the Melchizedek high priest was 'an eternity priesthood' (H. H. Meeter). It was established by the irrevocable oath of Yahweh. It was also more ancient. The Melchizedek high priest did not therefore have to establish his legitimacy by appeal to his ancestry. Indeed, all reference to Melchizedek's ancestry and life-span is omitted in Genesis, a point taken up in Hebrews. Moreover, the Aaronic high priest was a sinner, and he had first to be cleansed before he could assume office. A record is kept of appalling sins by Aaronic high priests. No sooner is command given concerning his assumption of office than Aaron himself accedes to Israel's idolatry (Ex. 32:1–6). Nadab and Abihu, his sons and potential successors, offer strange fire and are struck dead (Lv. 10:1–7). Eli's sons and potential successors live lives of open and scandalous sin (1 Sa. 2:22–25). Certainly Melchizedek must also have been a sinner like Aaron but in his case, in contrast, the biblical record refrains from all reference to sin. Indeed, he appears as a person of superior dignity to Abram. Moreover, the Melchizedek high priest of Psalm 110 transcends even David's capacities.

We may take this line of argument a stage further. In Genesis chapter 14 Melchizedek functions in a covenantal context. His blessing of Abram is parallel to Yahweh's blessing him in Genesis chapter 12. In that sense, Melchizedek can be seen as the one through whom the promised covenant blessings are channelled, even mediated. Consequently, he is the priest of the Abrahamic covenant, just as Aaron is the priest of the Mosaic covenant. Following Paul's argument in Galatians 3:15–22, the Mosaic covenant did not supplant the Abrahamic covenant. Rather, the two co-existed. The Mosaic covenant was temporary, coming to an end with the arrival of the promised seed of the Abrahamic covenant, Jesus Christ. In contrast, the Abrahamic covenant not only continued throughout the period of the Mosaic one, but reached full realization when Christ came. Therefore, the Aaronic high priesthood terminated with the coming of Christ. The Melchizedek high priesthood, however (since it was related to the Abrahamic covenant), was realized in Christ. The author of Hebrews had a sure sense of the structure and flow of redemptive history. As a result, it matters not that Christ was of the tribe of Judah, from whom no priests were taken in Israel. He was not an Aaronic priest at all. His tribe was based at Jerusalem, at which place Melchizedek had been priest–king.

Christ's qualifications as high priest

Jesus never claims for himself the office of high priest. Of course, since he was from Judah he had no right to the Aaronic priesthood. Yet he made no claim to the Melchizedek high priesthood either. The suggestion has been made that in the gospels Jesus makes no use of the ideas of priesthood.[5] Is this claim justifiable? There is much evidence to the contrary. Firstly, Jesus laid claim to a special relationship to the temple, where the high priest worked, which enabled him to transcend it and all that it stood for (Mt. 12:6; Mk. 14:57–58; Jn. 2:19, 21). Jesus even saw himself as fulfilling the temple and its ritual (Jn. 2:13–22). Thus, he placed himself and his task in a priestly context. Moreover, he assumed a place of centrality at religious feasts (Jn. chapters 7 – 8). His conflict with the incumbent high priests is seen by Cullmann as an implicit claim to the Melchizedek highpriesthood.[6] Secondly, Jesus' intercession is a prominent feature of his entire ministry. He prays for Peter (Lk. 22:31–32). He promises to intercede with the Father on behalf of his disciples so that the Paraclete will be sent (Jn. 14:16f.). John chapter 17 is an entire prayer of intercession to the Father on behalf of his people. Thirdly, he regarded his impending death as the shedding of new covenant blood and so parallel to the death of the Passover lamb. By seeing his death as sacrificial blood-shedding, he put it squarely in a priestly context. Fourthly, when he finally parted from his disciples it was with benedictions (Lk. 24:51; Jn. 20:19).

In the rest of the New Testament, Jesus' sinlessness is stressed in no uncertain terms (*e.g.* 2 Cor. 5:21; 1 Pet. 2:21–25; 3:18; 1 Jn. 3:5, 7). His death is constantly regarded as a sacrifice. Peter describes it as an unblemished offering (1 Pet. 1:19). He is the lamb of God (Jn. 1:29, 36; Rev. 5:6 – 6:5; 12:11; 14:1f.; 19:6–10; 21:9–14; 22:1–5), the Passover lamb (1 Cor. 5:7), a fragrant sacrificial offering to God (Eph. 5:2). In his exaltation, he constantly makes intercession for his people at the right hand of God (Rom. 8:34). He is our advocate (1 Jn. 2:1), the one mediator between God and men (1 Tim. 2:5). John thinks of him as the exalted lamb slain in sacrifice (Rev. 5:6), while Peter writes of his death and resurrection together as high priestly functions (1 Pet. 3:18). He has obtained access for us to God (Rom. 5:2; Eph. 2:18; 3:12). Believers share in his priestly and kingly role, but only because Jesus first is king and priest (Rev. 1:5–6).

In Hebrews Christ's qualifications as high priest are highlighted the most. He is himself fully human, having shared our flesh and blood. He suffered, endured temptation and experienced death (2:11–18). Thus he is in solidarity with those he represents. In 5:1–10 this is spelled out further. He was one with us in human weakness. His prayers were offered to God with strong crying and tears. He learned obedience through suffering (5:7–8). Therefore, he is able to sympathize with our own struggles (4:14–15). He is equipped to represent us before God, since he knows the problems we face (5:1–2). Moreover, just as Aaron, he was appointed by God. He did not seek the high priesthood out of a desire for self-aggrandizement (5:4–6). Moreover, he is able to discharge the duties of high priest perfectly, since he faced temptation successfully, emerging sinless from the ordeal (4:14–16; 7:26–27; 10:5–10). His learning of obedience through suffering (5:8) was not progress from disobedience to obedience but rather a lifelong development from one degree of obedience to another. As Luke stresses his obedience to his parents, his growth in favour with people and God (Lk. 2:39–52), so in Hebrews the implication is that of genuine growth as a human being, meeting each new challenge with obedience to the Father appropriate to the age he had attained.

111

Even more prominent in Hebrews is the fact that Christ, as a priest, offered a sacrifice for sins as the then Aaronic high priests did (5:1; 8:3; 10:11). It was a propitiatory offering (2:17)[7] involving the necessary bloodshedding (9:7, 18–22). One major difference between his sacrifice and theirs was that theirs were continual and ineffective (7:26–27; 9:12–14, 24–28; 10:2–4, 11–18) whereas his was once-for-all, because it was unique, unrepeatable and effective (7:27; 9:26–28; 10:11–14). The most crucial difference of all, of course, is that theirs were only animal sacrifices which had no intrinsic power to atone for human sins, whereas his was the sacrifice of himself, the Son of God who was simultaneously sinless man. As such he was both priest and victim, offerer and offering. The worth and value of his self-offering was infinitely superior to those offered by the high priests. Therefore he is now seated, his sacrifice complete and effective, while they were still standing (at the time Hebrews was written), continuing in unbelieving rejection of the true sacrifice to offer their now futile and always inherently ineffectual animals. So while the Aaronic high priest could alone enter the Holy of Holies, and that only once a year with a blood sacrifice, Christ's sacrifice has secured our continual access to God (4:14–16; 6:17–20; 9:23; 10:19f.). As such, he is our forerunner (6:20; cf. Jn. 14:1–3). We await the consummation of his high priestly work at the end of the age when he returns to bring salvation in its fullest sense (9:28).

Finally, not only has Christ done what the Aaronic high priest could not do but he has also annulled that priesthood. An alteration in the priesthood has taken place, the equivalent of a legal annulment (7:18). As the fulfilment of the Melchizedek high priesthood, the priesthood of Christ has total and definitive saving efficacy (7:19, 25; 9:12, 14, 15; 10:10, 14, 18, 22). He continues his high-priestly role in making intercession for us (2:18; 4:16; 7:25) and in benediction (5:9–10; 9:28; cf. Lk. 24:51; Acts 2:33; Gal. 3:29). All this demonstrates that there is ample evidence in the New Testament for Christ's priesthood. Christ has performed all the major functions of the priest's task.

Christ's vicarious obedience

The issue of Jesus' sinlessness has occasioned little controversy in the church for one obvious reason: the New Testament writers are unanimous in their testimony. We shall consider their handling of the question in what follows. Firstly, there is the comment of Luke on Jesus' infancy and childhood. In Luke 2:39–40, the evangelist recounts how Jesus was circumcised on the eighth day, as the law required. He was therefore a true member of the covenant community. The child thereafter grew in normal fashion. Most significantly, however, he also grew in wisdom in step with his physical development, and the favour of God was upon him. Evidently, even as a mere child, Jesus was singled out as bearing the grace of God in a quite remarkable way. In Luke 2:41–52, on the occasion when he remained behind in the temple debating with the rabbis, he is depicted as being concerned pre-eminently with doing his Father's business (verse 49). His theological ability impresses the rabbis (verses 46–47) and his conception of his vocation not only emerges prominently but also is beyond his parents' capacity to grasp (verse 50). Clearly, Luke does not regard this incident as a breach of his filial duty, for he comments that on the family's return to Nazareth he continued subject (*hypotassomenos*) to his parents (verse 51). The temple incident was the action of a child consumed by a desire to serve his Father, determined to sharpen his grasp of Yahweh's dealings with Israel. Thus it is hardly an act of disobedience to parents, but rather, it is a very human act, an act of obedience to his Father that is appropriate in a child: it was immature obedience. So much is underlined not only by Luke's comment in verse 51 but also by his concluding remarks in verse 52.

Jesus' further development towards maturity was one of rounded growth. He learned and grew in experience of life. No doubt he had to experience sorrow as well as joy, since we know that during this time his father Joseph died. Because Jesus was human, not all would have gone well for him or his family. On his father's death it would have been his task to provide for the family's needs, and his family, after all, was not rich (Lk. 2:6–7, 22–24). In the course of such struggles he grew in wisdom. Parallel with all this was social and spiritual growth. He developed and cultivated friendships. He was liked and respected. He grew in favour with God, a growing and maturing faith accompanying advancing age and strength. He learned to trust God in the rough and tumble of daily life, when things turned sour. He was learning obedience, progressing from one degree of faithfulness to another. Simply because he was human, his trust in God faced new and fresh challenges. And all this is couched in an enveloping framework of obedience to God.

Secondly, there is the record of Jesus' confident challenge to his opponents to convict him of sin (Jn. 8:46). The challenge of being without sin which Jesus issued to the Pharisees disqualified them from pronouncing judgment on the woman caught in adultery (in the disputed passage, Jn. 7:53 – 8:11).[8] Jesus's claim in 8:46, however, was one which his opponents found unanswerable. Moreover, the immediate issue concerns the truth. Jesus' challenge is for anyone to convict him of lying, of being false to the truth. As Raymond Brown indicates,[9] the background may be that of the Suffering Servant in whom was no deceit (Is. 53:9). Underlying Jesus' question is a deeper, more psychological point. To lay claim to sinlessness would require not merely abstinence from outward misconduct but also, what was far more important, a clear conscience. In the presence of disciples who knew him well and bitter opponents who were waiting for the least opportunity to destroy him, Jesus was nevertheless confident in himself that he had been faithful to God throughout.

Thirdly, there is the consistent witness of the New Testament to Jesus' sinlessness. We have already alluded to this above when reflecting on his qualifications as high priest. To a man, the New Testament writers regard it as beyond dispute. To be sure, Jesus is fully human: there could be no salvation unless the Word had become flesh. But did full and true humanity require sinfulness? The answer to that must be no. Just as Adam, when created, was fully human and yet sinless, so the second Adam who took Adam's place not only started his life without sin but continued so. Adam was tempted in a beautiful garden and succumbed. The second Adam was tempted in a bleak desert yet triumphed (Mt. 4:1–10; Lk. 4:1–12). Again, the ultimate goal of our salvation is seen as final deliverance from sin and its consequences. Life and righteousness will replace death and condemnation. Will we be less than fully human for that? In fact the reverse will be true. We shall be fulfilled as men and women, remade in the image of God. The assumption in the New Testament that Christ's true humanity involves complete sinlessness is in harmony with the basic anthropological and soteriological teaching of the whole Bible. Moreover, Paul's discussion of Christ as second Adam means setting him over against the first Adam as the head of a new humanity. He repairs the damage caused by the first. As such, he marks a new start every bit as much as the first Adam represented the beginning of the race. Hence, when the angel announces to Mary the impending birth of a son, it is presented in terms of a new creation (Lk. 1:34–35). The Holy Spirit was to come upon her, the power of the Most High would overshadow her. This is strongly reminiscent of the creation account in Genesis chapter 1, where the Spirit of God hovers over the face of the waters. The conception by the Holy Ghost is similarly a sovereign, divine act of creation, a radically new beginning as the inception of a new world (*cf.* 2 Cor. 5:17).

Fourthly, Jesus' obedience is more than simply the absence of sin. It is this, but it is much more. It is wholehearted fulfilment of the will of God as expressed in his law. Is that why Luke records even the events of Jesus' infancy as being 'according to the Law of Moses' (Lk. 2:21–22)? Certainly, by the time the cross loomed large Jesus was able to say in prayer to the Father that he had completed the work he had come to do (Jn. 17:4). His life had been dedicated to that task. It was his all-consuming goal, besides which everything else faded into relative insignificance:

> My food . . . is to do the will of him who sent me and
> to finish his work (Jn. 4:34).

Even when faced by the prospect of a death from which he shrank, Jesus submitted to the Father:

... not as I will, but as you will (Mt. 26:39).

The author of Hebrews cites Psalm 40:6–8 in reference to Christ:

Then I said, 'Here I am – it is written about me in the scroll – I have come to do your will, O God' (Heb. 10:7).

Jesus' whole life, and especially his death, is marked out as willing obedience to the will of God. Indeed, for Paul, Jesus' death on the cross is supremely an act of obedience: obedience that remedies Adam's disobedience and secures our justification and life (Rom. 5:12–21).

In this context it is helpful to see how Jesus' obedience fits into his priestly activity. Adam had been created good and free from sin. He lived in fellowship with God. He was given a law prohibiting his eating from the tree of the knowledge of good and evil. Apart from that, he had complete freedom of the beautiful garden he was to cultivate. The sad fact was that he broke that law. He disobeyed, and the penalty for disobedience was death. Consequently, he and his wife and all the race in union with him were thrust out of the garden, expelled from communion with God, and became subject to death in all its forms. When the second Adam appeared on the scene, it was necessary for him to repair the damage. This he could do only by making atonement for the sin of Adam and his race, an atonement which would be of no effect unless he shared human nature and also lived a life of willing and sinless obedience, not only for himself but also on behalf of the entire race he represented. Thus his priestly role was to be a whole work embracing both his incarnation and his atonement, his birth, life, death and resurrection, his suffering on the cross and also his entire life of faithfulness to God. Only a perfect sacrifice without blemish or spot could be sufficient.

Fifthly, Christ's human obedience is vicarious throughout. We are accustomed to thinking of the death on the cross as substitutionary. The whole of Christ's life, however, was vicarious too. His life was a unity, a whole. For example, at the start of his public ministry, he took Adam's place in the desert to face the temptation of Satan just as the first Adam had done in the garden. He was acting like Adam, not merely as a private person but as the head of a solidaric unit. His resurrection too is marked by a public, representational role in which he is vindicated in union with those who belong to him. 'As in Adam all die, so in Christ all will be made alive' (1 Cor. 15:22). This is the great insight Irenaeus had (for all its undertones of universalism), that Christ's whole history was a recapitulation of Adam's. Indeed, Irenaeus saw that more than a simple recapitulation took place, for Christ remedied Adam's deficiency, overcoming the effects sin had in the human race and raising us to triumphant vindication after he had made atonement on the tree. Christ therefore experienced every stage of human life, from embryo through childhood and adolescence to adulthood and eventual death. His entire experience was lived out both as a private person in his own right and also on our behalf and in our place. His whole obedience can be ours, since he obeyed God for us and in place of us.

Since our Lord's obedience reaches back over the course of his whole life, so every part and every facet of that life was lived for us. Not only did his redemptive suffering on the cross happen in place of us but so did his agonizing sorrow in Gethsemane, his wholehearted trust in God and his prayer to the Father. When, in chapter 2, we alluded to Christ's central place in God's covenant we hinted at the significance of his faithfulness for us. We will return to the theme in considering the relation between the atonement and justification in chapter 9. At this point we will merely indicate the role of his faith and piety. Of course, Christ had faith. He would not have been human, let alone faithful as a human, without it. In his case, it was not the sort of faith we exercise in repentance from sin, since he had no sin of which to repent. It was nonetheless true faith; a trust in God the Father that involved the commitment of his entire being. At the same time, when he was baptized by John the Baptist, a baptism of repentance for the remission of sins, he transparently did it on our behalf rather than on his own. It fulfilled all righteousness, being prospective of the cross itself. Thus his faith as well as his obedience was vicarious. His prayers were, of course, on occasions self-evidently made to the Father with a view to his blessing us. The prayer in John chapter 17, the request for Peter at the time of his denial, his continued intercession at the right hand of God, were all made so that God might send help to those in need. More, however, is meant than that. If Christ's whole life was vicarious, every aspect of piety was on our behalf and in our place. It is *his* faith, *his* obedience, *his* faithfulness, *his* prayer which avails for us. As our great high priest, he offers up worship and praise acceptable to a holy God, the fruit of a life of perfect faithfulness, flawless and pure. By virtue of that perfect intercession we are acceptable to God, having been brought by the grace of God to entrust ourselves into his hands. We therefore have full and open access to God precisely because Christ himself has full and open access to God. It is fully and only in Christ's mediation that we have such confidence to know that the way is open.

Because categories of priesthood seem so alien to modern Western thought, much of what we have said is somewhat strange. At root, we have neglected the theological significance of the incarnation. Since the Enlightenment attacks on the supernatural, the church has been forced to deal with questions surrounding the deity of Christ and the inspiration and authority of Scripture. As a consequence, a subtle docetic tendency has developed, so that we have forgotten the implications of the Word becoming flesh. That God made himself known to us as man, experiencing all that we experience, and experiencing it in human terms (so that the Son can represent us before the Father and so bring us to God in union with himself in the Holy Spirit) has no doubt been believed, but it has not been accorded the theological significance it deserves.

Perhaps this is due to the impact of the dualistic world-view of Kant which rendered the incarnation problematic. According to Kant, only that which can be observed empirically has the status of knowledge. Since the infinite God is beyond sensory experience, he is also beyond knowledge. Consequently, the appropriate field for theology is human religious experience:

Know then thyself, presume not God to scan;
The proper study of mankind is Man.
(Alexander Pope, *An Essay on Man,* II:1)

Since we cannot know things in themselves but only what we observe, the claim that God became man cannot be regarded as true knowledge. Behind this, is a radical dualism between the material and observable on the one hand and the spiritual and intangible on the other. As the nineteenth and twentieth centuries have largely been dominated by the Kantian world-view, it is hardly surprising that theological weight has shifted away from the incarnation in response to the prevailing climate of opinion in society. As T. F. Torrance has frequently indicated,[10] however, we have moved into an era in which philosophical dualism of the Kantian kind has been fatally undermined by developments in physics, which since Einstein have established the mutual interchangeability of energy and matter in the space/time metric field. Consequently, the observable is interpreted by the non-observable, theory and empirical evidence being mutually necessary. Now that the dualism between phenomenal and noumenal is obsolete, a world-view is in the process of emerging which no longer has to be inimical to the biblical doctrines of creation or incarnation. Therefore, it is not only theologically correct but culturally opportune to give the incarnation the weight that it deserves.

There can be little doubt that the neglect of the priesthood of Christ has had serious consequences for the church. After the struggles during the patristic period over the deity of Christ, the focus was on confessing Christ's deity to the neglect of his humanity. The net result was that his mediation faded into the background, leaving a gap for the sinner making confession and looking for compassionate and understanding assistance. Who better to step into the breach than the kind and loving mother of Christ, the Blessed Virgin Mary? The development of the cult of Mary met a real need in the church. The need was created by the church itself, however, by its neglect of the human priesthood of Christ, exercised in our place and continuing at God's right hand to meet our present need for grace.

The vital point to note is that Christ is utterly sufficient to meet us in our need. Since he has experienced temptation and suffering, he is able to help us (Heb. 4:14–16). This applies to us in every area of life, not only in our spiritual struggles but also in suffering and oppression of a tangible, material kind. After all, Jesus' sufferings were those of flesh and blood. He was tested to the uttermost, and his anguish and cries in Gethsemane are proof of it. His dereliction on the cross is something we cannot fathom. His teaching focused on good news for the poor. He himself knew something of the struggles of the distressed. His own family was poor, his parents able to afford only the cheapest animals to sacrifice (Lk. 2:22–24). He had no personal possessions and suffered the cruelest of deaths. He pronounced blessing on his disciples who were poor (Lk. 6:20), and he brought good news to the poor (*e.g.* Lk. 4:16–21). His continued intercession at God's right hand therefore includes strong and effective sympathy for the oppressed, born out of his own solidarity with the poor and undergirded by his concern for justice. Indeed, as his saving work encompasses the entire universe (see chapter 10), the righting of the social and economic wrongs of our fallen world is a key element in redemption.

Christ also helps us in other ways. Because he has known temptation, he is able to help us when we too are tempted. He knew the desolation of abandonment and betrayal. His sufferings were utterly intense. He knew bereavement and loss. Above all, he experienced death itself, the cruel death of the cross. He was described by Isaiah as 'a man of sorrows and familiar with suffering' (Is. 53:3). As the author of Hebrews put it, 'Because he himself suffered when he was tempted, he is able to help those who are being tempted' (Heb. 2:18). His prayer for Peter (Lk. 22:31–32) and the long prayer to his Father (Jn. chapter 17) are examples of his constant care for all who trust him. The book of Revelation is an example of his effective sympathy for the struggling churches of Asia Minor as they faced persecution from the Roman Empire. As the writer of Hebrews again stresses, 'he always lives to intercede' for those who trust him (Heb. 7:25). Christ's continued intercession is powerful and effective. It is virtually equivalent to the imparting of blessing in benediction, as we shall discuss at the end of chapter 7.

The sole priesthood of Christ

In reflecting on the priesthood of Christ we recall the idea of the priesthood of all believers that is so popular today. It traces its pedigree back to the Reformation, and particularly to Luther. Beyond that it finds its support in Yahweh's declared intention that Israel was to be 'a kingdom of priests' (Ex. 19:6), to Peter's declaration to the church that it is 'a royal priesthood' (*basileion hierateuma*: 1 Pet. 2:9) and to the doxology in Revelation 1:6, which states that Christ has made us 'a kingdom, priests to God and his Father' (*kai epoiēsen hēmas basileian, hiereis tō theō kai patri autou*). This idea was a liberating force at the time of Luther, when an autocratic hierarchy had eclipsed the liberty of the individual Christian. It highlighted the vital point that Christ had secured our access to God and so we had the privilege of being intercessors in his presence and offering up spiritual worship acceptable to him. Today the idea is frequently used by those who advocate 'open worship', and by those who reject ordination and an ordained ministry. It is argued that each individual believer is on a par and so each has access to God, freedom to approach him in prayer, and equal privilege to minister to the body of Christ. An order of specially chosen and ordained ministers is correspondingly seen as an infringement of the fundamental equality of believers, each of whom has been endowed with priestly privilege by Christ. This development was foreshadowed in many ways in the nineteenth century by the Plymouth Brethren.

There are reasons, however, why this teaching should be qualified. In the first place, its preoccupation with the individual is foreign to the Bible, in which the corporate has priority. Where the Bible talks of a priesthood for the believer the primary reference is in fact to the church. It is a corporate priesthood given by Christ to his church. The focus on the individual stems from late mediaeval nominalism, which maintained that reality existed exclusively in the particular and denied the existence of universals. This led to the development of an interest in individual piety, and in the role of the individual Christian, increasingly at the expense of the corporate solidarity of the community. Secondly, a stress on the priesthood of all believers can often undermine the biblical focus on the exclusive priesthood of Christ.

The clear message of Hebrews is that Christ is our great high priest to the exclusion of all others. He has no rival. He is supreme. If we place the priesthood of all believers in centre stage, Christ is displaced from his throne. His is the sacrifice, the intercession and the benediction, his the faith and worship acceptable to God. Our intercession and piety is accepted not in itself but solely by virtue of Christ. He represents us. We represent nobody.

On the other hand, a hierarchical view of the church can equally challenge the sole priesthood of Christ. If the ordained ministry is defined in priestly terms, the danger arises of human priestly intermediaries between God and his people. The Roman Catholic Church has historically veered in this direction.

Consequently, any doctrine of priesthood should begin and end with Christ. That is how the doxology in Revelation 1:5–6 runs. First, John points to the high-priestly work of Christ: 'To him who loves us and has freed us from our sins by his blood . . .'. This refers to his being both the priest who offers sacrifice and also the victim whose blood is shed. He himself, in his own person, fulfilled the whole ritual of the Day of Atonement. Only on that basis are we then described as 'a kingdom of priests'. We simply are enabled to share in Christ's own priesthood just as, being a kingdom, we share in his rule over the kings of the earth (verse 5). Moreover, our priestly role is a corporate one, as a kingdom, or, as Peter puts it, 'a royal priesthood'. The church is given to share in what Christ does because of its union with him. The Apocalypse was specifically addressed to the seven *churches* of Asia Minor, not to individuals. Consequently, we should learn to think of the priesthood of the church, rather than the priesthood of all believers.

As we do so, we should be careful to remember that it is a priesthood which exists only in Christ, in which the church is enabled to share. The individual is considered only in the context of Christ. He or she is not to be contemplated only as an individual. There is not the slightest biblical justification for thinking in terms of an aggregate of individual believers. That is nominalism. Instead, we should move from Christ to the corporate (the church) and it is there, and only there, that the individual fits. With such an understanding, office in the church can be seen as a way to share in the priestly work of Christ that is given to the church and not as an intrusion on the equality of all individual believers.

7

THE NATURE
OF THE ATONEMENT

The atoning death of Christ is at the heart of his work as priest. Before embarking on this subject it is important to recall the theological context which creates the need for atonement. Adam's sin plunged the entire human race into sin and condemnation. So humanity outside Christ is described as dead in sin, without God and without hope (Eph. 2:1, 11–12), destined for the judgment of God (Heb. 9:27) and eternal condemnation (Mt. 25:31–46; Rom. 5:12–21). Underlying this grim reality is the basic truth that God's justice requires the punishment of sin and the sinner. Adam was warned that disobedience would be met by death (Gn. 2:17). Yahweh made it clear to Israel that whoever sinned would die (Ezk. 18:4). Paul restates the theme: 'the wages of sin is death' (Rom. 6:23).

This is hardly a popular message and many have been the attempts to evade it. The whole concept of retributive justice is unacceptable in the Western world. In our criminal law, we have laid emphasis either on deterrence or on reforming the offender. Neither of these approaches is inherently just. The principle of deterrence almost requires that the penalty should be greater than the original crime. In the past, one could be hung for stealing a sheep. No greater deterrent exists than the death penalty and so it is no surprise that calls for its restoration focus on its deterrent powers. With simple deterrence, however, we tend to lose sight of the relative gravity of various crimes. On the other hand, if the stress is on reforming the offender, the plight of the victim is forgotten. What justice does he or she get? And how can the community be protected? Only if punishment is appropriate to the crime can the very different needs of community, offender and victim receive long-term justice.[1] In divine justice, the link between sin and punishment is vital. Could not God simply forgive us without sending his Son? Does he really need to punish the sinner? Does this teaching make him less gracious than a forgiving person? Is not God primarily love and is it not the nature of love to pardon and forgive rather than to punish? Is talk of the wrath of God a departure from the biblical revelation of God's character (especially in the New Testament) and thus a capitulation to pagan notions of arbitrary and capricious deities who can be angry and unpredictable?

The issues raised by these questions are not new. We will see in chapter 8 how Grotius designed his governmental theory of the atonement around the premiss that God was under no internal obligation to punish the sinner. He was answered by Francis Turretin.[2] In the nineteenth century, the American Presbyterian theologian, James H. Thornwell, found himself compelled to stress the foundational principle of the inexorable connection between God's justice and human sin.[3] Latterly, Leonard Hodgson expounded the point in an arresting manner as, in differing ways, have F. H. Bradley, C. S. Lewis and Leon Morris.[4] Morris and R. V. G. Tasker have also drawn attention to the biblical teaching on the wrath of God.[5]

How necessary was the atonement? According to Grotius and those who, with him, hold to its hypothetical necessity, it was necessary only in the sense that God saw it as the most prudent way of upholding his moral government. He could have done otherwise. It would have been in accord with his character to have issued a blanket pardon. That option, however, would not have highlighted sufficiently his authority as governor of the universe. Therefore, God sent his Son to the cross as a wise example of his morality.

The position we favour is that of consequent absolute necessity. That is the claim that while God was under no compulsion to save us (salvation in its entirety is an act of his free and sovereign grace) yet, having decreed salvation, there was no other way compatible with his nature by which we could be saved. We have already hinted at the grounds for this argument. First of all, there is the justice of God. That God will give to everyone his due is an axiom of biblical revelation. Of course, at present we see injustice on all sides but eschatologically we shall all be judged by God. The problem raised in the book of Job concerning the lack of correlation between sin and righteousness in humanity and the rewards and punishments of God is finally resolved as Job realizes that God will vindicate him at the last day. If this were not so, God would not be just. If he did not have a constant will to punish sin and the sinner, his holiness would have retracted in the face of human lawlessness. The second factor that underwrites the necessity of the atonement and so obviates the possibility of a free pardon is the nature of sin. Sin is an assault on God. It is enmity against God, and disobedience to his law. It is a human attempt to put ourselves in charge, to dispute the lordship of our creator; it is a contradiction of God's holiness. For these reasons, God must punish sin, not out of any external constraint but because of who he is and what sin is. If sin were to go unpunished it would be at the expense of God's own holiness. Moreover, the justice of our salvation would be undermined, for our forgiveness would then flow from the mere overlooking of sin rather than from a definitive and final settlement of it. In the remainder of this chapter we will discuss the major categories Scripture uses in its treatment of the atonement.

Sacrifice

The death of Christ is clearly portrayed as a sacrifice in many parts of the New Testament. Hebrews stresses it the most. In the face of encouragement to return to Judaism (possibly in

127

an idealistic form such as that of the Essenes[6]), readers are shown that Jesus offered a better sacrifice than any under the Mosaic economy:

> Day after day every priest stands and performs his religious duties; again and again he offers the same sacrifices, which can never take away sins. But when this priest had offered for all time one sacrifice for sins, he sat down at the right hand of God. Since that time he waits for his enemies to be made his footstool, because by one sacrifice he has made perfect for ever those who are being made holy (Heb. 10:11–14).

The Jewish priests continually offered sacrifices daily. They were still standing, going about their duties when the letter was written. As we have seen in chapter 6, their task was palpably incomplete. Their sacrifices were animals, incapable of atoning for the sins of humanity. Moreover, the high priest could enter the Holy of Holies only once a year, and only with the blood of the sacrificial animals. This is the light in which the writer of Hebrews considers the death of Christ. He, in contrast, offered only one sacrifice, never to be repeated. Notice how frequently the author uses the expressions *hapax* or *ephapax* (once for all) (Heb. 9:12, 26, 28; 10:10, 12, 14). His sacrifice is therefore effective, valid for all time, needing no succession or repetition. Christ is seen as seated, his work complete, at God's right hand in heaven.

Christ's sacrifice is perfect because of its nature: Christ offered *himself*. He is God's own son, and as such, he is superior to the prophets (Heb. 1:1–3), to the angels (Heb. 1:4 – 2:18), to Moses through whom the sacrificial system of Israel was introduced (Heb. 3:1–6), and to Aaron who was the first high priest in Israel (Heb. 4:14ff.), superior to anything that system had to offer. His one sacrifice is worth infinitely more than the multitude of offerings of the old economy. Again, Christ is both priest and victim. He is the sacrifice and superior to the sacrifices of the Old Testament. He is also the high priest who offers sacrifice and as such he is superior to Aaron. He offers himself to the Father through

THE NATURE OF THE ATONEMENT

the eternal Spirit.[7] All three persons of the Trinity are therefore engaged in his atoning death for our salvation.

The New Testament treatment of the atonement as sacrifice does not end with Hebrews. Frequently, we find reference to the expression 'the blood of Christ'. Usually this means his death.[8] So Peter describes him as redeeming us by his blood, like a lamb without blemish or defect (1 Pet. 1:19), and this in contrast to redemption by monetary means. Christ's sacrifice is of greater value than any redemption price expressed in gold. His blood purchased the church for God (Acts 20:28), and established the new covenant, as the blood of animal sacrifice ratified the Mosaic covenant (1 Cor. 11:25; Mt. 26:27–28 and parallels; 1 Pet. 1:2).[9] Paul also depicts Jesus as offering himself up to God as a sweet smelling sacrifice (Eph. 5:2).

To understand the death of Christ as sacrifice it is helpful to remember the nature and purpose of the Old Testament sacrifices. Although they have been superseded by Christ they can nevertheless shed some light on their fulfilment. After all, this is the context in which Christ's own sacrifice was made. First of all, the backcloth to the Old Testament ritual was always human sin. The offerer was pronounced guilty, and he was liable to the wrath of God. His sin and guilt were then symbolically transferred to the animal through the laying on of hands. Then the animal was killed and its blood poured out, to be manipulated by the priest. The offerer was thus cleared of his sin and guilt, the animal incurring it on his behalf. Of course, no intrinsic efficacy could attach to animal sacrifices as such. They were provisional, proleptic ceremonies that foreshadowed the coming reality. Secondly, the vicarious character of the Old Testament sacrificial system was fully evident. A person sins and is guilty; an animal dies; and the person is free because that animal is slain in his or her place. We too have sinned and are under the judgment of God. Christ takes our place and dies instead of us (vicariously), incurring our sin and its consequences. And so we are freed. That Christ's death is a sacrifice also points to other aspects of the New Testament doctrine of atonement to which we will now turn.

129

Obedience

When discussing Christ's qualifications as high priest, the writer of Hebrews stresses the wholeness of his life of obedience, as we saw in chapter 6. Christ obeyed God completely, willingly keeping the precepts of his law and ultimately suffering its penalties on our behalf. The factor of wholeness is important. Christ's obedience has commonly been considered under the dual headings of active and passive. His active obedience is thus his faithful fulfilment of all God's requirements as expressed in his law together with his complete freedom from sin. His passive obedience, in turn, is his willing submission to the curse of the law on our behalf. Of course, the passive element is not passive in the modern sense but derives from the Latin *patior* (to suffer) and relates to his vicarious sufferings. These, however, are simply theological tools. Christ's obedience was a whole. It is not as if he operated first in an active mode throughout his life, only to switch into a passive mode on the cross. Nor were these two elements interchanged at various stages throughout his life. Rather, his whole life and ministry consisted simultaneously of active discharge of his voluntary obedience together with submission to God's wrath on our behalf and in our place. Christ's whole life was one of obedience up to and including his death, thus forming the one obedience and righteousness, which is no more to be divided than is Christ's person.[10] Perhaps we would do better to speak of the one obedience of Christ as having both active and passive dimensions.

We should also be aware that Christ's was a willing obedience. His sufferings were voluntary, freely endured for our sake:

> I am the good shepherd. The good shepherd lays down his life for the sheep. . . . No-one takes it from me, but I lay it down of my own accord (Jn. 10:11, 18).

This is a theme stated by or of Jesus on several occasions (Mt. 16:23; Lk. 9:51; Jn. 4:34; Heb. 10:5–10). On the other hand, we must never forget that his obedience was worked out with a struggle. Not only was he subjected to the fiercely malicious attacks of Satan, but what awaited him was of such an order of suffering that it was repugnant to his human psyche. We can sense the turmoil and faintly discern the looming menace behind some of his pointers to the final sufferings at Calvary. His comments in Luke 12:50 and Mark 10:38, for instance, come into this category. The passage in Luke is heavy with emotion:

> I have a baptism to undergo, and how distressed I
> am until it is completed!

The verb *synechō* (to be distressed) indicates his state of oppression, of being hemmed in and left with no alternative. Yet the wider biblical and theological context makes clear that he freely chose this route.

In describing Christ's struggles in Gethsemane, we are at the limits of what human language can convey. 'He learned obedience through the things that he suffered', the author of Hebrews tells us (Heb. 5:8). This probably refers to Gethsemane, for he points to 'loud cries and tears' as accompanying the suffering, and to Jesus' prayer for deliverance from death (Heb. 5:7–10). The passages in the gospels are unambiguous. Jesus was sorrowful and greatly troubled. He faced death, the contradiction of all that he was. Death was the reward of sin. The Son of God had no sin and was utterly opposed to all that was sinful. Yet he faced death full in the face: 'Shall I not drink the cup which the Father has given me?' (Jn. 18:11). He found new resources of obedience even in this extremity. On the cross itself his final agony is expressed not to the Roman soldiers surrounding him, nor to the Jewish authorities nor to anyone standing by, but to God himself. Even in his appropriation of the Psalmist's cry of dereliction (Mt. 27:46), his faith does not falter: 'My God, my God' he cries. His last words are addressed to 'Father' (Lk. 23:46).

The atoning death of Christ as obedience is brought into sharpest focus by Paul (Rom. 5:12–21). Paul compares the sin of Adam and its effects with the righteousness of Christ and the consequences that result from it. In particular, in verses 18–19 he sees the righteousness or the obedience of the one

131

man as the basis for many people being accounted or constituted righteous. We shall be discussing this passage in
greater detail in chapter 9 in connection with the atonement
and justification, for it is clear that here we find the two are
closely, if not integrally, connected. At present, however, we
have to ask exactly what Paul means by 'the obedience of the
one'. The disobedience of Adam is a straightforward matter.
It is his first sin. It is by no means certain, however, that
Christ's obedience can be confined to one specific deed or to
one particular occasion. That which declares him righteous
or obedient is his whole life of obedience, including all that
we have seen to be involved both in his fulfilling the Father's
will and also in subjecting himself to the penalty of God's law
on our account. The cross, however, is not excluded from
view. In fact, it is especially at the cross that Christ's obedience is realized. It is there above all else that he suffers in our
place. It is there that he is seen willingly obeying his Father.
Consequently, the obedience of Christ by which the many are
constituted righteous, while involving all that he was and did
during his earthly ministry, includes most markedly his atoning death.

Penal substitution

At the heart of the biblical doctrine of atonement is the idea
of penal substitution. What do we mean by that? Firstly, when
we talk of its being penal, we mean that Christ endured
punishment. A penalty (Latin *poena*) was inflicted on him.
The obvious questions that arise from this claim relate to the
nature of the penalty and the one who exacts it. In the first
place, God's law has been broken and sin has been committed
against him. God is the one who prescribes the penalty and
exacts it. Secondly, the penalty God laid down for sin is
death, exclusion from fellowship with him for ever. For
human beings, this means eternal punishment (Mt. 25:46),
since if the life which the righteous enjoy is eternal (and
everlasting duration is part and parcel of what that implies,
for in what other categories can we understand eternal life?),
the torment to be faced can hardly be anything else since the
same words are used in the selfsame context. Secondly, when

we say 'substitution' we mean that Christ endured this penalty in our place. As Leon Morris has shown, the forms *anti*
and *hyper* both have a substitutionary connotation in the New
Testament.[11] Therefore, Christ himself willingly submitted
to the just penalty which we deserved, receiving it on our
behalf and in our place so that we will not have to bear it
ourselves, just as a substitute in a football match comes onto
the field and relieves a team-mate of the responsibility of
continuing to play.

An immediate question concerns the scope and severity of
the penalty inflicted on Christ. The death due to us from our
transgression of God's law is an eternal death that involves
everlasting exclusion from the presence of God, yet Christ
suffered on the cross for only three hours, and the sufferings
of his earthly life lasted for only about thirty years. Is there not
a huge disparity between the two? How can he be said to have
endured our penalty in our place if his sufferings are so
disproportionate to what ours were to be? In the face of
questions such as these we need to redirect our focus. The
reality is surely that Christ's sufferings were infinitely more
intense. The prime factor is that he is the Son of God. As Paul
put it 'God made him who had no sin to be sin for us' (2 Cor.
5:21). His experience on the cross is at once seen in a qualita-
tively different light. To fathom the depths of what Christ
endured we would need to spend eternity in hell. He was
rejected by humankind, abandoned by God, subject to the full
curse of the law and more besides. All this was undeserved for
he had been uniquely obedient to the Father. He was sinless.
He was righteous. He was pure love and wholesome goodness.
He was equal with God and the creator of all things.

The New Testament presents the atonement as penal substitution on many occasions. Once again, we can detect the
background of the sacrificial system of Israel. The occasion
for presenting sacrifice in Israel was sin. The offerer was
required to lay hands upon the animal to be slain, implying a
transference from the offerer to the victim. The victim was
killed and its blood placed upon the altar. The effect of the
offering was declared, namely that the offerer was forgiven
his sin (Lv. 1:4; 4:20, 26, 31; 6:7) Thus, the sacrifice was the
substitutionary representative and sinbearer of the one who

placed his hands upon its head. Consequently, the victim bore the penalty of the specified sin(s) and was the means by which the penalty was removed from the offerer. We saw earlier that the efficacy of such vicarious sinbearing did not rest in the animal sacrifices themselves but was dependent on the one great sacrifice of Christ who was to come.

In the New Testament itself, the theme of penal substitution is pervasive. 'God made him who had no sin to be sin for us,' writes Paul (2 Cor. 5:21): Christ was 'made sin' (*harmartian epoiēsen*). As Hughes says, 'There is no sentence more profound in the whole of Scripture.'[12] That Christ was not made a sinner or sinful is obvious from the rest of the New Testament and from the immediate context, where Paul stresses that he knew no sin. Nor does Paul mean that he was made a sin-offering, for such an idea would fit neither the parallel with righteousness (*dikaiosynē*) nor the use of sin (*hamartia*) in the same sentence. The meaning is that the sinless Christ was made to suffer for sin, that he was subject to the full brunt of the divine curse that hung over sin, the weight of which fell crushingly upon his innocent person. There is also the element of substitution: all this was 'for us' (*hyper hēmōn*).

1 Peter 3:18 presents a similar picture. There Christ is said to have 'suffered [or possibly died[13]] for sins once for all, the righteous for the unrighteous'. Again, Peter has stressed his sinlessness: he remained righteous even in his suffering (1:18–20; 2:21–25). Peter appears to see Jesus in terms of the suffering servant of Isaiah and as bowing obediently to the consequences of human sin. He also adds that this was on behalf of others. Jesus was righteous and suffered for the unrighteous (*dikaios hyper adikōn*). Earlier in 1 Peter 2:21–24 he is seen as having 'suffered for you' (*epathen hyper hymōn*). Against the backcloth of quotations from Isaiah chapter 53, Peter goes on to state that Christ 'bore . . . sins in his body on the tree', defining these sins as 'ours'. In Galatians 3:13 Paul describes Jesus as having become a curse, bearing the curse of the law against all who do not perfectly fulfil it. This ordeal was, again, on our behalf (*genomenos hyper hymōn katara*). In Hebrews 9:28 Christ is said to have been 'sacrificed once to take away the sins of many'. The sacrificial context is most

apparent in Hebrews and we note both the elements of suffering (bearing sin) and also substitution (the sin of many), both of which are set in a context where he has been described as 'holy, blameless, pure, set apart from sinners' (Heb. 7:26–27; *cf.* 4:15).

There are many other such passages, of which we can only mention a few more very briefly. There are the various texts in which Jesus is portrayed at the Last Supper, instituting the eucharist and defining it as 'my body, which is for you' (1 Cor. 11:24; Lk. 22:19), 'my blood, which is poured out for you' (Lk. 22:20; 'for many' Mt. 26:28; Mk. 14:24). Jesus talked of giving his flesh for the life of the world (Jn. 6:51). John records how the high priest, Caiaphas, unwittingly prophesied that Jesus was to die on behalf of the nation and the whole children of God (Jn. 11:51–52). In 1 John 3:16 John says 'he laid down his life for us'. Paul points to the Father delivering him up for us all (Rom. 8:32), to his love displayed in Christ dying for us (Rom. 5:8). He points also to Christ having died 'for our sins' as being the centre of the gospel (1 Cor. 15:3), to his having died 'a ransom for all' (1 Tim. 2:6), to one having died for all (2 Cor. 5:14), to his having delivered himself up for the church (Eph. 5:25) or 'for us' (Eph. 5:2). Jesus himself spoke of his role as a servant, to culminate when he would 'give his life a ransom for many' (Mt. 20:28; Mk. 10:45).

Martin Hengel has pointed out that the idea of substitutionary suffering was a familiar feature in classical antiquity. The idea of a hero dying for his city, for his friends or, indeed, for the sake of philosophical truth is often found in Greek literature. Such a death was commonly understood as a sacrifice of expiation whereby the anger of the gods was appeased. What made the Christian presentation of the atoning death of Christ so novel and, frequently, so repulsive to its hearers, however, was that Jesus did not die as a hero to deliver his community or his friends but as a condemned criminal sentenced to the repugnant fate of crucifixion. Moreover, he did not die for a limited and specific reason but for all human guilt. Therefore, although penal substitution was a category well known to the ancient world the biblical writers did not subordinate it to the tastes and pre-understandings of pagan culture.[14]

The concept of penal substitution has been the object of fierce attack over the years. In the first place, it has been regarded as inherently unjust that an innocent party should suffer and the guilty go free. In the normal processes of civil justice, such a situation would cry out for amendment. Two points, however, should be noted. On the one hand, the guilty do not go free; their guilt is fully recognized and they are punished with the full sanctions of God's law. The key issue is that they receive this penalty in Christ. The fact that he takes the burden of our sins upon himself and undergoes the sanctions God's justice requires should not blind us to the fact that in all he does, it is both as our substitute and as our representative. It is in the context of a real and vital union between him and us, which is at least as real and vital as that between us and Adam. Hence, we his people do indeed receive our just deserts for our misdemeanours inasmuch as Christ, having united himself to us in his incarnation, fully discharges the debt we owe. Our freedom which results from the atoning death of Christ is thus a just freedom, since the rightful claims God had against us have been fully settled on our account. The other point is equally significant. Due to the sin of Adam, we were plunged into ruin, estranged from God, 'without hope and without God' (Eph. 2:12). As Adam was expelled from the garden and from God's presence, so we shared in his condition. Had it not been for the coming of Christ and God's gracious covenant, we should have had no option but to face the just wrath of God. What kind of prospect is that? Jesus himself testified that there is no way to God apart from him (Jn. 14:6). Apart from the provisions of God's grace in the substitutionary atonement of Christ there is no salvation.

The second major attack on the doctrine of penal substitution has centred on its bearing on our view of God. What kind of God can it be that delights in an innocent suffering in this way? Is this not a picture of a God who is little better, if not a great deal worse, than a sadist, desiring to inflict crushing punishment on a guiltless bystander? The superficiality of such reasoning is seen, however, when we ask who exactly it was who had such accursed grief inflicted on him? It was Jesus Christ, who the church confesses to be consubstantial with the Father from eternity. Who was it who sent him there? Was it not the Father himself, who did not spare his only Son but gave him up for us all? Was this a suffering inflicted from without upon a grudging, resentful and unwilling victim? Not at all. We have already seen how Christ was a willing sufferer. His delight was to do the Father's will; he wept over Jerusalem; he prayed for Peter, at the moment he was betrayed by him; he loved his own, and loved them to the end; he was the good shepherd who freely laid down his life for the sheep. Rather than presenting a cruel and distorted picture of God, what penal substitution shows us is that God's love for us is such that he was prepared to pay the ultimate price that love can pay. 'God demonstrates his own love for us in this: While we were still sinners, Christ died for us' (Rom. 5:8). It tells us that God has identified himself with us in our suffering, that no situation of grief through which we may pass is outside his own experience or beyond his direct sympathy. When we remember the unity of the Son with the Father in the triunity of the Godhead, the scene is transformed.

A third class of objection to penal substitution concerns the place of God's law and its relation to the divine justice. We have alluded to that at the start of the chapter. Today there is almost universal distaste for thinking of God and salvation in legal categories. Such hostility to God's law is in strange contrast to Scripture itself. The Psalms are full of reflection on the perfection of God's judgments, ascribing wisdom to those who reflect long and hard on them (see Pss. 1:1–2; 19:7–12; 94:12–13; 119:1–176). Jesus asserted the permanence of the law and in the Sermon on the Mount even intensified its application to the thoughts, intentions and attitudes of the heart. Whereas it was common for the rabbis to concentrate on external applications of the Torah, Jesus was prepared ruthlessly to press its demands upon the entire person, requiring total and lifelong dedication to the service of God's kingdom. Paul, while asserting the law's inability to save, was careful to stress that he was in no way out to reject it (Rom. 3:31), calling it 'holy, righteous and good' (Rom. 7:12) and originating from the Holy Spirit (Rom. 7:14).

As an example of such objections, Colin Gunton, in an

interesting account of the christology of Edward Irving, recounts approvingly how Irving regarded penal substitution as 'stock-exchange divinity'.[15] There can be no doubt that, at times, this can be an impression conveyed by presentations of penal substitution. We have to recognize, however, that in talking of such vast and towering matters as the atonement our human language is inadequate and we have to use it after the manner of a scientist's use of models, or a cartographer's concentration on major points of significance in the construction of a map. Our knowledge is partial, so we use terms and analogues from our everyday experience to understand realities that transcend our full grasp. These models do not explain everything, just as penal substitution does not explain all that we can know about the atonement. But that does not mean that we do not know anything. We know partially but truly. Talk of penal substitution as 'stock-exchange divinity' is simply a coded message; its author means 'I do not like it'.

In connection with such criticisms, it may be helpful for us to see the penal substitutionary death of Christ in the context of God's loving provision for the deliverance of those who otherwise were without hope. After all, the biblical writers frequently stress this: 'God so loved the world that he gave his only Son', 'God demonstrates his own love to us in this: While we were still sinners, Christ died for us'. The atonement stems from the love of God and, since God's love is *just* love and his justice is *loving* justice, the cross is a demonstration *par excellence* of that love in a way that is commensurate with his justice. Similarly, his just requirements are fully satisfied in a manner which displays the amazing grandeur of his love and grace. Problems arise when the atonement is analysed in detachment from the frame of reference that the Bible gives it. It can then seem a cold, almost heartless, business transaction. When we recall the serious nature of sin and our hopeless condition apart from Christ, the sheer love of God in providing an escape thrusts itself, in all its magnitude, to the centre of our attention. When we remember that this was at the cost of his own Son, who willingly took our place, we are left with no words adequate to express our gratitude. In addition, we should remember that the primary issue in the atonement concerns the justice of God. As Paul puts it, in the foreground for God when he planned our salvation was the need to demonstrate and satisfy his justice:

> God presented him [Christ Jesus] as a propitiatory sacrifice through faith in his blood. He did this to demonstrate his justice, because in his forbearance he had left the sins committed beforehand unpunished – he did it to demonstrate his justice at the present time, so as to be just and the one who justifies the man who has faith in Jesus (Rom. 3:25–26, *my translation*).

God's amazing love had to be righteous love as well.

Expiation

By expiation is meant the removal of the guilt of sin. As a consequence of Christ enduring the curse of the law in our place, our sins are forgiven: he suffered the full penalty we incurred for them. The full sanctions of divine justice have been carried out, and nothing further is required. Christ has paid our debt and freed us from the burden which this entailed. This is taught or implied in many of the passages we cited in connection with penal substitution. For example, in 2 Corinthians 5:21 the result of Christ's being made sin for us is that 'in him we might become the righteousness of God'. According to 1 Peter 3:18, Christ's death is to bring us to God. In 1 Peter 2:24 its consequence is that we 'might die to sin and live for righteousness', while in Hebrews 9:28 Christ's high-priestly offering of himself will be followed by his reappearance from within the Holy of Holies to bring complete salvation to those who await him. In the background is the sacrificial event of the Day of Atonement, where the live goat was led away into the desert never to return. In so doing, it carried away the sins of Israel to a place from where it was impossible that they could ever come back (Lv. 16:20–22). Thus, the Psalmist reflected on the magnitude of the forgiveness of Yahweh: 'as far as the east is from the west, so far has he removed our transgressions from us' (Ps. 103:12; *cf.* Is. 44:22–23; Mi. 7:19). Hence, the problem of our sins has finally been removed by the death of Christ. Sin was the great barrier between us and God. By taking our place and suffering the penalty due to us because of our sins, Christ has overcome that barrier for us.

Propitiation

When the New Testament talks of the atonement as propitiation it points mainly to its relation to God himself. Paul makes clear that the first and main consideration is not our being justified but God himself being just (Rom. 3:25–26). Because he is just, our salvation had to be compatible with the claims of his own justice. Thus, Christ's death involves placating God's wrath that was directed against us. Christ himself endured it in our place. In one sense, penal substitution includes the ideas of both expiation (the removal of the guilt of sin) and propitiation (appeasing God's wrath). It is also helpful, however, to recognize these elements as different albeit inseparable.

The modern world is particularly hostile to the idea of Christ's death being propitiatory. C. H. Dodd crystallized much of this antipathy in a highly influential article published in 1931. He marshalled extensive linguistic and theological material to argue that in those places in the New Testament where verbs of the *hilaskesthai* group occur we should read 'expiate' and not 'propitiate'. Where the cognate noun *hilastērion* is found a similar result was claimed. Dodd regarded the concept of propitiation as pagan in origin, reflecting myths of capricious and arbitrary 'gods' who vented their anger in vindictive outbursts of rage. This, he maintained, was incompatible with the Hebrew view of Yahweh. The Old Testament did not present us with a god before whose arbitrary will we are helpless, a god ready to crush us under the weight of an immense anger. Still less is this a theme in the New Testament.[16]

It is not our intention to deal here with Dodd's linguistic claims. Not only would it take us too long but it would also be superfluous, since both Roger Nicole and Leon Morris[17] have produced abundant evidence that Dodd's argument rests on the claim that in the New Testament we find an unusual linguistic variant of the *hilaskesthai* group, which is a far more unusual use than the evidence can justify. In fact, the terms do mean 'to propitiate' and 'propitiation' and no amount of effort can evade this.[18] Nor do we dispute the obvious point that the biblical view of God is radically different from the pagan one. Dodd is absolutely right to reject any idea of God being capricious or arbitrary. Such conceptions are foreign to Scripture, which constantly stresses his faithfulness and reliability.

Leaving these considerations aside, there remain overriding theological objections to Dodd's position which destroy his argument even if the linguistic mistakes did not exist. That the wrath of God is his settled, personal antagonism to sin is a cardinal teaching of Scripture. For Dodd, passages which describe God as being wrathful are intended to teach that sin carries its own punishment by an inevitable and wholly immanent law. Sin does not pay, for it brings its own retribution. In no sense is there any transcendent personal anger on the part of God against the sinner. That would be to ape paganism. R. V. G. Tasker has disputed this argument, as has Leon Morris.[19] Essentially, God's wrath is his settled antagonism towards sin. It is the form taken by his holiness against sinful rebellion in the creature. If he did not have wrath in this context, he would no longer be holy. He would no longer be against sin, and so would no longer be God. Perhaps the word 'wrath' is not the happiest of terms. It may conjure up precisely those ideas against which Dodd warns us. God does not lose control as we often do when confronted by sin. Our wrath is at best mixed with sinful rage. God's wrath, however, is holy wrath.

Again, the question of propitiation is raised when it is asked who requires expiation for our sins. It is, of course, God who so requires it. Sin occurs before the eyes of God and it is in relation to God that the atonement takes place. Moreover, the testimony of Scripture is that the removal of God's wrath is an act of God himself. He himself provides the means of propitiation. Both in Romans 3:25 and in 1 John 4:10 it is his love that is displayed in the sending of Christ, his Son as propitiation:

> This is love: not that we loved God, but that he loved
> us and sent his Son as the propitiation with respect
> to our sins (1 Jn. 4:10, *my translation*).

Propitiation is the provision of the divine love. It is not harsh
and capricious but a manifestation of love, a loving action by
which God's gracious purpose comes into effect in accordance with his justice. It shows the cost that redemptive love
entails. It is not the case of a loving Christ appeasing a
wrathful Father, as if a division existed in the triune God.
Instead, the entire Trinity was engaged in providing our
salvation, and the death of Christ on the cross was itself the
loving act of Father, Son and Holy Spirit. Both expiation and
propitiation are therefore valid, biblical concepts and both
are aspects of the atonement. Those who stress expiation *in
opposition to* propitiation, however, have misread the New
Testament doctrine of the death of Christ.

In practice, what did this mean for Christ? It is at this point
that we face the most profound and amazing aspects of the
atonement. Christ's suffering in our place included his being
subject to the full force of God's wrath. We deserved that
ourselves. As Klaas Schilder showed so graphically, he took
the place of an *exlex*. Suffering outside the city gates, he was
cast outside the protective canopy of the law. In his trial and
what followed he endured not only the full sanction of the
Jewish law but also much more. The law prescribed death.
But by suffering outside the camp in the place where the
sacrifices were burned up completely (*cf.* Lv. 16:26–28; Heb.
13:11–13), Jesus was made to suffer as one upon whom the
law could exact only so much, as one ultimately delivered up
to a judgment and an ordeal that surpassed all the powers of
the law, to the fierce exaction of divine wrath.[20] That the trial
of Jesus was a travesty of justice simply reinforces the point.
It was not before the bar of human justice that he suffered.
He faced something immeasurably greater. He faced the
curse of God against the lawbreaker. He endured the holy
judgment of God against the unrighteous. He was made sin.
He experienced the fearsome fate of falling into the hands of
the living God, who is a consuming fire. He took our place as
the guilty, the accursed, the covenant breaker. He was

abandoned. He cried 'My God, my God, why have you for-saken me?' And he did so willingly because he did it for us.

Aspects of this scene have been presented to us in recent years by Moltmann, Jüngel and liberation theologians such as Sobrino.[21] The thrust of such discussion has been that God identifies himself with the outcast and oppressed. He has a bias to the poor. Jesus himself identified with the poor to the extent of suffering abandonment by God. His experience of dereliction on the cross identified him with the marginalized of society, who had been deprived of basic human rights by exploitative élites. Thus, the church has the task of being identified with Jesus in his solidarity with the oppressed, with those apparently abandoned to a dehumanized existence. Such reasoning has merit in directing attention to a neglected element of biblical teaching on the cross. Its weakness is that the biblical teaching on sin and the holiness and wrath of God is redefined into something other than Scripture itself regards it. God's wrath is no longer seen as his settled and holy antagonism towards sin and the sinner. Instead, sin is regarded primarily in corporate terms and consequently applied to social structures which the rich use to maintain their own positions and to deny human rights to the poor. The rich and powerful thus become the specific targets of God's hostility, while the poor receive his unqualified favour. There is little doubt that Scripture issues withering rebukes to the privileged. Corporate and social sin is a major factor that the church has for too long neglected. Aspects of these themes are important and need to be stated. But in liberation theology the death of Christ is not held to be propitiation in the sense we have described it, and which we believe the Bible to teach. Equally, the abandonment which our Lord experi-enced is seen in a different light.

Reconciliation

We now move on to a further aspect of Christ's death. By his propitiatory sacrifice on the cross, Christ has brought us out of a state of enmity with God into friendship. The original fellowship that Adam enjoyed with God before the fall has been restored. We are now at peace with him. This is the consequence of what we have been discussing. Because Christ took our place in obeying the Father and in suffering for our sins and because he appeased the wrath of God that stood against us, so he removed all barriers to a restored friendship with him. We are now in harmony with God through the atoning work of Christ.

This reconciliation is discussed in several places in the New Testament, chiefly by Paul. In Romans 5:10–11 he locates our reconciliation to God at the point of Christ's death, and looks forward to its ultimate consummation when Christ returns:

> For if, when we were God's enemies, we were reconciled to him through the death of his Son, how much more, having been reconciled, shall we be saved through his life! Not only is this so, but we also rejoice in God through our Lord Jesus Christ, through whom we have now received reconciliation.

In Colossians 1:19–20 reconciliation is seen to encompass the final renovation of the entire cosmos, but yet it is still the death of Christ that is its basis:

> For God was pleased ... through him [the Son] to reconcile to himself all things ... by making peace through his blood, shed on the cross.

In Ephesians 2:11–22, Paul has in mind the reception of the Gentiles into God's people and their unity with faithful Israelites in the new community of the church. This was a radical step, and one which took a while for some Jewish Christians to accept. Again, the point to note is that Christ himself is our peace (verse 14). He is the one in whom friendship is restored both on the vertical level in relation to God, and also on the horizontal level between Jew and Gentile. The enmity has been abolished through the cross. In particular the removal of the antagonism between Jew and Gentile was due to the atoning death of Christ destroying the ceremonial law of Israel. By fulfilling all that it signified, he made it obsolete. Since the ceremonial law was a barrier

144

between Israel and the Gentiles, the way was thereby opened for the two to be united in the church, God's new temple whose chief corner stone was Christ.

Finally, in 2 Corinthians 5:18–21 reconciliation is presented in the most forceful terms:

> All this is from God, who reconciled us to himself through Christ and gave us the ministry of reconciliation: that God was reconciling the world to himself in Christ, not counting men's sins against them. And he has committed to us the message of reconciliation. We are therefore Christ's ambassadors, as though God were making his appeal through us. We implore you on Christ's behalf: Be reconciled to God. God made him who had no sin to be sin for us, so that in him we might become the righteousness of God.

Again, the reconciliation is seen by Paul as already achieved. He as an apostle has an ongoing ministry of reconciliation, however, as he acts as an ambassador of Christ urging his hearers to trust him. The subjective reconciliation to which he urges his hearers is in turn founded upon the objective, definitive reconciliation achieved by God in Christ. God has reconciled us to himself through Christ (verse 18). This involved the non-imputation of our trespasses to us (verse 19) and is founded on the substitutionary suffering of Christ (verse 21).

That the atonement is seen as reconciliation is clear, and it is equally obvious that this involves and includes removing the problem of sin. A point not so immediately self-evident, however, is whether this reconciliation is purely one-sided. In other words, whose enmity is removed? The New Testament describes us as hostile to God by nature (*e.g.* Rom. 8:5–8). Is God, however, also reconciled? Much popular preaching proceeds on the premiss that God is purely loving, offering salvation and friendship, and that it is only human enmity that needs to be removed for reconciliation to take place. As a consequence, reconciliation is seen simply to involve removing our enmity to God, with God remaining constantly benign and friendly. Again we are indebted to Leon Morris, who has argued extensively and clearly that in all the passages dealing with the reconciliation Christ achieved, the primary reference is to removal of enmity on God's part. The change in attitude on our side is in fact the consequence of a reconciliation that God himself has undergone.[22]

In order to appreciate this, we must recall our discussion of propitiation. The wrath of God is a reality and not merely an impersonal law relating to sin and its effects. God's holy hostility to sin and the sinner is a fearful truth, which is fully consistent with his love and goodness. Reconciliation involves the removal of the enmity of the one offended by sin. With God's righteous demands satisfied, then and only then is his enmity withdrawn. Consequently, the primary reference in reconciliation is to God. By the atoning death of Christ, God is reconciled to us, since our sins are expiated and his wrath appeased. His justice and his grace are a harmonious whole. Our own personal reconciliation, our turning from enmity to love God is grounded on the decisive act of God in removing the enmity on his side.

In non-soteriological contexts, reconciliation has this meaning. It refers to the removal of enmity on the part of the person offended. Thus, when David is reconciled to Saul by the heads of the Philistines, it is the enmity of Saul that is in view, rather than his own (1 Sa. 29:4). It was Saul who, for whatever reason, was offended by David. In Matthew 5:23–24, the worshipper is to be reconciled to his brother before offering his gift. It is his brother who has something against him. It is he who was offended and who is the one to be reconciled:

> Therefore, if you are offering your gift at the altar and there remember that your brother has something against you, leave your gift there in front of the altar. First go and be reconciled to your brother; then come and offer your gift.

Again, in 1 Corinthians 7:11 the reconciliation between husband and wife has at the very least to be mutual, involving both parties to the marriage.

In the soteriological contexts we cited earlier the same principle applies. In Romans 5:10–11, the reconciliation has already occurred. God himself has brought it about in Christ. It is already operative. If it was seen in a 'manward' sense the argument would fall apart. Moreover, there is a parallelism between reconciliation (verse 10) and justification (verse 9). In effect, Paul is saying the same thing from two different perspectives. The argument in verse 9 is confirmed in verse 10 (note the connective 'for'). Paul regards justification here as a change of status, as forensic, as restoration to the favour of God. So too, therefore, with reconciliation. Additionally, reconciliation is seen as a gift (verse 11), which is objective in nature, rather than a subjective change in human beings.

In 2 Corinthians 5:18–21, we also noticed how the reconciliation is described as a work of God which has taken place in Christ. The ongoing ministry of reconciliation entrusted to Paul, whereby he exhorts men and women to trust Christ and so be reconciled to God, is grounded on the definitive work which God himself achieved in Christ. Certainly, the foundational act of reconciliation is not conceived as existing in isolation from the realization of reconciliation in humanity, any more than it is in Ephesians 2:11–22, where the horizontal dimensions are spelled out in great detail in terms of Jew–Gentile relationships in the church. The cardinal point is that God is the one offended but, unlike any human being, he has acted to remove the offence! The passage in Ephesians brings out very clearly that, while restoration of human relationships is of paramount importance and is an essential feature of what reconciliation is, the primary datum is that God himself has acted in Christ. It is this which definitively constitutes the nature of reconciliation itself.

This sovereign action of God in Jesus Christ is nowhere more evident than in the section in Colossians 1:20:

> God was pleased . . . through him [the Son] to reconcile to himself all things.

Only Christ could reconcile the cosmos. His death on the cross served not only to restore humanity to fellowship with God but also to renew the entire universe. No sense can be made of Paul if his language is taken to refer to our human response to Christ. This cosmic note alerts us to wider dimensions of the atonement. It is clear that human sin is the central problem which required the atoning death of Christ, yet there are other dimensions that result from what he did on the cross which call for further investigation. We shall consider these later.

Redemption

In speaking of redemption, the biblical writers bear witness to our deliverance from our bondage to sin and to Satan. This release is akin to being freed from prison. Moreover, it involves the payment of a ransom. In short, Christ's blood is the payment required to set us free from bondage and to make us God's own possession. Consequently, we belong to him and are under an obligation to live for him in all that we do.

Once again, sin and its consequences lie behind the need for atonement. We are also confronted, however, by demonic forces that are at work in the world and which enslave human beings, blinding them to the true light of the knowledge of God in Christ (*cf.* 2 Cor. 4:4). We will focus on deliverance from these in the next section. For the moment, we are still concerned with human sin. First of all, we note how commercial terms are used to describe our redemption. The verbal forms used in the New Testament, 'to redeem' and 'to ransom (*agarazō, exagorazō, lytroō*) and also the nouns 'redemption' and 'ransom' (*apolytrōsis, antilytron*) all customarily convey the idea of setting free by the payment of a ransom or by purchase in the market place, or something similar.[23] The New Testament makes it clear that this price was the life of Christ given up in death (Mt. 20:28; Mk. 10:45; Eph. 1:7; Col. 1:13–14). In 1 Peter 1:18–19 the price is explicitly stated: 'not with perishable things such as silver or gold . . . but with the precious blood of Christ'. Other relevant passages are Titus 2:14, Romans 3:24 and Hebrews 9:12. The common idea that redemption is to be equated with simple deliverance, without any commercial connotation, is foreign to the consistent teaching of the New Testament.

As we will see in the next chapter, many of the Fathers understood the ransom price to have been paid to the devil, perhaps with an element of cunning deception so as to trick Satan into trying to capture Jesus for his own, only to be left empty handed when he rose from the dead. The problem with those ideas was twofold. Firstly, Satan had no lawful rights over us; and secondly, the ransom metaphor is pressed beyond biblical bounds and used to answer a false question. The New Testament presents ransom as a figure expressing both the costliness of our salvation and also the enslavement which binds us to our owner. 'You are not your own; you were bought at a price', Paul is keen to stress (1 Cor. 6:20; 7:23). We should be careful not to press the idea further than this.

On the question of who requires the ransom price, the obvious answer is God himself, particularly in view of the Godward aspects of propitiation and reconciliation. Our deliverance was exceedingly costly to God himself but there was no other way to release us and to claim us for his own. It required the utmost expenditure. That Christ willingly undertook this enormous task, expending himself in the process, highlights yet again God's supreme love for us. Moreover, redemption involves our belonging to God: we are bought at a price. There is an integral connection here with sanctification. Christ died not only to expiate sin but to destroy it (1 Jn. 3:8). He purchased not merely(!) our forgiveness but our holiness, transferring us to God's kingdom and breaking the power of sin over us. Thus Paul, in Romans 6:1–23, stresses that we died to sin in union with Christ in his death and resurrection so that sin should no longer reign over us. Instead, we live to him so as to produce good and righteous fruit. If reconciliation and obedience bring the atonement into conjunction with justification, so redemption connects it to sanctification, and all by virtue of its being undertaken by Christ in union with us, his people.

Conquest

In tandem with the above, the atonement is also the occasion by which Christ conquers the rebellious principalities and

149

powers, the demonic world headed by Satan. Here the unity of Christ's death and resurrection are seen most clearly. Indeed, there are aspects of this victory which are related more specifically to the resurrection than to the cross. Possibly this is the most 'primitive' of all understandings of the gospel. The curse on the serpent in Genesis 3:15 includes the statement that the seed of the serpent would be dealt a crushing blow to the head by the seed of the woman. Paul, in Romans 16:20, takes this to refer to Christ crushing Satan under the feet of the church. He also understands the serpent to represent Satan (2 Cor. 11:3–4, *cf.* verses 14–15). Hence, the curse on the serpent is also a promise to humanity, a promise that one of the woman's descendants would one day deal a mortal blow to Satan. This theme is taken up by our Lord himself. He draws attention to the prince of this world being cast out of heaven and, in the same breath, to himself being lifted up so as to draw all people to him (Jn. 12:31–33). Here the connection between the cross and the overthrow of Satan is clear. Paul too sees the cross as being an open display of victory over the principalities and powers, whereby their power was disarmed (Col. 2:14–15).

In the difficult passage 1 Peter 3:18–22, Peter indicates that Christ, in his resurrection, proclaimed judgment on the fallen angels. Over the centuries there have been conflicting interpretations of this complex section. A common early view was that Christ went into Hades in the period between his death and resurrection. On the other hand, Augustine popularized the notion that the pre-existent Christ preached the gospel through Noah to Noah's contemporaries. Still others have maintained that Christ gives people a second chance to repent after death, a claim which would contradict the consistent claim of the rest of Scripture that this present life is decisive and that gospel proclamation here and now is of the utmost urgency. Again, a growing appreciation seems to be developing on syntactic, structural, semantic and theological grounds that what Peter is teaching is that Christ pronounced judgment on the spirits in his resurrection. Peter's readers were suffering persecution, Noah faced opposition and ridicule; Christ suffered. Consequently, just as Noah was publicly vindicated by the ark which saved him from the floodwaters while his adversaries drowned, and just as Christ was publicly vindicated in his resurrection in which he pronounced judgment on his adversaries, so Peter's readers, when confronted by the fiery opposition of a hostile world, could draw comfort from their baptism which saved them.[24] The progression from Christ's death and resurrection (verse 18) to his exaltation and enthronement over angels, authorities and powers (verse 22) is interrupted by the parenthesis (verses 19–21) describing his triumphant activity at his resurrection. Therefore, we have again a reference to Christ's subjugation of Satan and his forces which was achieved in his resurrection and as a direct result of his death and all that it entailed. The exegesis of this passage, however, will continue to be disputed.

There are a number of important features that this biblical perspective on the atonement brings to light. First of all, it brings the death and resurrection of Christ into a harmonious unity, an unmistakable theme of the New Testament. The shameful death on the cross, the suffering and dereliction that occurred there, are not the final word. For all the darkness, there is a bright side to the cross. Indeed, Jesus himself called his impending death the Father's glorification (Jn. 12:27–33; 17:4). Secondly, Christ's victory over Satan is decisive but, in the context of biblical eschatology, its full manifestation awaits his return. Therefore, we still see much damage done by Satan. It is essentially the same with the problem of sin. Christ redeemed us from the bondage of sin and bought us for God. Nevertheless, we still sin and will not be free from sin in a final sense until Christ returns and our salvation is brought to its consummation. The victory is a present reality but is not yet manifested fully. In the imagery of Revelation, Satan is bound, his power restricted, but within the limits of his leash he is still able to cause problems. Thirdly, Christ's victory over sin and Satan opens for us the prospect of the conquest of the various ills that have originated from those sources. Sin brought death in its wake and, with it, the decay and disease that are an endemic part of a fallen world. That is why Jesus' preaching of the kingdom of God was accompanied by healing miracles and by exorcisms. They were signs that God's rule was to result in the abolition of death, disease and sin. As Satan had provided the occasion for sin to enter, so he too would be dealt a mortal blow. In the context of biblical eschatology, however, the consummation of this victory awaits the *parousia*. In principle, it has been achieved. In practice, we wait in expectant assurance. We still get sick, we still die; Christianity is not a ticket exempting us from the consequences of the fall. It is, however, a pointer to a renewed and purified world and an assurance that the foundation of that world has already been laid.[25]

Moral example

Is the atonement also seen as an example? In short, did Jesus die to show us the love of God and thus compel a response of grateful love on our part? We will note the inadequacies of a purely exemplary theory of the atonement in chapter 8. Indeed, it may be asked how Christ's atonement can be an example to us since we certainly cannot copy it! It is literally unique. Again, any exemplary elements do not strictly belong to the atonement as such, but are consequences of it. In fact, it is more especially the self-giving love of Christ that serves as a model for us, insofar as we are urged to show the same kind of love to others. Thus, Jesus told his disciples to love one another as he had loved them. Indeed, this was to be the way they would be known as his (Jn. 13:12–17). Peter tells his readers that Jesus' patient endurance under unjust oppression was exemplary, for we are to follow his example (1 Pet. 2:18–25). The love which we are to show to one another, without which no-one can truly claim to know God, is defined by the love of God in giving his Son to be the propitiation (1 Jn. 4:7–12). All this does not relate directly to the atonement. It concerns the wider issues of the love of God towards us, evidenced by the entire process of salvation. Therefore to talk of Christ as our exemplar is of course justifiable, but the atonement itself can be exemplary only in an indirect and limited sense.

Conclusion

We have seen that the atoning death of Christ is an act of obedience to the Father and, as such, cannot be divorced from his entire life and ministry that led up to it. He fully obeyed the law of God and submitted to its sanctions on our behalf. His death was a sacrifice, in which he took our place and suffered the just punishment that was ours for transgressing God's law. Consequently, our sins were covered and expiated. With God's righteous and holy wrath now appeased, he is reconciled to us so that we are his friends. As a corollary, we have been delivered from bondage to sin and Satan, who in turn has been conquered and his power broken. All this is the provision of God's great love towards us. The full implications of what has taken place will be made known when Christ comes back.

In all the above models of the atonement both substitution and representation are present. Since the whole of Christ's life was lived in vicarious obedience, we cannot abstract any one part or any one period of time and say of it that this part, rather than others, was lived as our substitute and representative. At all times his whole life was vicarious. His obedience to the law of God was in our place, representing us. His human faith was for us and on our behalf. His worship of God was offered in place of us. Similarly, his whole obedient sacrifice, suffering the sanctions of the law, expiating sin, appeasing the Father, reconciling God to us and delivering us from the dominion of sin and Satan was undertaken in our place. It is ours because he did it in our place. It is ours because he did it on our behalf. It is ours because he did it in union with us. He took our wretchedness, sin and death while, in faith, we receive from him his righteousness and life.

Additionally, at all points Jesus lived and acted in union with us. We were chosen in him before the foundation of the world (we examined some of the significance of this in chapter 2). In his incarnation, by sharing our nature and living as man, he began to be from a human point of view in union with his people. Certainly, we do not experience Christ's salvation until we believe in him and are united to him by the

Holy Spirit. With the concentration of modern evangelicalism on the salvation of the individual, however, we
have tended to overlook the very strong focus of Scripture on
redemptive history. This is clear particularly in Paul and also
in Peter but it is a theme running throughout the Bible. As
we saw earlier, John Murray put it this way:

> This sustained introduction of the once-for-all past
> historical in a context that clearly [Rom. 6:1–11]
> deals with what occurs actually and practically in the
> life history of individuals makes inevitable the inter-
> pretation that the past historical conditions the con-
> tinuously existential, not simply as laying the basis
> for it and as providing the analogy in the realm of
> the past historical for what continues to occur in the
> realm of our experience, but conditions the latter
> for the reason that something occurred in the past
> historical which makes necessary what is realized
> and exemplified in the actual life history of these
> same persons.[26]

We recall that Christ is the second Adam. Adam represented the whole human race in what he did, particularly
when it came to his fall into sin (Rom. 5:12f.). So Christ from
beginning to end was starting a new human history. He took
Adam's place and ours and headed a new humanity. Therefore we miss the significance of the atonement if we forget
that Christ at all stages is to be seen as in union with us, his
own people. His birth announcement indicated the public
and solidaric nature of his task (Mt. 1:21). The outset of his
public ministry was a repetition of the temptation scene of
Adam, in a desert rather than a garden. Christ is portrayed
by John in the context of Israel, fulfilling the temple and the
feasts, as a greater Moses, replacing the old cultus. All that he
is and does is worked out in the context of solidarity with his
own people, the sheep in his flock. Therefore, that union is
especially expressed in his atoning death. On the cross he
dies for us and on our behalf but also we die with him
because we are in him (Rom. 6:1–9). That is why he brought
about such a radical break with the power of sin. The full

power of sin and Satan against us has been exhausted. We have died; sin and death can extract nothing more from us since the full penalty has been paid. In union with us, Christ has finally and ultimately blunted the edge of their weaponry. God in Christ has accomplished the reconciliation and we now await the full realization of what he has done. As in Oscar Cullmann's graphic analogy, our D-Day has already occurred. At present, we are embroiled in the sometimes messy mopping-up operations before VE-Day arrives.[27]

Finally, the atoning death of Christ is both unique and utterly sufficient. It is unique because no other way existed to rescue us. It is unique because of the unique person who died on the cross, Jesus Christ the Son of God. It is unique because no other atoning sacrifice could take away sins. It is sufficient because it blots out all our sins, because it achieved our salvation, and because it brings us into friendship with God. Christ's atoning work is complete: 'It is finished!'

> Here we have a firm foundation,
> here the refuge of the lost.
> Christ's the rock of our salvation,
> his the name of which we boast.
> Lamb of God for sinners wounded,
> sacrifice to cancel guilt.
> None shall ever be confounded,
> who on him their hope have built.
>
> *Thomas Kelly*

Excursus: Christs's continuing priestly work

We have given close attention to the cross. Our Lord's priestly activity did, however, not end there. On the third day he rose from the dead and he continues as our representative with God. His ongoing high-priestly role has a twofold aspect. Firstly, he makes intercession for us. As Aaron appeared in the Holy of Holies with twelve diadems in his breastplate, representing the twelve tribes of Israel, thus continually bringing them before the presence of God, so Jesus Christ is now at the right hand of God as our own representative. As we are united to him, so we are enabled to sit with him in heavenly places (Eph. 2:6). During his earthly ministry Jesus frequently prayed for his disciples. He prayed for Peter that his faith would not fail at the time he denied his master (Lk. 22:31–32). He prayed for his whole church, that it might be protected from the evil one, and exemplify the unity of God himself in the world into which he was sending it. His intercession is directed to very specific purposes. It is not indiscriminate. He does not pray for the world but for those the Father has given him (Jn. chapter 17).

This priestly work of intercession is said to continue after Christ's exaltation (Heb. 7:25; 1 Jn. 2:1–2). Of what does it consist? We can immediately say what it is not. Due to his work of atonement being a completed work he is not offering his shed blood in the presence of the Father. Westcott's view that the expression 'the blood of Christ' refers to the continued presentation of his life has been decisively refuted by Stibbs and others,[28] who have demonstrated that it is always used to mean his life laid down in death. Instead, his intercession includes prayer for his church; the prayer is less a petition for a matter on which the will of God is not decisively known but more a request concerning something which has been definitely settled. He is, after all, the Son of God. Moreover, the great turning point in the drama of redemption has already occurred, In fact, it is hard at this point to distinguish Christ's intercession from the second aspect of his ongoing priestly work, that of benediction. The priests in the Old Testament were charged with the task of blessing the people (Nu. 6:24–27). This was Jesus' parting action when he ascended (Lk. 24:51). Benediction involved not a pious wish that such and such blessings might be granted to the blessed but rather a declaration of a state of affairs that actually existed already. Jesus' parting benediction is inseparably linked to his finished atonement for sins. He is conveying to his people the blessing stemming from his death on the cross. In his ascension 'he led captivity captive and gave gifts to men' (Eph. 4:8–10), gifts which were provided by the Holy Spirit.

Indeed, the chief of these gifts was the Spirit himself whom Christ sent from the Father. On the Day of Pentecost Peter pointed out that the sending of the Holy Spirit was an action of the risen and exalted Christ (Acts 2:33–36). It was an act of benediction, whereby he sovereignly blessed his people in fulfilment of his atoning work on the cross. Therefore, all further ways in which Christ sustains and strengthens his church come into the same category. His messages to the churches (Rev. chapters 1–3), his continuing ministry to the church through the apostles (*cf.* Acts 1:1–2), his rulership of political affairs (Rev. 1:5; note here the overlap between his kingly and priestly functions) and his sending help to us in time of need (Heb. 4:14–16) all feature as ways in which Christ blesses his church as its priest. We see again how close this is to his intercession. In fact, intercession and benediction are really two sides of the same coin.

8

THEORIES
OF THE ATONEMENT

In this chapter we will survey the major ideas of the atonement in the history of the church. At the start, we mentioned that our study of Scripture is never done in a vacuum. Most new insights are variations on old themes. Others have blazed the trails before us. If we neglect the past we will be doomed either to reinvent the wheel or to reproduce old heresies, rejected by the church for their threat to our salvation.

The recapitulation theory

In chapter 1 we alluded to the famous recapitulation theory of Irenaeus. Irenaeus sets out his view in Book V of *Against Heresies*. He writes that Christ united himself with us in his incarnation so that we might become what he is (Preface). In the incarnation he united himself to humanity and so attaches humanity to God. By the Holy Spirit he unites us to God and so imparts God to human beings (V,1,1). Thus, there are two elements or 'moments' in this mutual union. The first stage is secured in the incarnation itself, while the second is achieved by the Holy Spirit working in us. In the first of these

moments, Christ became what we are, taking the place of
Adam. He crushed our enemy who had earlier led us captive
in Adam. Satan had led us to death. The only way we could
be brought back to life and Satan could be defeated was by
the Lord being born of a woman (V,21,1). As such, he obeyed
the Father and so restored humanity to the likeness of God.
He conquered Satan by obeying the Father's commandment.
Where Adam had been overcome through food, Christ over-
came Satan by hunger in the wilderness. Whereas Adam
disobeyed the command of God, Christ did not transgress
(V,21,2). In the end, he redeemed us by his blood in accordance with God's justice (V,1,1). Adam had disobeyed through
a tree. Christ obeyed on a tree and overturned man's disobedience (V,16,3). Thus, the whole of Christ's life was one
of obedience. It was also lived in counterpoise to that of
Adam. He recapitulated and annulled the disobedience of
Adam (III,21,10; IV,17,1–5; V,17,1). Consequently, Satan
was bound with the same fetters with which he had originally
bound the human race. Humanity was set free. Satan was led
captive since he had held human beings unjustly (V,21,3).

A number of comments are in order. Firstly, Irenaeus sees
the work of Christ against the backdrop of a sharp ethical
dualism. The human race has sinned and disobeyed God.
But behind all this is Satan, who led humanity astray. Satan is
the arch-enemy. Hence redemption is envisaged as a drama.
It involves conflict. The work of Christ is a conquest of Satan.
Secondly, the obedience of Christ is crucial and central. He
wins the victory over Satan by obeying the Father. If sin is
essentially disobedience to God's command, salvation is the
opposite. Thus, the death of Christ is in full accord with the
justice of God. The atonement is a ransom whereby
humanity is rescued from the power of the devil, but it is also
a sacrifice of obedience to God. Thirdly, the atonement is
seen in connection with the whole of Christ's life. The cross is
central, for it is there that the sin of Adam is overturned, yet
it is seen in unbroken connection with the life of obedience
that preceded it and with the resurrection that followed.

Irenaeus' view that the human race is transformed and
elevated by Christ's becoming man was to cohere well with
the dominant Greek idea that the chief impact of the fall was

moral corruption and death, and that the goal of salvation was that human beings might share the divine nature. Examples of Greek fathers who thought along these lines are Athanasius (*c.* 296–373) and Cyril of Alexandria (d. 444).[1] It seems that some form of realism is necessary to share such assumptions. In other words, the view requires the prior notion of human nature being a generic whole, and of the Logos uniting himself with this generic human nature. As a result, since individual people share in this human nature Christ can be said to have united himself with them and so to impart to them the divine nature which is his.[2]

The ransom theory

The ransom theory of the atonement, or the 'classic' theory as Aulén described it, enjoyed great popularity in the first thousand years or so of the church. In the East it dominated the field. Aulén argued that in this model incarnation and atonement stood in the closest possible relation.[3] At root is the same idea of ethical dualism. That is not surprising since Irenaeus himself included a form of the ransom theory in his own synthesis. The devil had humanity in his power because of the fall. Many Fathers went so far as to allow a certain authority to Satan. Consequently, the atonement is seen as a work of God. God himself came into the world in Jesus Christ. The Father handed him over to Satan. Satan fell into the trap, thinking that he had Christ in his grasp. Christ's divinity, however, concealed by his humanity, enabled him to overpower Satan and to rise from the dead, thus destroying 'him who had the power of death'. Thus, human beings are freed from Satan's power and Satan himself is now subject to death and condemnation.

Origen (*c.* 185 – *c.* 254) was an early exponent of this idea. He saw it more in terms of simple conquest, however, rather than as a transaction with the devil. The element of deception which was to creep in later was not present in his thought. Christ's death had as its aim to destroy Satan, who had the power of death.[4] Christ gave his soul as a ransom to Satan.[5] His resurrection spelled Satan's destruction.[6] God in Christ reconciles the world to himself by the conquest of his Son but

161

it is also a continuing process which will culminate when the last enemy is destroyed and when God is all in all.[7] The scope is cosmic, the work divine.

Later, crude and bizarre imagery was introduced into the picture. For example, Gregory of Nyssa (330 – c. 395) wrote of Christ as bait, with Satan being duped into swallowing what was on offer but being hooked by the hidden deity.[8] Ambrose (c. 339–97) also hints at such a theory.[9]

With the passing of time it was realized that Satan had no lawful rights over the human race. The ransom could hardly have been paid to him! Moreover, ethical questions were raised about the involvement of God in duplicity. Gregory of Nazianzen (330–89) dealt a powerful blow along these lines.[10] Yet crude imagery was still evident as late as the eleventh century in Peter Damian (1007–72), who thought that the devil went for Christ's body but was overcome by the divinity.[11]

Aulén stressed the following points in his polemic for the theory. Firstly, it proceeds on the assumption that atonement is a work of God. God is both author and object of reconciliation. Secondly, and consequently, the unity of redemption is preserved. Deliverance from sin, evil and the devil is at the same time deliverance from God's judgment on sin. The underlying theme that evil overreaches itself at the point where it appears to have triumphed rings true to experience.[12]

A number of serious flaws, however, are evident. Firstly, Aulén almost certainly overreached himself in his vigorous support for the idea. He claimed that Martin Luther (1483–1546) revived it after its eclipse by the Anselmic theory,[13] yet Luther's emphasis did not lie here. Certainly Luther regarded Christ as battling with and triumphing over the demonic powers (LW, 26, 281, 373; 53, 257). He saw these powers, however, as the agents of God's wrath. It was our guilt and the wrath of God that, in his estimation, was the immediate context of Christ's atoning death. He saw freedom from the power of the devil as a fruit of deliverance from God's wrath (LW, 26, 276–291; 27, 4)). His stress is on Christ's death as a sacrifice of substitutionary satisfaction for human sin (LW, 13, 319; 23, 195; 24, 98; 25, 45, 249, 284, 349). Secondly, there is a theological weakness that renders the theory at best incomplete. By viewing the atonement as essentially a work of God, little scope is given to Christ's humanity and a somewhat docetic picture is painted. Furthermore, since the framework of the theory is one of cosmic drama, conquest and reconciliation, it is not entirely clear how human sin fits into the picture. Yet sin is so central to the New Testament portrayal of the atonement that a theory which leaves it on one side is deficient. That is not to say that it should be rejected *tout court*. Rather, its validity is as one perspective among others, not as a controlling element.

Satisfaction / vicarious sacrifice

Anselm is widely credited with directing thought on the atonement towards the idea of satisfaction, of Christ's death being to meet the claims of divine justice on sinners. He was by no means, however, the first to do so. Tertullian had written of the Lord making satisfaction to God for the sin of man (*On Penitence* 5.9, *CCSL*, 1, 328–329; 7.14, *CCSL*, 1, 334; 8.9, *CCSL*, 1, 336). He said this in the context of penance, in a situation where a temporal penalty was accepted to avoid an eternal loss. Additionally, Tertullian could see Christ's death as a sacrifice in fulfilment of Isaiah chapter 53 (*Against the Jews* 13:21, *CCSL*, 2, 1388–1389). Cyprian (d. 258) too viewed Christ's death as having a surplus of merit which was paid to God as compensation or satisfaction (*On Penitence* 2, cited by Aulén, p. 82). Hilary of Poitiers (*c*. 315–68) writes of the eternal Son of God being condemned to death on the cross not by necessity of nature but for the salvation of man as a penal satisfaction (*officio ipsa satisfactura poenali*). He can even talk of God having suffered (*Passus ergo est deus, quia se subiecit voluntarius passioni*)! (*Treatise on the Psalms*, Ps. 53, *CSEL*, 22, 137, 144–145; see also his comments on Pss. 68:23; 135:15; 64:4; 129:9). Kelly calls him 'one of the pioneers of the theology of satisfaction'.[14] In the East, Origen wrote of Christ freely suffering for our sins, offering as a priest a sacrifice in which he himself was the victim (*Homily on Numbers* 24:1, *MPG*, 12, 755–759; *Commentary on John* 28:19, *MPG*, 14, 732–737). Cyril of Alexandria also thought of the atonement as a sacrifice of penal substitution (*On Adoration and Worship in*

163

Spirit and Truth 3, MPG, 68, 293f.; *On the Gospel of John* 2, MPG, 73, 192; *That Christ is One*, in MPG, 75, 1340–1341; *Discourse on the True Faith*, in MPG, 76, 1292; *Another Discourse on the True Faith*, in MPG, 76, 1344; *Letters* 50, in MPG, 77, 264). In fact, Kelly regards this motif as the mainstream in the East in the fourth century.[15]

Anselm, however, did not merely develop an idea. He founded an era. In a nutshell, this is what he said. If one person violates another he must repay what is owed plus an additional restitution for pain and injury. Therefore all who sin against God must repay their debt to him plus payment for the offence to his honour (*Why did God become Man?* 1:11). It is not fitting that God should forgive sins without payment received for humanity's debt, since God does nothing unjustly (1:12–13). If a sinner does not repay what he owes, God takes it from him. Therefore, sin is followed either by satisfaction or by punishment (1:14–15). To be saved, satisfaction must be made for human sin (1:19). Human beings cannot do this themselves (1:20–23); of necessity they are saved only through Christ (1:25), and God will complete his plans for them. But this requires that satisfaction for sin be made by someone who is not a sinner (2:4). God does not do this under any external compulsion. Any necessity arises from God's own nature; it is a necessity of honour (2:5). Only a God/man could make this satisfaction, one who is greater than anything other than God and one who is also human since it is a human responsibility to pay the debt – hence the necessity of the incarnation (2:6–7). The God/man is not obliged to die, since only the corrupt have to die. Sin will be impossible for him since he is God. Thus, he dies from his own free choice, as a voluntary act of the will (2:7–11). Primarily, then, Anselm sees the atonement as a payment of the human race's debt to God by a substitute whom God himself provides. It is a satisfaction of divine justice. It is also a conquest of the devil (6:7) but the striking thing is that nothing is owing to the devil. All that is owed is owed to God (2:19).

Anselm has been heavily criticized on a number of counts, including the following. Firstly, it has been said that he introduces necessity into God, thereby reducing everything to logic. The atonement is seen as an event which had to happen out of sheer logical necessity. The approach is one of the utmost rationalism. As we have indicated, however, the necessity is seen by Anselm as arising out of the nature of God himself and not from any source extrinsic to him. Moreover, Anselm's approach is dictated by the context of his work. He was writing to his fellow-monks in dialogue form, on the assumption that his colleague was 'taking the part of those who will believe nothing unless it is first proved by reason' (1:10). Since this was in any case undertaken in a monastic context, it falls under Anselm's own overriding view of theology as *fides quaerens intellectum* (faith seeking understanding). Secondly, the claim has often been advanced that Anselm saw the atonement through the eyes of mediaeval feudalism and so imported the notion of honour on to God, thus distorting the focus of Christ's death. The context is more the penitential system, however, than the feudal one. This was the original locus for both Tertullian and Hilary. Whatever the defects of the evolving doctrine of penance, it did at least rest on the biblical doctrines of sin, the justice and grace of God, and the necessity for repentance and good works. Besides, Anselm integrates incarnation and atonement well. He sees the reparation by Christ as a work of the undivided mediator, both God and man. There is no placating of an angry Father by a kind and loving Son, for the atonement is the provision of God from first to last.

Luther, as we have already noted, viewed Christ's death as a sacrifice (*LW* 13, 319; 23, 195) in which he took on himself all our sins, and obtained forgiveness and reconciliation. It was a satisfaction to the justice of God (*LW* 25, 249; 36, 177; 12, 365; 51, 92). Christ was our substitute. He 'shed his blood for me', for 'we can and must say: "God was crucified and died for me". And if anyone projects a god who did not suffer and die for me, I will have no truck with him' (*LW* 24, 98). Christ died for us so that we will not die for all eternity (*LW* 25,45; 51,92; 34,119; 53,219f.). His death secures our forgiveness, righteousness and eternal life (*LW* 25, 284, 349).

Calvin also taught that the atonement was a satisfaction to the justice of God. The passage cited in chapter 1 (pp. 24–25 above) is a good example, where the entire course of Christ's career as mediator reaches its goal in his offering our flesh to God as a satisfaction to divine justice (*Institutes*, II,12,1–2). His obedience was the ground of all he did on the cross (II,16,5; II,17,3). Our sins were transferred to him (II,12,2–3; II,16,5–6) and his suffering for our sins involves a penal element. The atonement is a propitiation of the wrath of God (II,15,5–6; II,16,6; II,17,2–4; *Commentary on Romans* 3:24–25). It is not a case of an unwilling God being placated by a loving Jesus, however, for the propitiation is the provision of God's love. Christ came because God loved us (*Institutes* II,12,1; II,16,1–4; *Commentary on 2 Corinthians* 5:19).

The classic confessional documents of Protestantism all follow this line. The *Formula of Concord* (1576) refers to Jesus Christ as having expiated all our sins, having made satisfaction for them and thus obtaining remission of sins, righteousness and eternal life (V:iv). The Thirty-Nine Articles of the Church of England (1563, 1571) state: 'The Offering of Christ once made is that perfect redemption, propitiation, and satisfaction, for the sins of the whole world, both original and actual; and there is none other satisfaction for sin, but that alone' (Art. XXXI). The Westminster Confession of Faith (1647) speaks of Christ the mediator 'by his perfect obedience and sacrifice of himself . . . once offered up unto God, hath fully satisfied the justice of his Father' (VIII:v). We have already examined some criticisms of this position in chapter 7.

The moral influence theory

The claim that the atonement was principally a demonstration of the love of God, its power residing in a moral and subjective change in us as we contemplate what Christ did, is most frequently described as the moral influence theory. Peter Abelard (1079–1142) has been identified as its founder. This is false on two counts. First, a purely exemplary cast had been suggested for the atonement long before Abelard. Clement of Alexandria (*c.* 155 – *c.* 220) had taught that Christ was an illuminator whose task involved the impartation of knowledge (*Protrepticos* 11, 114, 4, GCS 12, 80–81; *Paedogogus*

1, 5, *MPG* 8, 261–280; *Stromatum* 2, 22, *MPG* 8, 1079f.).
Second, the claim for Abelard rests on one passage in his
writings, in his *Exposition of the Epistle to the Romans*, in particular his comments on Romans 3:19–26. In fact, the case
rests on just one sentence, which states that redemption is
'love in us'. Earlier in the selfsame context, however, Abelard
has unequivocally spoken of redemption by the blood of
Christ, which he sees as his death. He rejects a ransom paid to
Satan for it is properly paid to God. Hence, the atonement is
in reality a Godward phenomenon and not a subjective moral
change in us. Recent scholarship has recognized this to be
so.[16]

The real genesis of the idea appears to be in Enlightenment Germany. In Britain, Hastings Rashdall attempted
belatedly to popularize it in 1915 but by then it was too late,
for the First World War was to shatter optimism about the
nature of humanity and to encourage a recovery of the idea
of sin and depravity. This indeed was the Achilles heel of the
theory. Its basic predicate was that human beings have the
power to improve themselves morally. The doctrine of
original sin and any ensuing depravity was viewed as intoler-
able, hence the attempt to empty the atonement of ideas of a
divine transaction concerning sin, wrath and judgment. That
this was a naively complacent view of human nature was
demonstrated beyond question by the horrors of the decades
after Rashdall. Two world wars, Auschwitz, Hiroshima and
countless revelations of human wickedness have rendered
the position untenable. Of course, Christ's death does produce a subjective moral change in those who contemplate it in
faith by the power of the Holy Spirit. Where the theory goes
wrong is in seeing this change as the atonement.

The governmental theory

The Dutch jurist Hugo Grotius (1583–1645) expounded the
idea that salvation by the atoning death of Christ was undertaken by God for the purpose of safeguarding his moral
government of the universe. In his work *Defence of the Catholic
Faith concerning the Satisfaction of Christ*, Grotius opposed the
Socinians who argued that to punish is not suitable for God.

He insisted, in contrast, that it is appropriate in order to prevent the corruption of human morals. God's wrath serves as an example to human beings and God uses punishment to promote the common good (*Works* [1679], 3:306–309). There are reasons given us in Scripture why God has chosen to punish Christ and why he did not choose some other way to save us. Firstly, he chose this way out of goodness, his foremost characteristic. Secondly, he did so because of his wrath against sin. Thirdly, he chose to do so in his wisdom. He wisely chose to uphold his law and its authority. He relaxed the penalty of the law against us but only by transferring it to someone else. He did this not so much in order to display his wrath but rather to deter us from sin (*Works* 3:315–317). At root, the atonement was a free decision of God made for strictly prudential reasons. His decree was not a necessary outflow from his nature. God could have chosen otherwise, but all told, it was the best and wisest course of action in the circumstances. Acts of God's goodness stem from his free will which always functions according to his wisdom.

There are several reasons why this approach is untenable. Firstly, it adopts a limited and truncated view of God's justice. The focus throughout is on the rectoral justice of God at the expense of his retributive justice. God is seen as a wise administrator, weighing up alternatives to arrive at ends most conducive to morality, exactly like a seventeenth-century Dutch jurist! Little consideration is given to the biblical connection between sin and punishment, or judgment in strict accord with human actions, due to God's being a just judge (*cf*. Rom. 2:5–11). Secondly, following from this, the connection between sin and punishment is severed. This lies at the root of all attempts to evade the classic Protestant understanding of the atonement as satisfaction of divine justice. Certainly, according to Grotius God does punish human sin in Christ. But such punishment comes not because God's righteous, holy and just character requires it but because he freely chooses to punish in order to govern the human race more effectively. Moreover, thirdly, the view introduces an element of arbitrariness into God. He could have chosen some other way to save us if he had thought it wiser. The wisdom and will of God have been elevated over his justice. Instead of God's wisdom being in accordance with his retributive justice, the two are abstracted and separated. It is a weakness of John Stott's treatment of the cross of Christ that he approaches Grotius' viewpoint uncritically, even citing B. B. Warfield in support, despite Warfield's own consistent opposition to it as a halfway house between an objective view of the atonement and outright rationalism.[17]

Vicarious sympathy/repentance

In the middle of the nineteenth century, a number of writers stressed the vicarious nature of the atonement but wished to eliminate any notion of Christ having suffered the penal sanctions of the law of God. Two of the most significant of these were John McLeod Campbell and the American, Horace Bushnell.

We have already encountered Campbell in chapter 1. Writing from a pastoral situation in which many of his parishioners lacked assurance of salvation, Campbell wrote a sustained and critical attack on the theology of Calvinism as exemplified by John Owen (1616–83) and Jonathan Edwards (1703–58). Owen saw a fixed link between sin and punishment, arising from the inflexible justice of God. Both he and Edwards consequently considered Christ to have suffered what the elect deserved to suffer and what the non-elect will endure in hell. Campbell opposed this on a number of grounds. First, he saw it as a limitation on the warrant of the gospel, which calls all who hear it to trust Christ. Second, under this approach the work of Christ is no longer a revelation of the nature of God. God's justice has been made an essential attribute of God but his love has been relegated to an arbitrary attribute. God is of his own necessity just but exercises his love strictly in accordance with his free will. Campbell held that in the theology of Owen and Edwards, the cross does not make known the love of God. Third, in such a view the atonement was seen in legal rather than filial terms. It represented a truncated view of God and his work.

Instead, Campbell proposed that the atonement be seen in its own light. Christ's sufferings were not penal so much as the sufferings of incarnate holiness and love. Christ came into the world to live a life of self-sacrificial love. So he bore our burdens in love and, of necessity, cared for all humanity. He endured pain in sympathy with God, responding to God's judgment on sin with a perfect 'Amen' in his humanity. His confession of our sins was a perfect human repentance for the sins of man. As God, he grieved over our sin. Peace with God is spiritual before it is legal.[18]

Campbell's argument can be criticized as follows. Firstly, in opposing what he regarded as an excessively legal doctrine of atonement and in attempting to do justice to the filial, Campbell tended to go to an extreme and divide up the attributes of God on a basis to his liking. Consequently, the wrath of God against our sin (the focus of Owen and Edwards) was replaced by love and holiness. As a result, Christ was not held to have undergone penal suffering on the cross but, instead, to have repented on our behalf in loving sympathy with us.[19] Campbell considered such a view to be pastorally preferable. One is hard pressed, however, to avoid the conclusion that he allowed the pastoral situation to dictate to his view of God. Secondly, the larger question which undermines his entire thesis flows directly from what we have just said. If all that was necessary for atonement was vicarious repentance, why did Christ have to die the cursed death of the cross? Is there not something more at stake? Campbell leaves us with the overwhelming centre of the Christian faith (the cross) as little more than a frightening charade.

Horace Bushnell, in his book *Vicarious Sacrifice* (1866), expounded a position not dissimilar to Campbell's. Christ did not submit to a penalty which we had deserved. Such a substitution would be offensive to our strongest sentiments, besides being revolting to God himself. Rather, Christ, in love and at the expense of great suffering and even death, brings us out of our sins and the penalties attaching to them. Love is essentially vicarious, identifying with others and taking their burdens. So Christ identified with us in friendly sympathy. He did not take our sins or suffer their punishment; that would be gross injustice. Atonement is a change produced in us, a subjective reconciliation. As a result, God is set in a new relation to us, one of peace. For Bushnell, the atonement is

170

essentially subjective. He moved close to the moral influence theory. He lacked the more strongly objective cast of Campbell, yet shared his stress on the vicarious nature of the atonement. Both rejected the idea that Christ suffered the penalty of the wrath of God for our sins. Both denied a necessary connection between sin and punishment.

Karl Barth

We have already referred to Barth's distinctive treatment of the atonement in chapter 1. We indicated how he saw the incarnation as decisive, insofar as the union of deity and humanity in Christ is the covenant made by God with man and the locus of atonement. Barth goes on to develop his doctrine of atonement at length in *CD*, IV/1, pp. 211ff.

According to Barth, Christ's life and ministry demonstrate that God is for us. He came to save us, but he saved us by pronouncing sentence on us as judge. This sentence was taken by Christ as our substitute. He became sin for us and was both judge and judged on our behalf. As such, sin was punished and we are reconciled to God. The justice of God was made known: Jesus took our place as judge and judged, he was judged and acted justly. The resurrection which followed was an act of God, his verdict acknowledging that his wrath was fulfilled in the death of Jesus. It demonstrates that God is ours and we are his. From this standpoint Barth then proceeds to discuss the nature of the sin which had occasioned Christ's work.

In many ways, Barth presents a vigorous and ingenious exposition of the penal substitutionary view of the atonement. What distances it from previous formulations of the doctrine is the strong colouring given by his masterful doctrine of incarnation. That is what encourages the frequent claim that Barth was a universalist. The atoning work of Christ is thoroughly objective. It is an historical event. It has taken place, it is finished. Yet since Barth's view of God, humanity, election and covenant is so pervasively dominated by the momentous event of the incarnation, the overwhelming impression is conveyed that Christ atoned for all people and that all are therefore saved. Barth, of course, denied that

171

universalism was a necessary conclusion from his teaching (*CD*, II/2, p. 417). Such a denial, however, appears to be despite what he says elsewhere rather than because of it.

Abandonment by the Father

In recent years a new and distinctive perspective has emerged in discussions of the atonement. This has come about through the work of Jürgen Moltmann and Eberhard Jüngel, and has been taken up by liberation theologians such as Jon Sobrino and adapted to the social and political context of Latin America. The new approach focuses on the crucified Jesus as abandoned by God. Much of the impetus for this view derives from the horrific experiences of the twentieth century. Events such as the Holocaust, the bombing of Hiroshima and the ensuing spectre of mass destruction and contamination by nuclear weapons, dire predictions of ecological disaster, starvation and the brutal oppression of marginalized groups in the two-thirds world have all directed attention inescapably to the problem of suffering in situations where there is apparently no hope of relief. Many are forced to endure life in subhuman conditions; whole population groups have been subjected to genocide; the entire human race is threatened with possible extinction; the greed of irresponsible élites threatens many. How far is God involved and concerned? What has Christian faith to say that is meaningful?

In connection with questions such as these, Moltmann took up a theme present in Luther, that of the *theologia crucis* (theology of the cross), and went on to speak of 'the crucified God'. At the cross God himself participated in the suffering and desolation of the world. He endured the curse of abandonment which only the outcast and deprived would undergo. In Jesus' cry of dereliction, 'My God, my God, why have you forsaken me?', Moltmann detects a trinitarian revelation. The Son suffers abandonment and so identifies with those who themselves are abandoned by God. The Father, in turn, suffers the Son to be delivered up to abandonment. The Spirit who justifies the ungodly, proceeds from this event. It is a bold and breathtaking insight that, far from being aloof from human suffering and anguish, God himself freely and directly identifies with it and suffers himself.[20] For Sobrino, the death of Jesus represents God's identification with the poor and marginalized in their suffering and struggle for justice. Jesus' proclamation of the kingdom of God and his own solidarity with the poor ended when his mission terminated in failure and abandonment. The cross was a tragedy. As the poor were dispossessed and destitute so Jesus died in the knowledge that he had shared their marginalization and abandonment. Sobrino is critical of the history of reflection on the cross insofar as it has avoided the scandal of failure and has understood it in the light of the resurrection. Instead, suffering must be seen as part of the being of God, in contrast to Greek epistemology. The death of Christ is the result of the incarnation being situated in a world of sin and injustice. On the cross God himself is crucified. The Father suffers the death of the Son and takes on himself all the suffering and pain of human history. In so doing, he makes himself known as a God of love.[21]

It is clear that this perspective offers a fruitful insight into the reality of God's love and his identification with suffering, providing it is held that he determined to take our sorrows freely without any external necessity laid upon him. It is, however, an incomplete picture of Christ's death. Firstly, the focus is on social and corporate sin to the virtual exclusion of the personal and individual. Christ's death was occasioned by sinful social and economic structures with their concomitant oppression and injustice. As a result sin against one's neighbour is accorded priority over sin against God. In turn, sin against God is said to consist in sin against one's neighbour. The horizontal is absolutized. As such, the perspective fits into a thoroughgoing neo-Kantian framework in which eternity is eclipsed by time. Secondly, the view is based on the premiss that God has partiality to the poor or to the abandoned. This is especially clear in liberation theology. Sobrino stresses it,[22] as do Gutiérrez,[23] Miranda[24] and Segundo.[25] It is hard to see how these assumptions are compatible with the gospel call to personal faith and repentance, irrespective of the social or economic class to which a person belongs. Without doubt, the gospel and therefore the atonement has direct reference to the affairs of life, to economics and power relationships, otherwise redemption has been abstracted from creation. Yet the assumption that God has a preferential love for the poor (who are the poor?) appears to short-circuit the need for a transition from wrath to grace. Besides, the priority placed on praxis over faith, of doing over knowing, creates a kind of Pelagianism, a form of salvation by works that renders the cross little more than an example of doing justice in a world of oppression, rather than an act of God for redemption from sin and a sacrifice of propitiation occasioned by humanity's rebellion against its maker. Thirdly, the prior hermeneutical commitment to advocating the case of impoverished social classes raises inevitable questions as to how far the immediate context in society is governing the understanding of the death of Christ and, consequently, how far the intrinsic nature of the atonement is itself being allowed to govern reflection. Indeed, the exponents of this perspective claim that action, not reflection, is primary. Only by involvement in the struggle for social change can we learn the true nature of Christ's work. The liberation struggle quite self-consciously governs the proposal on the atonement.

Conclusion

This survey of the history of thought on the atonement shows that no one theory has ever commanded universal support. Moreover, no one viewpoint appears to answer all the questions that surface when we reflect on what Christ came to do on the cross. At least some of the above positions claim to exclude others in a hegemonistic sense. The moral influence theory and the view of vicarious sympathy were both forged in opposition to objective formulations that stressed the atonement as penal suffering of the wrath of God. While the ransom theory could coexist with other perspectives, Aulén tended to advocate it as a competitive alternative to the more legal ideas of Anselm. On the other hand, the idea of satisfaction or penal substitution does not exclude other theories. It is compatible with the conquest theory and can also see subjective change occurring in human beings as a consequence of what Christ did on the cross. As such, the penal substitutionary theory, while maintaining that the essence of the atonement lay in Christ suffering the penalty of God's wrath for our sins, can also admit that this does not exhaust its meaning, whether on the individual, corporate or cosmic levels.

9

ATONEMENT
AND JUSTIFICATION

The connection between atonement and justification

We now turn our attention to something often overlooked in discussions of the atonement. The lines of connection from the death of Christ to our justification are too significant to ignore. Traditionally, the work of Christ has been regarded as a topic separate from the application of salvation by the Holy Spirit. As a result, the affinity between justification and the atonement has often been missed. A glance at standard works of systematic or dogmatic theology will show just how frequent such a separation can be. It is a classic case of an imposed model, useful for a particular purpose, inhibiting the development of the inner connections and ramifications of theology. All models have limitations. A common method has existed in systematic theology of proceeding from one discrete topic to the next in linear progression. This has produced great clarity and the impression of logical progress from one point to the next. There are dangers, however, of being trapped by the limitations of the model or models we use. In this case, the separation of the work of Christ from the work of the Spirit (since they appear from one perspective to follow in logical sequence) has led to the loss of other connections that exist between them, such as between the atonement and justification. These connections can often be seen only if we take another perspective.

Before we begin, we must remember that in discussing justification we are concerned with the situation of a law court, an objective and forensic matter. What is at stake is the question of our status before God in terms of his law. By his sin, Adam plunged the race into guilt. We had infringed God's righteous and holy law and were guilty before God. The penalty was death. Paul makes that clear in Romans 5:12–21, where he traces the effect of Adam's one act of disobedience, showing that it resulted in condemnation and death for all. On the other hand, justification brings into view the possibility of acquittal from guilt, being declared righteous and so receiving life. At root are categories derived from the court room. We have seen how such terms are used in connection with the atonement.

Perhaps the clearest demonstration of the connection between atonement and justification is that of Paul in Romans 4:25f. Christ was 'delivered over to death for our sins and was raised to life for our justification'. Here, Christ's death and resurrection are seen, as usual, by Paul in unbroken unity. Yet, there are distinct consequences flowing from each. The death of Christ dealt with the question of our sin and guilt. His resurrection secured our justification. These are not separate but rather parts of a whole, however – a unity that is every bit as real as the death and resurrection itself. Justification, as we shall see, consists for Paul not only in pardon for sins, due to the removal of guilt, but also in the imputation of righteousness. Hence, the atoning death of Christ secures one side of our justification, that of pardon or forgiveness, while his resurrection obtains for us the other element, righteousness. As death and resurrection stand together as twin aspects of the central accomplishment of Christ, so too do atonement and justification. The death of the cross was not the end for Jesus. Indeed, it would have been a tragic charade if the empty tomb had not followed. In turn, it was the resurrection that gave meaning to the death and cast light for the disciples on all that had gone before. After all, the very idea of resurrection requires death first, or it is not resurrection. As much then as death and resurrection are inseparable and mutually necessary, so also justification cannot take place without the atonement for sins, for people cannot be accounted righteous if they are under the wrath of God. Neither, on the other hand, can the atonement be understood without its inseparable corollary, receiving righteousness, which enables us not merely to be brought into a state of innocence, but makes us fit to be friends of a just and holy God.

We will now look at this from another perspective. As it appeared at the time, Christ was condemned to death as a criminal. He died in disgrace, abandoned by his disciples and forsaken by God. He faced the edict of the law that all who died upon a tree were accursed. With this as the backcloth, the resurrection was nothing less than a full public vindication of Jesus. It was a declaration by God that in his sight Christ was righteous and just, a declaration that was made publicly and proclaimed across the world. In short, Jesus' resurrection was his justification. We know that we who trust Christ are united with him in his death and resurrection, since he is and was at all stages our representative and substitute. Consequently, we share in his ignominious death, and our sins really are transferred to him. Christ endured the full penalty we have incurred. In the same way, we also share in his resurrection, his public vindication and his justification by God. He took our sin and guilt, and so we receive his righteousness and justification. He suffered in our place there and then on the cross. His justification in his resurrection will be ours in a final sense when we also are raised from the dead at the last day and receive full public vindication in the judgment. Because of our union with Christ, however, that justification is anticipated here and now and we receive it through faith.

We shall now examine this relationship between atonement and justification in more detail. Firstly, we recall the character of the atonement as obedience. We saw in chapter 7 how Paul describes Christ as having, by his obedience, secured for

179

us righteousness and life. Paul is directing us particularly to his one act of obedience which stands in antithesis to Adam's act of disobedience (Rom. 5:18–19). We saw, too, how Christ's whole life was one of consistent faithfulness to the Father. We saw also how he suffered the just consequences that were due to us for our sins. This passage of obedience included all that he underwent up to and including the cross. It involved both his suffering the penalty due to us for our sins and also his positive fulfilment of the law of God on our behalf. Since Christ's entire ministry was vicarious in nature, all this was done for us. Our sins were laid to his charge, while his righteousness is put to our account. Because he is united with us as the second Adam, the penalty that was ours has been fully discharged in him, while we in turn are truly invested with his righteousness. Thus, whereas we were by nature guilty before God and deserving of condemnation and death, Christ's obedience secures for us acquittal of our guilt and additionally gives us a right status in the sight of God. The atonement is thus an integral part of the movement of God's grace which results in our being justified.

Secondly, Christ is therefore the sole ground of our justification. In ourselves we are guilty before God. We have sinned, all of us, in Adam. In practice, all who have survived infancy have gone on to commit sins freely and voluntarily. The only way out is by the atoning death of Christ in our place. Only the sinless and obedient Christ could step in on our behalf and make atonement for our sins. By doing this, he obtained pardon for us and applied his righteousness to us. As atonement is on no other basis than that of Christ, so is our justification. That is why we are justified by grace alone, for it is by the righteousness of another that we are made right with God. It is not our own doing, it is the gift of God, the result of Christ and all that he has done. It is undeserved, a work of God's goodness and mercy. As a consequence, we are justified also by faith alone, for saving faith is abandoning trust in ourselves and commitment to Jesus Christ. By entrusting ourselves to him we are confessing both our own sinfulness and the righteousness of Christ alone which is sufficient to enable us to live with God.

The nature of justification

We now turn to consider the biblical teaching on justification. Obviously, Paul's letters to the Romans and Galatians, together with the Letter of James are of primary interest. We should not forget the Old Testament background, however, especially in the Psalms and Job.

In the Psalms, there is frequently a plea by the psalmist for vindication by Yahweh (*cf.* Ps. 13:1f; 43:1). He regards himself as faithful but persecuted by the ungodly and so looks to Yahweh to set matters right. The scene is that of a courtroom, with Yahweh the judge who is expected to pronounce the verdict in favour of the suffering but faithful suppliant. Often it is Israel herself who pleads for vindication (Ps. 135:14). As her sorrows increase with exile along with her exploitation at the hands of pagan nations, Israel looks ahead to Yahweh's coming to bring final deliverance to his people and to vindicate her openly in the sight of the nations (*e.g.* Is. chapters 24 – 27). On both the corporate and individual levels, the verdict of Yahweh in vindicating his people runs counter to the current life situation, which on the face of it would spell abandonment by God.

The classic case in this regard is Job. According to the conventional theological view of his day, Job is a wicked man. Since God is just, he rewards the righteous and punishes the wicked. Since Job is suffering deeply, having been stripped of his wealth, health, reputation and social standing, the acceptable conclusion to his friends is that he has sinned in serious ways. Job, on the other hand, knows he is righteous. Eventually, he comes to see that God's justice is to be made known fully only in the future. He clings to the expectation that he will be vindicated then. After his friends are progressively silenced, God speaks. The mere fact of his addressing Job personally demonstrates that he regards him as righteous (a fact known to the reader from the start but hidden from Job and his friends). He publicly owns him as his servant, restores to him double what he had lost and as a result Job is cleared of all charges and triumphantly vindicated in the sight of all. Here we are close to an embryonic doctrine of resurrection. Job's revival of fortunes is analogous to a resurrection from the dead.

Elsewhere in the Old Testament, vindication occurs in the context of God's covenant (Pss. 13:5–6; 43:3–5; 135:13–14; Is. chapters 24 – 27). Yahweh is faithful to his covenant people and so will bring vindication and deliverance to them accordingly, no matter what the obstacles that appear to lie in the way.

In a complementary way, the experience of Jesus follows these lines. He was the faithful servant of God who was subject to suffering and eventual death. His crucifixion appeared to represent the end of the road for him and all that he had taught. He died abandoned by God, condemned by the Jewish authorities. In that context, his resurrection was a public vindication both of his claims and also of his person. Where human beings had condemned him, God declared him righteous. Where it appeared that he had failed miserably, God intervened by raising him to his right hand. Christ's resurrection was his justification.

Moreover, all this took place because of God's covenant. We saw in chapter 2 how the promises of each successive historical covenant came to a focus in Christ. The servant about whom Isaiah wrote was himself described as the covenant, given to enlighten the Gentiles and to bring deliverance to the captives and sight to the blind (Is. 42:1–7). Jesus understood this to refer to himself. As such, the varied lines of Old Testament expectation of Yahweh coming into the world to fulfil his covenant and thereby to vindicate and justify his own people all came to fruition in the death and resurrection of Jesus Christ. It is here that God justifies his people. It is here that they are acquitted from all guilt. It is here that they receive righteousness. This is so because it is here that Jesus Christ himself is justified by God, declared to be righteous in the sight of all. Since the people of God are in union with him, they too are justified in him in his death and resurrection: 'He was delivered over to death for our sins and was raised to life for our justification' (Rom. 4:25).

This is what provides the background for Paul's discussion of justification. Because our justification is grounded squarely in the death and resurrection of Christ, it is both objective and gratuitous. For Paul, to be justified means to be acquitted from the guilt of sin and to be clothed with the righteousness of Christ, a righteousness that is imputed rather than imparted. Since it is the righteousness of Christ, received by faith (a faith directed to Christ alone) and thus wholly of grace, it is the righteousness of someone else and not inherent to ourselves. It is the righteousness of Christ, made known publicly in his resurrection.

Popular Protestant interpretations have considered Paul in Romans and Galatians to oppose Jewish attempts to establish favour with God by their own works (*cf.* Rom. 9:30 – 10:4). As E. P. Sanders has shown, we have no evidence that any Jewish group in the first century attempted such an exercise. These later viewpoints misunderstand Paul by reading him in the light of the late mediaeval controversies. The Jews, in fact, considered themselves to be in covenant with Yahweh already. Indeed, Paul himself in Romans chapters 9 – 11 denies that God had cast them off forever. The law was given at Sinai not in order that the people could enter into covenant with Yahweh by obeying it but because he had taken them into covenant already: 'I am the Lord your God, who brought you out of Egypt' (Ex. 20:2). The principal problem appears to be that there were some Jews who insisted that Gentile converts submit to the full Jewish ceremonial. They were seeking to establish a requirement for covenant membership additional to faith in Jesus Christ, thus destroying grace and basing justification on some human achievement. Such a view would have undermined the sole sufficiency of the work of Christ for justification. Underlying this attitude of the Judaizers was the wider and more prevalent pride in the law among the Jews generally. It was seen as distinguishing them from the Gentiles and as demonstrating their membership in the covenant.[1]

Thus, because of the sole centrality of the work of Christ Paul so strenuously insists on justification by faith. Faith in itself is nothing. It is self-abandonment. By faith we entrust ourselves to the keeping of Christ. We rely exclusively on him and eschew all dependence on ourselves. Moreover, faith has an eschatological side to it. Paul can say we are justified by faith (Rom. 5:1) but he can equally talk of our being saved in hope (Rom. 8:24–25). Hope is oriented to the future, to the return of Christ, to the redemption of our bodies. Consequently, in faith we look ahead to the time when all God's promises will reach their ultimate fruition. We wait with eager expectation for his final verdict, given at the last judgment, when we will receive open, public and universal acquittal, vindication and justification. That absolutely definitive judgment will be entirely gracious for, again, it will be grounded unequivocally on the work of Jesus Christ on our behalf. So here and now, in faith, we are enabled to anticipate that verdict. At the same time, since that verdict will be christologically based, from God's side it is anticipated at the present moment, since the self-abandonment of saving faith matches the christological basis of justification. Put another way, justification by faith in the present mirrors the gracious vindication on the last day.

How does sanctification fit this picture? Does God's grace not impart what it imputes? What of the rigorous teaching of James that we are, after all, justified by works? Firstly, we will consider the relationship between justification and sanctification. We have noticed how for Paul union with Christ is an overarching soteriological concept. He regards all the blessings we receive in salvation as existing in Christ (1 Cor. 1:31; Eph. 1:3–14; 2:1–10). Thus, we benefit from the work of Christ by being united to him by the Holy Spirit. In union with Christ we are justified, sanctified, adopted as God's sons and redeemed from the power of Satan. Thus, both justification and sanctification are received in union with Christ. Whereas justification refers to our status, sanctification relates to our moral condition and nature. Both have present, past and future dimensions to them.[2] Justification affects our legal standing, however, while sanctification concerns our transference into God's possession and our consequent ethical renewal. Therefore, they are distinct soteriological elements. Nevertheless, in practice it is not possible to separate them. A justified person who is not at the same time set apart as God's and thereby being renewed into his image just does not exist. Again, there is no such being as a person who is being sanctified but is not also justified by faith. While the wider theological context of justification requires us to recognize its objective, christological nature and so view it in terms of imputation rather than impartation, we are compelled to acknowledge that the one justified by grace through faith alone is, at the same time, made God's own possession and is in the process of being renewed in his image. The perfect righteousness of Christ is imputed to one's account in justification. Indeed, by virtue of union with Christ this is not a legal fiction but is a reality, since union with Christ is not only a legal union but also a personal, real, spiritual union effected by the Holy Spirit. In that sense, the righteousness of Christ is graciously conferred by virtue of that union (*cf.* 2 Cor. 5:21; Rom. 5:19).[3] In sanctification, righteousness is imparted to us but it is never perfect or complete, however, since we will never be free from sin in this life.

Secondly, the question of the relationship between the teaching of Paul and James on justification is best understood in terms of the differing contexts in which they wrote. Paul, as we have suggested, was insisting that Christ alone is the ground of justification and that there are no additional requirements for covenant membership. Attempts to include additional rites of the Jewish law as mandatory for all, Jews and Gentiles alike, were in practice destroying the gratuitous nature of salvation. For James, however, the danger was the claim to a faith that was devoid of practical outworking. Christian faith is inseparable from good works. If there are no works flowing from faith it is not true faith at all. The works of faith which James commends differ from the works of the law which Paul condemns. As has often been said, we are justified by faith alone but faith is never alone. Moreover, Paul and James cite different examples. Paul refers to Abraham being justified by faith when he believed God and it was reckoned to him as righteousness (Gn. 15:6). James points to Abraham's offering of Isaac on the altar (Gn. chapter 22) and says that his faith was demonstrated by his works (Jas. 2:21–22). As he indicates, faith works together with actions; living faith is active faith. This is no different from Paul who, after pointing to salvation being entirely of grace (Eph. 2:8–9), immediately declares that we have been created in Christ Jesus to do good works, which God prepared in advance for us to do (Eph. 2:10). The Christian life is a unity. Its beginning is an act of God's pure mercy and goodness, while its continuation is no less a work of his grace, even when it requires and involves our most strenuous efforts:

But by the grace of God I am what I am, and his
grace to me was not without effect. No, I worked
harder than all of them – yet not I, but the grace of
God that was with me (1 Cor. 15:10).

Justification in the history of theology

Only very limited attention was given to justification in the
early church. The Reformation threw it into centre stage. By
that time, however, there had been a great deal of theological
development. Alister McGrath has summarized this in his
outstanding work, *Iustitia Dei*. What follows is an extremely
brief survey to set our discussion in historical context. Any
readers interested in pursuing the history of justification
further should begin with McGrath.

In many ways, Augustine is the first major landmark in the
historical treatment of justification. He was to have a great
influence on the mediaeval period. As McGrath demonstrates,[4] Augustine's wide-ranging treatment of justification
included elements that would be distinguished very clearly at
the time of the Reformation. His primary understanding of
the verb *iustificare* (to justify) was 'to make righteous', implying a doctrine of justification by imparted righteousness,
righteousness based on the work of the Spirit within the one
who is justified. This was to become dominant in late mediaeval Catholicism and the Reformers opposed it vehemently.
In fact, justification was for Augustine both an event and a
process. It was an event, in which God initiates human beings'
justification by giving them a will capable of seeking good. It
is also a process, whereby humanity (now possessing a will
released from its previous captivity to sin) co-operates with
God in acquiring merit through his grace by doing good.
This process stems from God himself and is not seen as a
purely human attempt to earn God's favour. Thus, for
Augustine, in justification God makes human beings righteous. When Paul speaks of our being justified by faith,
Augustine sees this justifying faith as faith working through
love.[5] The justified person has an inherent righteousness, not
an imputed one. Justification therefore embraces and
includes what Protestant theology later came to regard as

sanctification. It envelopes the whole process of the Christian life and opens out to include within its scope the entirety of our personal, social and civic life. All is seen in the context of the grace of God.

The influence of Augustine on the entire mediaeval period was, of course, all pervasive. By the time Luther appeared on the scene a variety of theologies of justification had developed, all traceable in some respect or other to Augustine. There is strong evidence, however, that Luther himself had most pointed contact with the *via moderna,* particularly with the teaching of its prominent representative, Gabriel Biel (1420–95).[6] From this perspective God, who can do anything he pleases *de potentia absoluta* (by absolute power), has freely bound himself to act within certain limits *de potentia ordinata* (according to his ordained power) by establishing a covenant (*pactum*) on the terms of which human salvation is to be worked out. According to this *pactum,* God has in grace promised to regard certain human actions as worthy of salvation even though they are not so in strict justice. The qualifying criterion for acceptance of such works and the consequent infusion of grace was that one had 'done one's best' (*facere quod in se est*). This was a semi-Pelagian doctrine of justification that allocated the first step to humanity and the next to divine grace. The big issue that loomed for Luther was the obvious one of how it was possible to be sure that he had done his best? If we were justified, in part at least, on the grounds of something present within us, then justifying righteousness was based on remunerative terms. For anyone troubled by an awareness of sin, problems of doubt and lack of assurance were unavoidable. It was against such a background that the breathtaking discovery was made by Luther that the righteousness of God made known in the gospel (*cf.* Rom. 1:17) was the revelation of the righteousness of Christ made available freely for sinners.

The characteristics of Luther's understanding of justification are well known. They arose, as we have said, largely from his own experience, limited as it was to one strand of current teaching. As a result, Luther strenuously insisted on its objective, *extra nos* (outside ourselves), character. The righteousness involved in our justification is that of someone else. It is the righteousness of Jesus Christ. We are sinners and we remain sinners after justification. Therefore, Luther parts company with Augustine who had stressed the imparting of righteousness and consequently it being inherent in the human race. With Augustine, however, he sees justification as not only an event experienced at one time but also as a continuing process thereafter. It is a process by which, although we are sinners, God is enabled to overlook our sinfulness in view of its ultimate removal.[7] We are justified because of Christ; our justification is not due to anything in ourselves. In fact, the righteousness of Christ is the antithesis of human attempts at righteousness. Luther was therefore something of a bridge between Augustine and Protestantism. He departed from the former on the nature of justifying righteousness but did not adopt the position of the latter on the separation of justification and sanctification. He was not as violently at odds with Rome as he thought. The *via moderna* was not to be identified with the whole church. There were, in effect, a cacophony of opinions on justification in the church at the time, some of which (such as the *schola Augustiniana moderna*) were a lot closer to his own thinking.[8]

Moreover, Luther's theology of justification did not command the scene in Protestantism, Lutheranism included. Melanchthon developed a strong emphasis on imputed righteousness but simultaneously introduced a note of ambiguity by also referring to righteousness as impartation. In the years that followed, Lutheranism was racked by discord over whether justification included the indwelling righteousness of Christ's divine nature (Osiander) and whether justification is a new ability to fulfil the law (Melanchthon). Eventually, the Formula of Concord (1576) consolidated the Lutheran doctrine of justification and in the process brought about some significant modifications of Luther's own position, notably by affirming Melanchthon's development of Luther's objective doctrine in terms of legal imputation. Luther had used legal terminology but had not taken the further step of regarding justification overall in categories of the lawcourt.[9] Additionally, there was a marked difference in outlook in the Reformed camp. Zwingli, for instance, approached justification from a primary interest in regeneration and transformation in the life of the Christian. Justifying righteousness is not only extrinsic but is also imparted.[10] Bucer, in turn, spoke of a two-stage justification, the first a forensic justification of the ungodly, the second a more moralist justification of the godly on the basis of good works.[11] Calvin, however, maintained Luther's stress on the external and objective nature of justification and, unlike Bucer, distinguished justification from sanctification. For him, union with Christ was the primary datum in soteriology, with both justification and sanctification seen as the primary benefits of salvation received by virtue of such union. Hence, they could be distinguished while at the same time held in inseparable conjunction and still regarded as purely gratuitous due to their thoroughgoing christocentricity.[12]

Perhaps most striking is the difference in emphasis on justification between Luther and Lutheranism on the one hand and Reformed theology on the other. For the former, justification is central to the whole of theology. It is the doctrine by which the church stands or falls. It functions as a kind of critical methodological tool by which any aspect of theology, or theology as a whole, is to be judged. McGrath wishes it to function in precisely that way today.[13] It is not hard to see why this claim is made. Justification by faith alone is the affirmation of salvation by grace *par excellence*. It directs us to Christ and away from all forms of self-salvation. As such, it is the hallmark of a truly Christian theology. However, there is hardly an instance of Reformed theology placing justification in the centre. Not that Reformed theologians opposed justification by faith alone, or salvation by pure grace. On the contrary, they saw salvation in its entirety as a display of the sovereign and free mercy of God. The explanation lay in the fact that, for Reformed theology, everything took place to advance the glory of God. Thus the chief purpose of theology and of the whole of life was not the rescue of humanity but the glory of God.[14] The focus was theocentric rather than soteriological. Even in the Heidelberg Catechism (1563), where soteriological concerns are more prominent (one of its authors, Zacharias Ursinus [1533–87] was formerly a Lutheran) the famous first question 'What is your only comfort in life and in death?' is

answered with reference to the action of the Trinity, beginning 'I am not my own but belong . . . to my faithful saviour
Jesus Christ'.

Following from this was an attempt by Reformed theology
to grasp the unity of creation and redemption. The whole of
life was seen in the embrace of God's revelatory purpose. With
the covenant at its heart, the whole of life was to display God's
glory. Naturally, that included at its heart the restoration of
sinners to fellowship with God. It also entailed, however, the
reconstitution of both civil and ecclesiastical affairs. Lutheranism, in contrast, showed less developed interest in the application of the gospel to political life and focused more narrowly
on soteriology. Possibly, this stemmed from Luther enjoying
the patronage of his Elector, which freed him from having to
safeguard the Reformation in a political sense in quite the same
way as his Reformed counterparts. The net result was that
while for Lutheranism justification by faith was the heart of
theology, for the Reformed theologians it was subordinate to
an overarching sense of the centrality of God and his covenant. Yet for both, the underlying concern for the gratuitous
nature of salvation, its objective reality *extra nos*, was the same.

It is important to realize that the response of Rome at the
Council of Trent was not a monolithic one, any more than the
Reformation itself produced a single theology of justification.
Essentially, the Council rejected the idea that the Christian life
did not involve inner transformation. It found itself opposing
a notion of justification that made sanctification irrelevant and
unnecessary,[15] a position adopted by no responsible Protestant but one which the Roman Catholic Church evidently
believed was entailed in the Protestant doctrine. In contrast, it
affirmed that justification involved transformation and
renewal, an impartation of righteousness rather than an
imputation. Calvin and Reformed theology generally saw this
as confusing justification with sanctification. In practice, a
range of theological opinion was represented at Trent, symp-
tomatic of the complexity of the late mediaeval church. There
were the Thomists, who at this time were fairly close to
Augustine and denied that any merit was possible prior to
justification; the Franciscans, who covered a variety of positions, from the *via moderna* (with the semi-Pelagianism that

Luther had encountered) to others who opposed prior merit; and a variety of other perspectives, about which little is known.[16] What Trent did, by opposing its view of the Protestant position and leaving the variety of its own viewpoints without comment, was to legitimize this range of opinion within the church.

McGrath outlines in some detail developments in justification since the Enlightenment. For our purpose, it is sufficient to draw attention to three attempts to bridge the great sixteenth-century divide between Catholic and Protestant. The first such attempt at rapprochement was that of Hans Küng, in his dialogue with Karl Barth in his book *Justification*.[17] Küng simply accepted Barth's recognition of the distinction of justification and sanctification, however, with both as aspects of the one work of salvation in Christ. In this Barth was structually in agreement with Calvin and the consensus of Protestantism.[18] Küng, however, had no evidence whatever that the Roman magisterium had moved to adopt this position. At Trent it had followed Augustine's understanding of justification as infused righteousness, received by faith working through love. That declaration had never been changed. It was not Rome, but Küng, that had reached agreement with Protestantism.

The second example of attempted rapprochement between Catholic and Protestant is the joint discussions between scholars appointed by the US Roman Catholic Bishops' Committee for Ecumenical and Interreligious Affairs and the Lutheran World Ministries (the USA National Committee of the Lutheran World Federation). These discussions are encapsulated in the volume *Justification by Faith: Lutherans and Catholics in Dialogue VII*.[19] It consists of a common statement and a range of scholarly papers on justification. Our focus is the former.

The statement rehearses the historical disagreement between Catholicism and Lutheranism and then moves to a discussion of hermeneutical and theological areas of continued difference or convergence. Its major affirmation, repeated, states:

> ... our entire hope of justification and salvation
> rests on Christ Jesus and on the gospel whereby the

good news of God's merciful action in Christ is made
known; we do not place our ultimate trust in anything other than God's promise and saving work in
Christ (pp. 16, 72).

It is acknowledged that this does not necessarily involve full
agreement on justification but it does raise the question of
whether such differences should divide the church once the
overriding priority of the grace of God in Christ is confessed.

The report is honest in the areas of disagreement that still
exist, despite the convergences brought about by the modern
openness in the Roman Catholic Church to historical-critical
study of Scripture. Differences in hermeneutic are present as
we outlined above and, with them, disagreement over
whether justification is to be the test of theological orthodoxy
(pp. 49f.), and whether justifying righteousness is imparted by
the Spirit or is purely imputed (pp. 50–51). Significant differences exist on the sufficiency of faith (pp. 52–54) and on
merit, where, although the respective positions may now be
compatible, it is difficult to find a common language (pp.
54–55). On the question of satisfaction, while outstanding
divergences are difficult to pinpoint their effects are far-
reaching (pp. 55–56). Contrasting theological perspectives
between Catholic and Lutheran continue. Both sides recognize these perspectives. 'Some of the consequences of the
different outlooks seem irreconcilable' (p. 57), however, and
both sides need to think jointly about the problems. Meanwhile Catholics now realize that justification is a more common theme in the New Testament than they thought, while
Lutherans see that it is more nuanced than they supposed.
Both understand Scripture to have a christological centre
from which other elements should be interpreted. Still there
remains the core question of how far justification is imputed
or imparted (p. 71). All told, the report's honesty is commend-
able. It does not sweep genuine differences under the carpet
and so is able to point to real convergences in both a realistic
and positive way.

The third attempt at agreement we shall consider is the
report published in 1987 by the second Anglican-Roman
Catholic International Commission (ARCIC II), *Salvation and*

the Church. In this document there is a realization that the controversies over justification in the sixteenth century arose largely due to fear. Rome feared that Protestants were undermining the need for good works by an objective and legal doctrine of justification. Protestantism, on the other hand, was concerned that Rome had destroyed the distinction between justification and sanctification with its stress on justification by infused grace and so had undermined the gratuitous nature of salvation. Rome saw Protestants as espousing an unduly individualistic doctrine of salvation, and so marginalizing the church and sacraments. Protestants, for their part, saw Rome as placing church and sacraments so much in the centre that the sole mediation of Christ was thereby threatened. All this is no doubt correct. The Commission sees salvation (correctly, in my judgment) as inseparable from the church. After all, we are none of us saved as isolated individuals but in the context of the community, as part of the church of Jesus Christ, in union with Christ. The document seeks to see union with Christ as the heart of soteriology, again correctly. As such, justification and sanctification are distinct but inseparable gifts we receive in union with Christ. This is none other than Calvin's view, taught by the Reformed church, and reaffirmed by Barth.

At this point, the Commission has made some significant headway, contrary to McGrath,[20] who argues strongly that the Commission made a serious mistake by adding a section on salvation and not considering justification purely in itself. Not only Rome but the Reformed churches too held that justification was to be seen in a wider context than that supplied merely by its most immediate connections. Neglect its hermeneutical underpinning in relation to church and soteriology and a gathering of minds on justification can take place only among those (such as Lutherans) who see it as central, towering and in many respects self-standing. All this is not to say the Commission is clear or helpful in its discussion of these wider issues, and here McGrath's criticisms are pointed and accurate. Moreover, in its concern to reconcile the two sides and to express the unity of justification and sanctification it is unclear exactly what the Commission means by justification. It involves the removal of our condemnation and a new standing before God but, at the same time, it is also 'indissolubly linked' with our sanctifying re-creation. God's grace 'imparts what it imputes'. When God pronounces us righteous he also makes us righteous.[21] These statements are of such ambiguity as to be capable of being understood in a way acceptable both to Trent and to Calvin. Is the sanctifying re-creation of us in grace part of justification or not? Is justification both imputation and impartation? Or is it purely legal yet not to be isolated from the imparting of grace that occurs in sanctification? These questions leave one with the uneasy impression that the Commission has simply found a convenient form of words, leaving the prime point at issue unaddressed. This is the danger, when the upheavals of the Reformation are seen merely as misunderstandings, rather than disagreements.

Part Four

CHRIST AS KING

10

THE MEDIATORIAL KINGSHIP OF CHRIST: THE COSMIC DIMENSION

We turn now to consider the kingship of Christ. As we indicated earlier, Jesus never explicitly claimed to be king. That is no reason, however, to deny that he exercised kingly functions and prerogatives. For one thing, his consistent proclamation of the kingdom of God is evidence that he saw his task in relation to kingship. Additionally, it was only at the resurrection that his full authority came into view. It was then that he was installed by God at his right hand and given full rights over the entire universe. As he said to his apostles 'All authority in heaven and on earth has been given to me' (Mt. 28:18), pointing to his being invested with the legality and right of God himself. We shall return to the theme of the connection between the resurrection and Christ's kingship later. At present, it is enough to note that the synoptics' stress on the kingdom of God is absent from the other New Testament writers' references to the post-resurrection Christ. In its place we find the mediatorial kingdom of Christ. He is the one who is seen to exercise the royal prerogatives of God, and he does so as our mediator, as the one who was slain on the cross for our sins.

In these discussions we will be examining the relation between Christ and creation and also that between creation and redemption. These connections have frequently been overlooked in Western Christianity, which has instead concentrated its attention on personal, individual salvation. That this is vital almost goes without saying. Yet, by its general retreat from culture since the Enlightenment, the Western church has tended to isolate itself from the wider community and has come to be seen increasingly as an anachronism. The unfortunate irony is that this has, in part, been due to its own neglect of important aspects of biblical teaching concerning creation, incarnation and resurrection. To these we now turn.

Christ as the creator, director and goal of the universe

With the unfolding of redemptive history, awareness grew of the trinitarian nature of God. In the Old Testament God revealed himself as one, in contrast to the pagan polytheism of the Ancient Near East. In the New Testament there is a growing realization that, as our Saviour, Christ is equal with God and that the Holy Spirit is, in the unity of God, distinctly personal. As this understanding emerges, so the realization dawns that creation involved all three persons of the Godhead. Even in Genesis chapter 1, creation is seen as the work of God (verse 1), his Spirit hovering over the waters (verse 2) and his word issuing creative fiats (verse 3f.). The doctrine of the deity of Christ supports the claim that, as God, he shared in the creation of the world. Moreover, there are several explicit statements which make this claim even clearer. Perhaps the most significant of these is by Paul in Colossians 1:15–20,[1] the major themes of which we will now examine:

> He is the image of the invisible God, the firstborn over all creation. For by him all things were created: things in heaven and on earth, visible and invisible, whether thrones or powers or rulers or authorities; all things were created by him and for him. He is before all things, and in him all things hold

together. And he is the head of the body, the
church; he is the beginning and the firstborn from
among the dead, so that in everything he might have
the supremacy. For God was pleased to have all his
fulness dwell in him, and through him to reconcile
to himself all things, whether things on earth or
things in heaven, by making peace through his
blood, shed on the cross.

First of all, God's beloved Son (verse 13), who is both King
and Redeemer (verses 13–14), is seen as pre-existent and
possessing the nature of the invisible God (verse 15a). A
strong body of opinion, including Barth, understands this to
refer to the incarnate Christ, to the exclusion of any idea of
pre-existence.[2] Paul, however, elsewhere writes of Christ as
eternally equal with God (Phil. 2:6–7), so such ideas were not
foreign to him. James D. G. Dunn claims that Paul is simply
thinking in terms of Wisdom literature in which personal
pre-existence was not yet articulated. Thus, pre-existent Wisdom comes to its fullest embodiment in Jesus Christ. On the
other hand, as C. F. D. Moule has argued, Dunn overstates
his case.[3] We shall see why in a moment. Moreover and also
contrary to Dunn, S. Kim sees Paul's whole christology,
including a full-blown doctrine of pre-existence, as arising
from his encounter with the risen Christ on the Damascus
road. Kim does not mean that Paul received his entire theology
and christology there and then. His thought did develop.
What Kim argues is that on the Damascus road the essential
lines of Paul's christology were formed and the full implications of that revelation were more or less completely form-
ulated soon after. Thus, the pre-existence of Christ was not
an idea that came only very gradually and therefore was not
quite taught by Paul. It was there effectively from the start of
his Christian experience.[4] The context in Colossians supports
Kim's claim that Paul did teach Christ's pre-existence. The
Colossian church was struggling against heresy. Whatever its
precise nature, the heresy evidently included a denial of
Christ's absolute supremacy. The Wisdom language alone
could hardly answer such a challenge if it was divorced from
a corresponding personal reality. As a consequence, we may

say that Christ (as in Heb. 1:3) reflects the glory of God both in the time of revelatory history but also too in the eternal relations of the Godhead.

Secondly, the Son (eternally co-equal with God) is Lord of creation since as pre-existent Son he created it (verse 15b). The first-born in Israel had priority over all other members of the family. He inherited a double share in the family property (Dt. 21:15–17). Consequently, as first-born of all creation, the Son is heir to the entire cosmos. The point here is priority and supremacy. Since in verse 16 he is said to be creator, he is, therefore, in terms of his personal identity, not simply the chief part of creation but is rather superior to it as its maker.

Thirdly, the Son is creator and ruler of the universe, in all its multi-faceted diversity (verse 16). 'All things' is a comprehensive statement, excluding nothing. Tangible and non-tangible, spiritual and material, angels and human beings: everything owes its existence to the Son. The universe was created *in him*. Not only did he originate it but it was made in union with him as its head. All things were made *through him*, as the agent in the actual work of creation. This is paralleled in Hebrews by the comment that God made the ages through the Son (Heb. 1:2). In the background is the Genesis account where God shaped and structured the dark, watery and empty world by his word (*cf.* Heb. 1:3). Moreover, the Son is the goal of creation: everything was made *for him*. The reason the universe exists is found in Christ. The goal to which it is directed is conformity to Christ. Its unity is in him.

Fourthly, as creator the Son maintains in being what he has made (verse 17). As in Hebrews 1:3, where the Son is said to uphold all things by his powerful word, there is a strong teleological note. There is no idea of passivity, of the Son supporting the universe as a dead weight. The stress is on progress, on a dynamic movement towards a goal. It is intriguing how such a claim is paralleled in modern physics, where the structure of the universe is disclosed as dynamic rather than static. According to Paul, it is Christ who provides its order, coherence and dynamic directedness.

Fifthly, the Son has become the redeemer of his church and thereby renews and completes his creation (verses

18–20). As creator of the world he is also head of his church. Therefore he sustains a dual relationship to creation and church. This is not a dualism, however, for church and universe are mutually interdependent. Paul assumes a unity between the pre-existent Son and the incarnate Christ. This unity, in turn, lends biblical support to the dogma of *enhypostasia*, with its claim that the personal identity of the God/man Jesus Christ is that of the eternal Logos; in other words his human nature has been assumed into union without any independent, autonomous existence apart from that personal union.[5] Thus, the head of the body (the incarnate Christ) is identified with the creator of the universe (the pre-existent Son). Nevertheless, the very fact that the church exists, testifying to deliverance from sin by the blood of the cross (verse 20), indicates that something new has occurred, something in continuity with the original creation but yet which assumes a disruption that had to be put right. Thus, there is a distinction or perhaps a parallel, between creation and redemption. As the Son is the first-born of all creation (verse 15) so he is the first-born from the dead (verse 18) by his resurrection, the one establishing his headship over creation and the other his headship over the church.

The connection between incarnation, atonement, creation and redemption is outlined further in verses 19–20. In the first place, the incarnation involves the full presence of God, so that Jesus Christ incarnate is truly the embodiment of God (verse 19, *cf.* 2:9). Thus reconciliation took place between God and the human race. Additionally (and in the same way), reconciliation also occurred between God and his creation, since humanity is not only part of that creation but also the chief part as God's image and representative. The incarnation was therefore a reaffirmation by God of his creation and the beginning of creation's redemption and renewal. Secondly, attention swings forwards to the atonement where this reconciliation is formally and decisively accomplished, for it is 'through the blood of his cross' (verse 20, *my translation*) that all things are reconciled. Nevertheless, we have already observed that incarnation and atonement are part of one great reality and cannot be divorced without prejudice to both. That which was begun in the incarnation came to full

expression in Christ's death and resurrection. Thirdly, we
note that this reconciliation includes the entire cosmos (verse
20). The scope of 'all things' here in verse 20 cannot be less
comprehensive than the 'all things' that the Son created
(verse 16) and holds together (verse 17). The church is
central in the reconciliation (verse 18) yet we must never lose
sight of the fact that Christ has brought about a cosmic
reconciliation. Our redemption is a microcosm of that of the
whole universe, a central, key microcosm since the redemption of the whole is achieved by the Son becoming man. Once
again, the author of Hebrews parallels Paul. In Hebrews
2:5f., he indicates that 'the coming world', the world introduced by the Son in his death and resurrection (Heb. 1:2–3),
is under the authority of the human race. Originally, God
gave us the responsibility of governing the earth as his personal representatives. Sin entered, however, and we misused
our charge. We do not yet see the human race in full
authority. We have been deeply affected by sin, and so too
has the creation. Today we are only too aware of human
abuse of the environment, diabolical weapons of mass
destruction and our enormous propensity for carnage. However, we see Jesus (Heb. 2:9), who as man is now seated at
God's right hand, crowned with glory and honour, all things
under his feet. Hence, our salvation ultimately consists in the
administration of God's renewed creation, in union with
Christ. We 'groan inwardly', awaiting that liberation, the time
when our bodies will be redeemed. So too does the creation
as it awaits the manifestation of the children of God (Rom.
8:18–23). As Athanasius put it:

> We will begin, then, with the creation of the world
> and with God its maker, for the first fact that you
> must grasp is this: the renewal of creation has been
> wrought by the self-same Word who made it in the
> beginning. There is thus no inconsistency between
> creation and salvation; for the Father has employed
> the same agent for both works, effecting the salva-
> tion of the world through the same Word who made
> it at first.[6]

Sin, the resurrection and the creation mediatorship of Christ

We have recognized a twofold aspect to the relationship between Christ and creation. As eternal and pre-existent Son he created the universe and continues to sustain its existence. On the other hand, as the incarnate Son and our mediator he is now risen from the dead and, in his place of supreme authority he is renewing us and will ultimately redeem both us and the whole created order. The connection between these two poles concerns how we relate and prioritize creation and redemption. This is the theme of Chul Won Suh's book, *The Creation Mediatorship of Jesus Christ.*[7]

Dr Suh considers that, broadly speaking, there have been two main ways of construing this relationship. On the one hand, there have been those who have argued that God's principal goal is the renewal of the cosmos. As such, the incarnation was merely a means to a greater end. In fact, if (hypothetically) Adam had not sinned, Christ would still have become incarnate, since it would have been a necessary step on the way to the elevation of creation, humanity centrally included, to a higher status. This is an essentially supralapsarian position, with the primary concentration on the ultimate end of election, the destiny to which all things are directed, the renewal of the cosmos. Suh terms this 'elevation-line' theology. On the other hand, there is the argument that the incarnation is solely concerned with putting right the problems surrounding human sin. Restitution of the created order is simply a byproduct; the atonement and the removal of sin is primary. In Suh's categories, this is 'restitution-line' theology, regarding the work of Christ as centrally concerned with restoring what went wrong due to sin. It is an infralapsarian perspective.[8]

There are, of course, weaknesses with both approaches, corresponding to the infralapsarian and supralapsarian debate. The 'elevation-line' theology tends to minimize the impact of sin, almost making it a necessary part of a divinely ordained progression towards bringing creation to fruition. Again, questions over the final judgment can easily arise when such a synthesis is adopted. Moreover, can one avoid implicating Christ in human sin? Many of the exponents of such thinking have posited the incarnate Christ as the mediator of creation to the exclusion of the pre-existent Son (Barth is one). One wonders if this is not something of an absolutization of time, in Kantian fashion. Moreover, the biblical centrality of the death and resurrection of Christ is missing.

The shortcomings of the 'restitution-line' theology centre on a lack of interest in creation. By narrowly focusing on redemption from sin on the human and personal level, its exponents may have ignored the cosmic scope of Christ's work. Again, such a dualism points to Kantian or even Greek roots. It is an excessively individualist attitude. In today's world, where the health of the environment is such a pressing matter, it appears restrictive, pietistic and irrelevant to cling to a theological model which does not address such questions. Moreover, to separate creation and redemption is, so to speak, a Nestorian position. Just as Nestorianism held the two natures of Christ apart without doing adequate justice to the unity of his person, so this model has difficulty integrating the renewal of the created order. There is potential for a disruption in understanding the works and ways of God, which has serious implications in a host of areas.

The biblical witness is clear as to Christ's role in and over creation. As the eternal Son he made all things (Jn. 1:1–5; Heb. 1:1–2). As the incarnate Son he is renewing and will restore all things (Eph. 1:18–23; Heb. 1:2–3; 2:5–9). It is preferable to hold these two aspects together for two very good reasons. In the first place, we have already noted the identity and continuity between the eternal and incarnate Son. In terms of personal identity, it is the pre-existent Logos who assumed human nature into personal union. The scene and context is different, the personal actor is the same. In short, there is an ongoing personal identity between the pre-existent Son of God and Jesus Christ. Secondly, we must avoid a dualistic split between creation and redemption. God is creator and redeemer. Both the universe he made and the redemption he has provided are his works. If we were to conceive of salvation as affecting only the purely spiritual or personal dimensions, we would be left with a severely truncated gospel. Such a view would be akin to the Greek denigration of the material in favour of the spiritual. Moreover, we could hardly then do justice to large sections of the Bible which speak of creation and its renewal on the material level. Hence, we should see the twin foci of Christ's role as mediator of creation as parts of a greater, unified whole.

Nevertheless, the resurrection does function in a special way, marking the entrance of something new. After all, Christ's work has unashamedly historical roots. The incarnation is nothing other than an affirmation by God of the value and validity of his creation and thus of space/time. Consequently, the resurrection itself is the affirmation of Christ's renewing and restorative work in and upon the creation. It is striking how often the New Testament reflects on this. It is the point at which he is given 'all authority in heaven and on earth' (Mt. 28:18), at which he is 'appointed heir of all things' (Heb. 1:2–3). God's mighty power raised him from the dead and seated him at God's right hand, far above all principalities and powers, all things being placed under his feet, Christ filling all the creation (Eph. 1:18–23). Made alive in the Spirit, he has gone into heaven, angels being in subjection to him (1 Pet. 3:18, 22). He now reigns, till all his enemies are put under his feet (1 Cor. 15:20–26). In turn, Paul describes our salvation as being made alive with Christ (Eph. 2:5). Again in Ephesians, Paul describes the mystery of the inclusion of the Gentiles in Christ's church (following the resurrection) as something to be made known by the church to the principalities and powers in the heavenly places (Eph. 3:8–11), a mystery previously hidden but part of God's eternal purpose.

We are close here to the perspective of the atonement as conquest. One of the great strengths of that view is its relation to creation. We shall explore further the relation between Christ's resurrection and ours in the next chapter on the corporate dimension of the mediatorial kingship of Christ. At the moment, the point to note is that sin and the fall disrupted creation. In particular, the human race fell into guilt and misery, plunging the universe itself into bondage. In no way did this take God by surprise or force him to

205

change his plans, as Suh implies.[9] God's actions are free, unconstrained from without. He is hardly taken by surprise by events which he did not expect. Rather, the incarnation and redemptive work of Christ were planned by God from eternity with the purpose of remoulding the entire created order, having removed human sin and guilt and conquered his enemies in the spiritual realm. Because of the personal continuity between the pre-existent and the incarnate Christ, Christ's mediation of creation is now essentially similar to that in the beginning. There is continuity between them. Any distinctions arise out of the changed condition of the creation itself. In the first place, the cosmos is subject to bondage on account of human sin. Secondly, the Son assumed human nature in the incarnation. However, in no way was there a change in his personal identity.

The doctrine of the creation mediatorship of Christ has important bearings on the continued relevance of his work. How, it can be asked, can something done so many years ago be of effect for the human race in an ongoing sense? How relevant to us today is the atoning death of Christ 2,000 years ago? How can the death of the one have any significance for the many? On the one hand, there is a huge historical and cultural gap between now and then. Can it be bridged? On the other hand, how can our situations now and in the future be eternally affected by only one person living somewhere else? Here, as Colin Gunton has helpfully indicated, the creation mediatorship of Christ assures us that the historical gap between then and now is no barrier. Christ himself has cosmos-wide significance in his own right. He made the universe. He is Lord of space and time.[10]

The mediatorial kingship of Christ and the eschaton

Creation and redemption are inextricably connected. From one perspective, creation exists for the sake of redemption; redemption will be nothing less than the restoration, renewal and completion of creation, humanity centrally included. From another angle, redemption depends on creation; the cross itself required the prior existence of the world, the

206

human race, Jerusalem and wood, while the ongoing task of the church demands that the nations of the world continue in existence so that they can be discipled.

This holds true also from the perspective of the end. When Christ returns it will be to bring complete salvation to his church, focusing on the resurrection and redemption of the body. At the same time, the cosmos itself will be liberated (Rom. 8:18–23). Paul brings these elements together in Philippians 2:5–11: Christ, having emptied himself and submitted to the death of the cross, is now exalted and given the supreme name of 'Lord' (*kyrios*). His installation at God's right hand is in view. Following this, every knee will bow before him, doing homage and confessing him as 'Lord', to the glory of God the Father. Paul pictures a united universe: its central focus is the exalted Christ, and all things are seen in the light of Christ. The unity and harmony of the cosmos will be realized through its creator, sustainer, redeemer and mediator, who provides all things with meaning. Moreover, this unity and fulfilment is itself grounded on the unity in God himself. The universal homage to Christ as Lord will be to the glory of God the Father. There is no competitiveness within the Godhead: ''Tis the Father's pleasure we should call him Lord'.[11] God is relational, in his unity living in a fellowship of love and communion. So his creation will be brought to its fruition, in a harmony and unity that in its essential dynamism brings honour to Christ and thus glory to humanity. We have yet to see what God will make of the human race.

In 1 Corinthians 15:25–28 Paul provides us with another glimpse of the consummation:

> For he must reign until he has put all his enemies under his feet. The last enemy to be destroyed is death. For he 'has put everything under his feet'. Now when it says that 'everything' has been put under him, it is clear that this does not include God himself, who put everything under Christ. When he has done this, then the Son himself will be made subject to him who put everything under him, so that God may be all in all.

At his parousia, when the dead are raised, all Christ's enemies will have been subjected to him. Then he will hand over his kingdom to God, his mediatorial task achieved, creation restored, death destroyed, humanity triumphant. Ephesians 1:9–10 puts it like this:

> ... the mystery of his [God's] will ... which he purposed in Christ, to be put into effect when the times will have reached their fulfilment – to bring all things in heaven and on earth together under one head, even Christ.

It is a case of all things being headed by Christ, God's eternal plan achieved, all in their proper place in the grand design: the love, goodness, wisdom and grace of God self-evidently displayed throughout.

The mediatorial kingship of Christ is from one perspective a time-related phenomenon, lasting from resurrection to parousia. At the latter point it merges into the eternal state in which God reigns. From another angle, it will never end, since Christ is and will always be our mediator.

At present, we are alert to the pressing issue of the environment. If Christ is creator and sustainer of the universe, and if he is to remould it, then car exhaust emissions, ozone layer depletion, nuclear waste disposal, toxicity in the atmosphere and the widespread problem of garbage removal are matters of integral concern to the church and to theology. This world belongs to our Saviour, and we have been given custodial charge of it. We are responsible to him for how we use it. The problem of sin includes not only questions of personal morality but also the careless use of Christ's environment. A host of matters, in the personal, political and social arenas, are transformed when we see Christ's mediatorial kingship in this way. Moreover, as another direct implication, no realm is out of bounds to the Christian faith. All things – education, politics, business, sport, the arts, family life, economic conditions such as inflation and unemployment, scientific enquiry, the legal system and so on – are to be seen from the perspective of the creation mediatorship of Jesus Christ. This represents not just one way of looking at the world. Since he made it, to view the universe from any other perspective will result in distortion.

11

THE MEDIATORIAL KINGSHIP OF CHRIST: THE CORPORATE DIMENSION

We have seen that, by his resurrection, Christ now rules the cosmos as its mediator. We will next examine how his authority as king relates to the salvation of his church. There is an important point at stake in treating the cosmos-wide dominion of Christ first. While our place as human beings, made in the image of God, is central to God's plans, it is crucial to put our own salvation in context. God's purpose embraces his entire creation. It is as a part of that creation that he made us, to govern and take care of it. It is also as part of his creation that he intends to deliver us from sin. The end result is that his church is to be the spearhead of a renovated and restored cosmos.

Christ's resurrection and the church

When Christ rose from the dead, he was installed in supreme authority over creation. We have seen that already. Insofar as his disciples were concerned, it was the prelude to their being constituted his church. He had told them to wait in Jerusalem until the promised Holy Spirit would come. Only a few days after Christ's ascension, the Spirit suddenly came to the waiting disciples on the Day of Pentecost. From that point on, the disciples were no longer simply a group of individuals who followed Jesus. They were a collective unit. They became the *church*, the body of Christ, united personally to Christ himself in a profound and deeply mysterious manner, empowered beyond their own strength to witness to what God had done in and by his Son.

If ever there was a palpable demonstration that the church owed its origin and existence to God, it is the events before and after Pentecost. Prior to Pentecost, the disciples simply waited, passive, inactive, powerless. There was simply nothing for them to do other than to remain together in hiding. This was not the passivity of failure, a case of inability or unwillingness to do what they ought to have done. Rather, they were obeying the instruction of Jesus himself to wait in Jerusalem until the promise of the Father should come. This was the activity and attitude appropriate to the time. Then, when the Spirit came, the situation was totally transformed. From that day on, the disciples were active in proclaiming the gospel, bold in the face of persecution, generous in their concern for the poor and underprivileged. Moreover, the Spirit achieved what no human agency could have done. He bound the disciples together not simply into a united group of individuals like a sports team with a high degree of team spirit but, far more than that, into an organism with a life of its own. Paul describes the church as a body, each part united to the others in an organic spiritual manner. Each part is thereby inseparably affected by the behaviour and health of each other. In turn, the body and all its parts are united to the head of the body, Jesus Christ (1 Cor. 12:12–26; Eph. 4:1–16). This far exceeds the unity experienced by a cricket team or even a nation. It is not a physical union as a human body nor a social union such as a 'body politic'. It is a union effected by God and indwelt by God the Holy Spirit himself (*cf.* Jn. 17:21).

As Peter made clear in his speech on the day of Pentecost, the Spirit was sent by the risen Christ (Acts 2:33–36). Consequently, the church was established by the Spirit at the behest of Christ himself. The connection between the risen Christ and the Holy Spirit becomes so close that Paul, for instance, could equate the two. 'The Lord is the Spirit', or 'the Spirit of the Lord' (2 Cor. 3:17) are not untypical of his comments. The risen Christ works through the Spirit; the Spirit testifies of Christ. Christ sends the Spirit as an act of benediction to his church. Indeed, there is evidence that in Paul there is a gradual narrowing of focus as time passes so that in his later letters the work of the Spirit is increasingly understood as an aspect of the work of Christ himself, probably due to this close unity which he expresses. As a corollary of this apostolic tradition, the church itself is widely seen as Christ's church (e.g. Mt. 16:18; Acts 20:28; Eph. 5:25), not only empowered by him but belonging to him as well. This relationship is grounded on what happened at Pentecost but it also continues permanently (e.g. Eph. 6:10f.). In the words of Geerhardus Vos, the Spirit is 'the circumambient atmosphere' which the church breathes for its very existence,[1] for the Spirit himself is the deposit guaranteeing the full future inheritance. There is thus a past dimension, based on Pentecost, a present and continuous dimension by which the Spirit is continuously sent to the church by Christ, and a future dimension in which the full measure of the Spirit will be made known at the eschaton. All these dimensions, however, are dependent on the exalted Christ who, with the Father, sends the Spirit.

There are a number of different ways in which the term 'the church' can be used. First of all, in its widest sense it refers to the whole company of the redeemed, all who have received and will receive the salvation of Christ. In this sense, the church is identical to God's elect. Ultimately, the church in this sense will be known as it really is only at the end of the world at Christ's parousia. In a second sense, we can speak of what is often described as the 'visible' church, the institution that is present here and now in our own world and those who belong to it. As such, it consists of all who profess faith in Jesus Christ. Some go further, believing that Scripture warrants us to regard the children of believers as members of the church, but this has not met with universal acceptance, least of all by those of Baptist persuation.[2] In many cases, parts of the church may be living in a state of doctrinal or moral decline, so much so that it may even be doubtful if an allegiance to the biblical Christ really exists. We recall that the church at Corinth, however, for all its glaring sins and misdemeanours, was still regarded by Paul as Christ's. In this sense, we include the structure and government of the church as it comes to expression at local, regional and national levels. A third meaning refers to the church historically. In part this involves its past dogmatic pronouncements, in which we can trace its attempt to witness to the grace of God in diverse historical and cultural situations. Of course, not all the past activity or dogma of the church may be considered acceptable. The church may progress or regress. It can also digress. For example, the dogmas of transubstantiation, the immaculate conception and the bodily assumption of the Virgin Mary may all be seen as digressions from the teaching of Scripture and thus as invalid developments.

In all the various levels described in the previous paragraph, despite whatever qualifications we make (which reflect the very human and consequently sinful condition in which it finds itself), the church is indisputably a resurrection community. It is the fruit of Christ's atoning death on the cross and of his victory over the grave. Since the sending of the Spirit is historically dependent on the death and resurrection of Christ (Jn. 7:37–39) and the Spirit brought the church into being and continues to animate it, the church's life is itself the direct outflow of all that Christ did for its salvation at Calvary and the empty tomb.

The church and personal salvation

The mediatorial kingship of Christ as it extends to his church includes the salvation of the individuals within it. As a resurrection community, the church is both the locus and the bearer of salvation. It is the locus of salvation insofar as there is no place where salvation is to be found other than in the church. It is the bearer of salvation because it is to the church that Christ has committed the gospel and there is no other way we or anyone can hear that message apart from the instrumentality of Christ's church. Here we use the term 'church' in a wide and perhaps loose sense. A person can come to faith in Christ simply through reading the Bible and perhaps have no personal contact with the church, either as an institution or as a body of believers. Still, it is only through the message of the apostles and prophets (the foundation of the church) that salvation has reached that person. Even elect infants and other elect persons unable to hear or understand the gospel (*cf.* Westminster Confession of Faith 10:3) are saved only through Christ, the same Christ to whom the church bears witness. We shall first enlarge on this theme and then see how the salvation of the individual fits into it.

It is fairly easy to see the church as the *bearer* of salvation. It is from church pulpits that the gospel has traditionally been preached. God has ordained that we hear the gospel from the lips of others. He has not arranged to bring the message himself. Angels are not employed for the task: it is we who are co-workers with God (2 Cor. 6:1). Even if we came to faith simply through reading the Bible alone, it was the word of the apostles and prophets that we read, the testimony of God's people in old or new covenant. Scripture itself is a covenantal document, a testimony of human faith as well as a word from God, recognized by the church as God's provision for its life in this world. On the other hand, if we trusted Christ through a personal introduction by a friend then it was equally through the instrumentality of an individual who was part of the church in one of the senses described above. If our faith does not fit the picture defined for us in the word of the apostles and prophets we have good cause to question whether it is Christian faith in the first place. The New Testament makes it clear that the apostles envisaged a continuing transmission of apostolic doctrine from one generation to another (2 Tim. 2:2), with faithfulness the key quality required in those responsible, so that the message could be passed on unimpaired. Frequently, the church is urged to uphold the truth; it is made aware that its message must be preserved intact, and exhorted to fight off those who would distort or dilute it (2 Tim. 3:1f.; 2 Pet. 2:1f.; Jude 3–4).

Next, the church is also the *locus* of salvation insofar as there is no other place where salvation is to be found. Jesus Christ is the only Saviour (Jn. 14:6; Acts 4:12). He alone is the hope of the world. But where in the world can one go to find him? If the church is the bearer of the good news of salvation it must be to the church that we are to go for salvation. It is not a case of the church having saving efficacy in itself. Christ alone saves, but Christ is to be found in the church. Therefore the church is the place where salvation is to be found, in all the senses of the word 'church' discussed above. In the first meaning of the word, we find salvation in Christ through the testimony of God's elect people, those who themselves have found deliverance through his cross and resurrection. In the second place, we find salvation through the ministry of the visible church in word and sacrament, as it points us to Christ who alone saves. Thirdly, we find salvation as we take our place in the historic church, confessing our faith in harmony with the church of past ages as, for instance, in the Nicene Creed, recognized in East and West alike as expressing the substance of the trinitarian faith (how else can we claim to share the church's faith if we cannot share its confession?).

Cyprian (c. 200–58) wrote, 'You cannot have God for your Father unless you have the church for your Mother'.[3] Calvin was in essential agreement:

> I shall start, then, with the church, into whose bosom God is pleased to gather his sons, not only that they may be nourished by her help and ministry as long as they are infants and children, but also that they may be guided by her motherly care until they mature and at last reach the goal of faith. 'For what God has joined together, it is not lawful to put asunder' [Mk. 10.9], so that, for those to whom he is Father the church may also be Mother.[4]

And again:

> But because it is now our intention to discuss the visible church, let us learn even from the simple title 'mother' how useful, indeed how necessary, it is that we should know her. For there is no other way to enter into life unless this mother conceive us in her

216

> womb, give us birth, nourish us at her breast, and
> lastly, unless she keep us under her care and
> guidance until, putting off mortal flesh, we become
> like the angels .... Furthermore, away from her
> bosom one cannot hope for any forgiveness of sins
> or any salvation . . .[5]

The church does not compete with Christ for the very
good reason that the church belongs to Christ, is animated by
Christ, is indwelt by the Spirit of Christ and proclaims the
word of Christ through his apostles and prophets. Salvation
therefore takes place *into* the church, *in* the church and *in
connection with* the church. Both the church and the salvation
it proclaims and bears are together grounded on the saving
efficacy of the cross and resurrection of Jesus Christ.

From all this, it is clear that soteriology and ecclesiology are
integrally connected, both being outflows of the accomplishment of Christ. In this we are distancing ourselves from two
prominent positions, those of traditional Roman Catholicism
and of much modern Anglo-Saxon evangelicalism. In the
first place, Roman Catholicism has traditionally subordinated
soteriology to ecclesiology. The church has been accorded a
status comparable to Holy Scripture inasmuch as Scripture, it
was claimed, could be interpreted aright only by 'holy mother
church'.[6] Even Vatican II, with a far more prominent and
nuanced doctrine of Scripture and tradition, has not resolved
that question without a mountain of ambiguity.[7] In essence,
the authority of the church hierarchy was such that other
areas of church life and doctrine were in practice subordinated to its authority. Consequently, or perhaps we should
say concurrently, personal salvation was to be received only
as a direct result of participation in the prescribed channels
of sacramental grace. The sacraments, working with *ex opere
operato* (automatic) efficacy, were indispensable to salvation.
For instance, to die without baptism was to imperil one's
salvation. God, in effect, operated via sacramental means. Put
bluntly, to be saved one had to join the church. First is
ecclesiology, second soteriology.

Modern evangelicalism in Britain and North America has
gone to the opposite extreme. Soteriology comes first and

ecclesiology straggles far behind. The key thing is to have Christ as your personal Saviour and Lord. The individual is paramount. The post-Renaissance focus on the individual person has come to dominate in the church to such an extent that entire areas of crucial biblical teaching on corporate solidarity sound strange and alien, if they are ever heard at all. Yet Paul describes salvation in fundamentally corporate terms, as being in Christ and being raised with Christ. Following from that, church membership has in practice been seen as little more than an optional extra on far too many occasions for comfort. Trust Christ? Yes. Join a church? Maybe, later, when the time is right. Allied to this has been a neglect, even an undermining of the sacraments. Baptism is frequently seen as an act of personal obedience to Christ, as a testimony to others, as a step on the road of discipleship and therefore as something which can come later on, somewhere down the road. The persistent New Testament practice of baptizing at the very point when a person can first be regarded as a Christian (whether at conversion or at birth to believing parents) is often lacking. In modern evangelicalism, soteriology and ecclesiology have been separated radically. Together with this disturbing trend, there has been a proliferation of extra-ecclesial organizations active in preaching and teaching the faith, areas which the New Testament commits to the church. Many of these bodies have done sterling work in spreading the gospel, ministering to Christians and serving human need. Their existence, however, has brought together people from very diverse church backgrounds. This has for the most part been a wonderful way of restoring a focus on the central themes of the gospel. It has also fostered a biblical ecumenicity. In order to achieve this co-operation, however, questions of church and sacraments have often been forced to one side. The message conveyed is that these are purely secondary issues. At the same time, there can be little doubt that the very existence of so many extra-ecclesial organizations is testimony to the malaise of the institutional church, and to the indisputable fact that an individualistically oriented soteriology has severed the cord that ties church and individual together under the mediatorial kingship of Jesus Christ.

It follows that individual soteriology and ecclesiology are integrally connected and that this connection should be given renewed expression again in our own day. One way of doing this is to pay close attention to the biblical doctrine of covenant as it comes to fruition and to full expression in the work of Christ. In the covenant of grace, the individual finds his or her place in the community of the people of God. Corporate solidarity is most prominent, yet it is a solidarity that does not ride roughshod over individual liberty. The godly person, by definition, belongs to the community. Moreover, as we indicated in chapter 2, the covenant itself is fulfilled for us on all levels by Christ. He is the promised mediator, his is the required response. He is our God, we are God's people in him. Individual liberty and collective solidarity are together harmonized in Christ, and in him soteriology and ecclesiology find their unity.

Classic Reformed theology grappled long and hard with these connections. We have referred to Calvin already. It is remarkable how he is able to develop the implications of the Christian life at great length in Book III of the *Institutes*, and to integrate such a discussion into an equally detailed treatment in Book IV on the church as the means by which God introduces us to the society of Christ and holds us there. There is no sense of the two strands, the individual and the corporate, as rivals with one far less important than the other. It is heartening to see a renewed appreciation of these connections emerging in recent years, as is exemplified in the title of the ARCIC II report, *Salvation and the Church*.

In the same way, the family is also integral in soteriology and thus in the mediatorial kingship of Christ. Western tradition has increasingly concentrated on the individual and his or her decisions. 'One man, one vote' is a slogan the West has spread far and wide, and we have forgotten how central the family unit is in God's redemptive plans. 'As for me and my household, we will serve the Lord' was a wholly natural thing for Joshua to have said in the setting of the household structure of God's covenant (Jos. 24:15). In a congregation which takes Scripture seriously I recently heard a preacher on the same text read 'as for *me*, I will serve the Lord'!

Because the church is an instrument of salvation, the

219

ministry of the Word and the sacraments are the twin central foci by which Christ's mediatorial kingship is advanced. They are both functions of the continuing ministry of Christ. They are ways by which God brings us into his church and thus to salvation. They are also means by which our union with Christ is cultivated on an ongoing basis. We recall how, for Paul, Christ and the Spirit are conjoined in the administration of baptism as we are incorporated into the body of Christ (1 Cor. 12:13). The one Spirit baptizes us into the one body and thereafter enables us to drink of himself on an ongoing basis. Theologically, the Spirit is therefore connected with baptism. This does not mean that the Spirit's grace is automatically present in baptism. Nor does it imply that there is necessarily a temporal identity between baptism and the Spirit baptizing us into Christ's body. It is a theological connection. The Spirit makes us living members of Christ's church, its theological counterpart being our baptism with water. The two are part of an integral whole, two sides of a coin. Each person who is a Christian is incorporated into the church of Jesus Christ by the Spirit in baptism. This statement is without prejudice as to when such a person may become a Christian, other than that it is by the Spirit and in baptism. Christ and Spirit, individual and church, are in harmonious congruity.

Christ's resurrection and ours

The relation between christology, soteriology and ecclesiology is fully evident when we look to the future and to the resurrection. Our resurrection at the end of the world will mark the completion of the church's salvation. It is grounded on the resurrection of Jesus Christ. Thus, Christ's own resurrection marks the commencement of his reign as mediatorial king, a reign which is to culminate in the total vanquishing of death and the resurrection of his church in the power of the Spirit.

In 1 Corinthians chapter 15, Paul develops these themes at length. Underlying his comments is an assumption that Christ's resurrection and ours are, in essence, one reality. He argues backwards and forwards from one to the other in a

220

manner which presupposes that there is an organic connection between the two. Thus, in verses 12–19 he indicates that if Christ was not raised from the dead we cannot be raised either. Again, if there is no general resurrection of the dead it is impossible that Christ himself could have been raised in the first place. In both cases, the whole edifice of the Christian faith would collapse. Therefore, the relation between the resurrection of Christ in AD 30, and ours at the end of the world is so close, so unbreakable that if one part were not true the other would also be false. They are parts of the same reality, much like a piece of cake sliced into two, or as identical twins are two segments of the same fertilized egg. In post-Einsteinian physics it has been demonstrated that the parts of a tiny sub-atomic particle, split in two and separated by infinite space, will behave identically. In a somewhat analogous manner, the resurrection is a single phenomenon, its parts separated by indefinite time. Thus the nature of the resurrection body is the same both for Christ and for us (verses 42–49). As Adam was the one who initiated the race, 'a living being', bequeathing a body subject to weakness, corruption and death, so the risen Christ, 'a life-giving spirit', is the firstfruits (*cf.* verses 20, 23) of those who belong to him and who will share in the resurrection body which is powerful, glorious, incorruptible and under the impetus of the Holy Spirit. Once again, the salvation of the individual and the church are inseparable, while the resurrection of Christ, in which we share, is empowered by the Spirit, the post-resurrection Christ being 'a life-giving Spirit' (that close connection between the risen Christ and Spirit again!) with the resurrection body a 'spiritual', a pneumatic, body.

The resurrection marks the completion of the church. Christ gave himself for the church and now nourishes and cares for it. Ultimately he will present it to himself free of sin and full of glory (Eph. 5:25–27). The resurrection, at the same time, is the point at which our redemption is complete (Rom. 8:23). It is the goal for which we yearn with powerful emotional force (2 Cor. 5:1–5).

> Meanwhile we groan, longing to be clothed with our heavenly dwelling . . .

Christ's parousia, when we will be raised, will realize our salvation as individuals and the church's fruition as the bride of Christ.

In the interim, Christ in his mediatorial reign will progressively subjugate his enemies, his Spirit working through his church. Death itself is the last enemy to be destroyed, having been dealt a death-blow by the cross (Heb. 2:14; 2 Tim. 1:10), but awaiting its final abolition at the parousia (1 Cor. 15:23–26). In the context of 1 Corinthians chapter 15, which we cited above, Paul argues that when death is put away, all other enemies of Christ will already be overcome. Death is the last enemy destroyed. The mediatorial kingdom of Christ is therefore a progressively advancing tide of conquest. As leaven hidden in a lump of dough gradually leavens the whole, or as the tiny mustard seed grows into a large shrub, so Christ's kingdom, at first hidden like a seed thrown down by the sower, ultimately spreads and permeates the whole:

> For as in Adam all die, so in Christ all will be made alive. But each in his own turn: Christ, the first-fruits; then, when he comes, those who belong to him. Then the end will come, when he hands over the kingdom to God the Father after he has destroyed all dominion, authority and power. For he must reign until he has put all his enemies under his feet. The last enemy to be destroyed is death (1 Cor. 15:22–26).

The individual, the church the cosmos will all be brought under the headship of Christ. This final great salvation has already begun! Christ's own resurrection is the firstfruits, the first instalment, and as such the guarantee that the full reality will come into effect.

In summary, the reign of Christ as king extends over the entire universe. In a narrower sense, it is focused on his church and the individuals within it. Individual salvation ought not to be separated from the church which brings the message of the gospel and to which Christ has committed the means by which the gospel is cultivated. Both individual and church are nurtured to salvation by the Holy Spirit, whom

Christ himself has sent. Ultimately, this salvation will be consummated at the resurrection, when Christ returns. Our resurrection, however, is part of the same reality as Christ's. It is impossible to understand the gospel aright in detachment from the overarching reign of Jesus Christ our king, to whom we are united by the Spirit.

Conclusion

In summary, Jesus Christ is unique. He alone is God incarnate. Fully human, he is simultaneously one with God in status and personal identity. Thus, his work 'for us and our salvation' is complete and utterly effective. God's eternal purpose in election focused in him, and we were chosen in Christ before the creation of the world. God's covenant was made in Christ, and all God's promises come to expression in him. He is the sole mediator between God and humanity. In Christ, God is our God; in Christ, we are God's people. As prophet, Christ spoke the word of God during his earthly ministry since he was and is the eternal Word; through his appointed apostles, he speaks to us today in holy Scripture. As our high priest, his death on the cross atones for our sins and brings all who trust him into a living relationship with God as his own children. Raised from the dead, 'he sits at God's right hand 'til all his foes submit' (Isaac Watts). He is king, renewing the cosmos and ruling his church. When he returns, his believing church will be raised to serve God in the life of the world to come. Every knee shall bow and every tongue confess that Jesus Christ is Lord, to the glory of God the Father.

Appendix

THE INTENT
OF THE ATONEMENT

A question discussed frequently and sometimes heatedly over the years is that of God's intent in the death of Christ. Just what did God intend to do by giving up his own Son to such a cruel death? The traditional term for this issue is the extent of the atonement. This phrase, however, is misleading for a number of reasons. *Extent* normally denotes area, some physical or geographical space or considerations of size. Translated into debate on the atonement, the focus becomes that of *number*: how many, or what proportion benefit from Christ's death? Did Christ atone for the sins of all or simply for those of the elect? Did he atone for the sins of all in a provisional sense? Or, from quite another direction, is the atonement of limited or unlimited value? If the idea of *intent* is the central theme, however, the principal point at stake becomes that of *purpose* or *design*. In short, the issue crystallizes into the place of the atonement in the overall plan of God for human redemption. The spatial and mathematical yields to the teleological. In reality, categories of intention have defined the nature of the discussion. Did God plan the cross to save his chosen people or, rather, did he allow it as a provisional payment for the sins of all, to come into effect for those who repent of sin and trust Christ?

This topic has at times been fraught with controversy. Either the question is faced, with resultant dangers of contention, or it is ignored. But there are few theological issues, however arcane, which do not have important underlying differences of perspective which need to be understood. We are tackling this question because we believe it comes into this category. Behind differences over the intent of the atonement lie disagreements concerning the nature of the atonement. For that reason, it may help future discussion if these are clarified.

At the same time, it is important to remember that we are to focus on positions rather than people. When certain views come under criticism, we must bear in mind that scholars, preachers and theologians are never entirely consistent and often have a happy instinctive knack of avoiding the pitfalls into which their own theories might lead them. We shall examine the strengths and weaknesses of the main alternative positions and seek to indicate some major boundaries within which discussion should take place. It is possible that there are additional nuances which we do not have time to cover.

Historical background

The post-Reformation period saw the lines of division on this issue most clearly drawn. Before then, there had been two main trends, the majority position being that Christ had died for all people. While there were some, such as Origen, who leaned towards a form of universalism, for the most part there was little attempt to consider how it related to the design of God in the atonement. There were some notable figures, however, who maintained that Christ died with the intention of atoning for God's elect only. The great Augustine was one,[1] and Prosper of Aquitaine was another.[2] So also was Gottschalk.[3] Peter Lombard meanwhile produced the formula 'sufficient for all, efficient for the elect',[4] that was to play a significant role in the discussions that followed. The question was thrown into the foreground by the Reformation's defence of the sovereignty of God. Oecolampadius, Bucer and Vermigli[5] all taught that Christ died for the elect. But it was not until the Colloquy of Montbéliard (1586) that it became a matter for controversy, when Theodore Beza (1519–1605), Calvin's successor at Geneva, clashed with the Lutheran Jacob Andraeus. Beza held firmly that Christ died to save the elect only, while Andraeus maintained universal atonement. When Arminius appeared on the scene, the battle lines were firmly drawn. Arminius regarded God's election as conditional on his foreseeing who would believe. In short, God did not give faith to people because he had elected them. Rather, he elected those he foresaw would repent and believe. Therefore, since election was conditional so also was the atonement. Christ suffered on the cross. His death was therefore available for all, conditional on their believing him. The Synod of Dort was forced to make a major pronouncement. In a wide-ranging declaration following a tense and potentially divisive debate behind the scenes, the Synod stressed the infinite value of the death of Christ, moved on to spell out its universal scope (insofar as its context in the gospel promise is to be proclaimed indiscriminately to all people without exception), before indicating finally that it was God's intention that his Son atone for the sins of his elect.

Effectively, four positions of substance are clear, within which there may be varying nuances discernable. In the first place, there is *universalism*. This is the assumption that Christ died with the intention of atoning for all people without exception and that the outcome of his saving work is that all without exception are saved. Thus, God's intent is achieved. The intent is identical with the result. Overall, the view has the merit that purpose and achievement are in harmony. However, it fails to do justice to the testimony of Scripture that not all will be saved (Dn. 12:2; Mt. 25:46; 2 Thes. 1:8–10; Rev. 20:7–15). Jesus spoke more of hell than heaven. If all are to be saved, why the urgency in gospel proclamation that we see in Acts?

Secondly, the view of *Arminius* and those who followed him was that Christ died with the intention of saving all people without exception. Not all, however, are saved. Therefore, he did not secure an actual atonement on the cross but rather underwent a provisory suffering for all which is ratified by believers when they trust in Christ at conversion. Christ's death permits the Father to forgive all who repent and believe. Consequently, the cross is not a direct satisfaction by Christ of divine justice in the place of those he represents. Instead, divine justice is satisfied for those who choose to believe. This is an indirect and provisional satisfaction of God's justice. The intent of the atonement is not secured, since all people without exception are not actually saved.

Thirdly, there is the view known as *limited atonement*. The modifier was used to indicate its claim that the efficacy of the atonement was limited to the elect. In short, Christ died with the intention of atoning for the elect only. As such, intention and outcome are in harmony but, in contrast to universalism, account is taken of the fact that not all will be saved. In the eyes of advocates of the Arminian and Amyraldian (see below) theories, this position does not do justice to a number of biblical passages that speak of Christ dying for all, nor does it allow room for God's offer of free forgiveness to all who believe.

Fourthly, with the French theologian, Moyse Amyraut, there arose the idea which became known as *hypothetical universalism*. Amyraut (1596–1664) maintained that Christ died for all without exception. God in his foreknowledge, however, recognizing that all would not trust Christ, decreed to save a certain number. Consequently, the Holy Spirit applies salvation to the elect while Christ dies for all. The intent of the atonement thus differs from the application of salvation. Again, since Christ dies with the intention that all be saved, his death is not the suffering of divine wrath against the sins of his people.

The historical controversies have been bedevilled by emotive terminology. The use of the term 'limited atonement' is a case in point. The opposite of limited is unlimited. An atonement free from all human limits is clearly a far more attractive option. With such language, the one position is handicapped from the start and clear thinking immediately clouded. An alternative sometimes used has been to rename 'limited atonement' as 'definite atonement'. The result of that is that universal or unlimited becomes indefinite, conveying an impression of fuzzy thinking or doctrinal indifference. Once again, one position is adversely affected by the choice of terminology. The issues are perhaps most fairly assessed by the terms 'effective' and 'provisional'. The one position argues that Christ actually made full satisfaction for sins on the cross and secures, too, the response of faith on the part of his people; the other (in varying ways in both Arminian and Amyraldian forms) holds that he simply suffered, and that this suffering does not intrinsically achieve what it was intended to do since it is dependent on a response on the part of human beings which, in very many cases, fails to materialize. On the one hand, it is said that God saves sinners. On the other, it is claimed that God makes provision for sinners to be saved but at the same time leaves it up to their own decision since his provision is contingent and provisional.

The issue at stake: the nature of the atonement

At first sight, these seem to be rather recondite and speculative questions. Underlying them, however, are issues of great importance. At root lie differences over the nature of the atonement. The effects flowing from the atonement are dependent on what actually happened at Calvary and on what God himself intended to be the outcome. If Christ died with the intention of atoning for all and if he actually secured the salvation of all, then all will be saved. A universalism will follow because of what the purpose of the cross is conceived to be. The same observations apply to other views of the atonement. The nature of the atonement is of one piece with its intent.

In chapter 7 we saw that the New Testament stressed the atonement as penal substitution. Christ suffered in our place, on our behalf. He suffered to bear our sins, and endured the penalty we should have undergone ourselves, the just wrath of God on account of our sin. He did this to the full. He cried 'It is finished!' He was openly vindicated by God in the resurrection, public evidence that his atoning work was complete. Because of his submission to the justice of God on our account there remains no further reckoning for us to face.

Since Christ made atonement for sins on the cross, we are faced with the following alternatives. Either he suffered in place of all people, in which case all will be saved, or he suffered in place of God's elect, in which case only they will be saved. The first alternative is ruled out by the consistent and unrelenting testimony of Scripture that some will be lost. If we start from the nature of the atonement, we are left with the second alternative, that Christ died on the cross to secure the salvation of a vast community, beyond number, drawn from every nation on the face of the earth (Rev. 7:9).

It appears to follow that if we wish to maintain that Christ died for all without exception while rejecting universalism, we will have no alternative but to redefine the nature of the atonement. Christ's death will then have secured the salvation of no-one in particular. It will simply be a provisional suffering, dependent for its effect on a believing response by the sinner. This is seriously deficient for a number of reasons. In the first place, the fulcrum of atoning efficacy then belongs to human beings. It is our response which brings the atonement into effect. Christ on the cross did not fully and exhaustively pay the penalty for all the sins of anyone. Therefore, it is the point of repentance and faith on our part that brings the atonement into actuality. Until that time and apart from the fulfilment of that condition, Christ atoned for the sins of no-one. Faith is the hinge on which the atonement depends. The suffering of Christ on the cross is purely contingent and provisional. It seems impossible theologically to hold to the penal substitutionary nature of the atonement and at the same time maintain that Christ died provisionally for all without exception. Moreover, since we have seen the apostolic testimony to penal substitution throughout the New Testament, we are forced to conclude that the idea that Christ died with the intention of atoning provisionally for all without exception is without foundation.

What we are discussing here is the classic Arminian theory of atonement. Of course, it is true that Arminians have been among the staunchest defenders of penal substitution: their place in the evangelical world is secure. Modern followers of Arminius may often diverge on this point or that, but present-day Calvinists and Arminians both recognize that historic Arminianism does not cohere with penal substitution.[6]

Since this may sound rather startling, we will now note some other points concerning the Arminian view. Firstly, how does the Arminian doctrine of the atonement relate to the grace of God? We recall that the decisive point of atonement is that at which a person repents and believes. Whatever God has done for our salvation in Christ is in the end made to depend upon what someone does in response. If faith is seen as a gift of God, then confusion is introduced into God, for he intends Christ's death to be for all but does not give faith to all. If, however, faith is not seen as a gift of God then human beings are very obviously co-authors with God in their own salvation. Saving faith is then a purely human activity independent of God's grace. How does this relate to the witness of Scripture that salvation is a work of the Lord alone? How needy are human beings on such reckoning, if they still retain the ability to do what is right in the eyes of God apart from the exercise of his saving grace? Are they really dead in sin (Eph. 2:1), so requiring to be created anew? By enlarging the natural capacity of sinners to do what is right, the grace which God displays in their rescue is constricted.

Secondly, how does a provisional atonement resolve the problem of sin? The Arminian view of the atonement holds that Christ's sufferings on the cross are accepted by God in lieu of a full satisfaction of his justice for the actual sins of his people and, additionally, their atoning efficacy is contingent on a believing response to the gospel on our part. What basis is there for this in divine justice? How can we have assurance that all our sins, each and every one, have received full, complete and entire punishment as God's justice requires and so we have been freed from all possible condemnation by God both now and for ever? As Toplady wrote, 'Payment God cannot twice demand, once at my bleeding surety's hands and then again at mine'. According to the Arminian view, Christ did not make payment for my actual sins. He simply suffered. Forgiveness is free, but it has no basis in divine justice. The connection between human sin and the justice of God in punishing it ('the soul that sins, it shall die') is removed and so there is no corresponding connection between the forgiveness of sins and the justice of God. This position has close historical associations with the governmental theory of the atonement (Grotius, the author of the governmental view, was an Arminian), the weaknesses of which we saw in chapter 8.

The criticisms above also apply to the Amyraldian theory of atonement. This too argued that Christ died with the intention of atoning for all without exception. Hence, this position cannot consistently hold to penal substitution either. More than that, it openly betrays an internal collision in the mind of God, with an intention that Christ's atoning death should be for all being countered by a decree to save some. We will consider these theological implications below.

The issues at stake in the relationship between the intent of the atonement and its nature are well summarized by the Puritan, John Owen:

> To which I add this dilemma to our Universalists:- God imposed his wrath due unto, and Christ underwent the pains of hell for, either all the sins of all men, or all the sins of some men, or some sins of all men. If the last, some sins of all men, then have all men some sins to answer for, and so shall no man be saved .... If the second, this is it which we affirm, that Christ in their stead and room suffered for all the sins of all the elect in the world. If the first, why, then, are not all freed from the punishment of all their sins? You will say, 'Because of their unbelief; they will not believe'. But this unbelief, is it a sin, or not? If not, why should they be punished for it? If it be, then Christ underwent the punishment due to it, or not. If so, why must that hinder them more than their other sins for which he died from partaking of the fruit of his death? If he did not, then did he not die for all their sins. Let them choose which part they will.[7]

Or as a more recent writer puts it, 'If we universalize the extent we limit the efficacy.'[8] We will discuss some of the criticisms of this view later. Universal atonement cannot be effective atonement, unless we go the whole way to a full-blown universalism. Universal atonement is, in practice, limited in efficacy.

The theological context

Our investigation thus far can be summarized as follows: only effective atonement does justice to the biblical insistence that the cross was a work of penal substitution. In the section below we will consider the view of effective atonement from a number of different theological angles. It will be important to see if it fits into the overall picture of God's dealings with us in Jesus Christ. A valid theory of this nature ought to be compatible with what we know of other contiguous theological areas. We will examine a number of spheres in which effective atonement appears compatible with its theological environment and then turn to discuss some areas where it looks rather weak.

First of all, we should observe that it is perfectly congruent with the wider biblical framework in which the atonement is discussed. Whether we consider the cross as obedience, as sacrifice, as conquest of Satan, as reconciliation, or as propitiation, all of which we have seen to be elements of the whole, the point that Christ dies as a representative of his own people is not only compatible but is positively demanded. How else can reconciliation have been achieved on the cross (and Paul talks of reconciliation as accomplished) unless those who were reconciled actually are reconciled? Since some continue forever in a state of enmity with God, this reconciliation which Christ effected is evidently intended for his chosen people. Moreover, Christ's conquest of Satan is experienced by those who have turned from darkness to light, from the power of Satan to God. This is not for one moment to deny that Christ's death has objective cosmic dimensions distinguishable in some sense from the more immediate concerns of the salvation of his church, as we discussed in chapter 10. Nor should we forget that his atonement is of infinite value. (We will discuss this shortly.) He was God's own Son. That puts his death beyond all calculation.

233

Secondly, effective atonement can be seen as a direct outflow of the electing purpose of God. If God has chosen his
people in Christ unconditionally before the foundation of the
world, it follows that he sent Christ into the world to atone
for their sins and to secure their salvation. Given the premiss,
the conclusion follows. Similar issues arise here to those we
discussed above. If we universalize the scope of election, we
end up with universal salvation. Barth's doctrine of election
has this colouring to it: for him, Christ is both electing God
and elect man; humanity is elect in Christ while God in Christ
takes on reprobation in our place. We noted in chapter 2 that
Barth tries to avoid committing himself to universalism. Yet
his disclaimer is significant in itself; he was aware that this
might be a criticism of his position.

If we make election conditional, on the other hand, we will
probably have a provisional atonement. Arminius did that.
His view of election was that God chooses believers. His
choice is on the basis of his foreseeing that some will repent
and believe. It is an election conditional on his foreknowledge. Since the centre of gravity has shifted from God's
decree to human response, what results is that the weight in
the atonement is similarly felt at the point of believing appropriation. True, it could conceivably be held by followers of
Arminius that since the atonement was provided for those
God foresaw would believe, it is not therefore provisional in
intent. This would not correspond, however, to the classic
Arminian theory. In liberation theology, on the other hand,
with its tendency to absolutize time by focusing almost exclusively on the economic and political realms, election is in
some ways replaced by God's attitude of partiality towards
the poor. The cross is correspondingly seen as Jesus suffering abandonment by the Father in solidarity with the poor
and oppressed. Again, the nature of God's determination has
direct bearing on what is considered to happen in the death
of Christ.

Therefore, the crucial point at issue is the nature of election: is it unconditional? The claim of an election conditional
on God's foreknowledge of human faith rests on exegesis of
passages such as Romans 8:29, where Paul states that 'those
God foreknew he also predestined to be conformed to the

likeness of his Son'. At first sight, it would appear that Paul is indeed supporting a conditional form of election and that God consequently chooses those whom he foresees will repent and believe in Christ. A merely advance knowledge, however, is hardly in view. After all, it is *persons* who are the objects of this knowledge. God not only knows things about them, he knows *them*. The kind of knowledge here is more akin to the deep, personal knowledge of a covenant bond such as marriage. Just as Adam knew Eve his wife (Gn. 4:1) or as Yahweh said of Israel 'You only of all the families of the earth have I known' (Am. 3:2, *my translation*), so here we are moving in the intimate context of God's love for his own, seen in his working all things together for their good (verse 28), in clearing them of every charge (verses 33–34) and in preserving them from every danger that might threaten to tear them from his keeping (verses 35–39). It is the context of 'that special taking knowledge of a person which is God's electing grace'.[9] Moreover, the question of God's foreknowledge of the faith of human beings simply begs the question as to the source of that faith. If it is from God (and since humanity is depicted as dead in sin it can hardly come from anywhere else) then it is God's foreknowledge of what he himself is going to give and so is hardly different from fore-ordination.

Thirdly, effective atonement is most compatible with the doctrine of the covenant and of Christ as second Adam. When Adam sinned the entire race sinned in him (Rom. 5:12ff.). He was head of the race in a twofold sense. On the one hand, all are related to him organically. As an acorn has in itself the potential of an oak tree, so that the oak which eventually develops can be said to exist in the original acorn, so the whole race was existent in the person of the first Adam.

Again, as the head of the race, Adam was its representative. Consequently, his actions were simultaneously those of the people he represented, like a Member of Parliament who acts in his official capacity on behalf of his constituents. In this sense, the relation is legal and representative rather than organic. Similarly, Christ is the head of the new humanity as the second Adam, and he imparts a real personal union to his people. His life is communicated to them by the Holy Spirit.

Additionally, he is also their representative as Adam was of those who were related to him. His actions were done on their behalf and in their place. Thus, his death on the cross was a representative death undergone on behalf of those united to him.

In view of this, a provisional and universal atonement would undermine the vital union with Christ that lies at the heart of biblical soteriology. If we are united to Christ then we surely are united in his death and resurrection. Indeed, a case can be made for this being the heart of the Pauline theology.[10] If, however, his death was faced with the intention of atoning for everybody in a provisional sense, contingent on their own believing response, then Christ's union with his own people is somehow suspended. He is no longer anybody's representative. He is not acting vicariously. In practice, if he is in the place of everyone provisionally, he is in the place of no-one specifically. At the heart of these questions is the influence of nominalism. If reality consists exclusively in the particular, then one will think inevitably in categories concerned with the individual and salvation will be seen as a purely individual matter. Scripture holds before us, however, the corporate nature of humanity and of its salvation. We belong in Adam by nature and, as Christians, in Christ by grace. Therefore, it is not first and foremost a question of Christ dying for certain individuals. He died for *his people* (Mt. 1:21). That heads us in the direction of effective atonement where Christ dies for his people.

Fourthly, the unity of Christ's high-priestly work is compatible with effective atonement. Christ's role as high priest is a whole. It is one unified movement of grace towards humanity whereby he takes our place in obeying the Father, in atoning for our sins and in bringing us to God. He makes very clear that he prays for us besides dying for us. This is a dominant theme in his great high-priestly prayer to the Father in John chapter 17. In that prayer he says to the Father that he does not pray for the world but for those whom the Father had given him:

> I pray for them [those the Father gave him]. I am not praying for the world, but for those you have given me, for they are yours (Jn. 17:9).

236

His intercession is limited. He prays for his own and not for the world. It follows that his atoning death is intended for those the Father had given him and not for all in an indiscriminate fashion. If we see the intercession as particular and the cross as universal, we are positing a disruption in the heart of Christ's high-priestly work. This was the outcome of the Amyraldian doctrine of atonement. Christ dies for all without exception but he intercedes for the elect, to whom the Spirit grants faith. There is consequently a fracture between atonement and intercession as also in the person of Christ himself as he dies for all but prays only for his elect. There is also disruption in God as the Father chooses some on seeing not all will believe, as the Spirit applies salvation to these elect and Christ prays for them, while Christ goes to the cross (presumably in pursuance of the Father's plan) with the intention of atoning for all. This leads us into a further issue.

The doctrine of the Trinity requires, fifthly, effective atonement. According to Scripture, the author of election is principally the Father (Jn. 6:37–40; 17:2, 6, 9–10; Eph. 1:4), who chooses some but not all. Again, the Holy Spirit applies salvation to some but not to all, for many persist in unbelief and ultimately will perish. From this background, universal atonement maintains that the Father chooses some (conditionally), the Holy Spirit applies the gospel to some but the Son dies for all. This is by far the most serious problem with provisional atonement. It threatens to tear apart the Holy Trinity. It introduces disorder into the doctrine of God. The Father and the Holy Spirit have different goals from the Son. The tendency is towards tritheism, and the unity of the Godhead is undermined. Ultimately, the doctrine of the Trinity will be blown apart. Historically, the emergence of a provisional universal atonement was followed by moves in precisely that direction. In the wake of the Arminian controversy, the leader of the Remonstrants at Dort, Simon Episcopius (1583–1643), held that only the Father had deity of himself, the Son and the Holy Spirit being subordinate in terms of essence.[11]

Moreover, the problem deepens once we remember the principle *opera trinitatis indivisa sunt* (the works of the Trinity are indivisible). In all God's works and ways, while some are more appropriately seen as effected by one of the trinitarian hypostases rather than the others (only the Son died on the cross, for example), yet all three are in some way involved in all that he does. Thus, while it is the Son who submits to the cross, the Father delivers him up. In turn, the Son offers himself to the Father through the eternal Spirit (Heb. 9:14). Hence, the confusion is worse if, on the one hand, in election all three persons of the Trinity determined to choose some and to apply salvation to the elect through the Spirit's work and then, on the other hand, changed to providing an atonement which is only provisional. Not only is the unity of God ripped apart but the faithfulness of God is undermined. Where is the firmness and reliability of his purpose? What assurance can be had from a God who decides first one thing, then another? Issues such as these are not peripheral but reach right to the nerve centre of the Christian faith. The substance of the gospel is at stake.

In illustration of this last point, the recent attempt of James B. Torrance to revive the theory of John McLeod Campbell is illuminating. Campbell argued that historic Calvinism, represented by John Owen and Jonathan Edwards, had made justice an essential attribute of God while relegating love and mercy to the status of an arbitrary attribute. In short, God was said to deal with all people according to his justice but to exercise mercy only to some according to the decision of his will.[12] This is said to be contrary to the biblical view that God is essentially love. This argument has been answered by Paul Helm. Helm challenges Campbell's historical claim, arguing that the evidence that Owen and Edwards held the position ascribed to them is unsubstantiated. Then he points out that 'A justice that could be unilaterally waived would not be justice, and mercy which could not be unilaterally waived would not be mercy.'[13] In short, justice, by nature, cannot be offset but must be applied to all. On the other hand, mercy is a free gift, unexpected and undeserved, and by its very essence cannot be required as an obligation but instead is exercised sovereignly by whoever dispenses it. We speak of the prerogative of mercy but of the necessity of justice. The universal atonement of Campbell thus inverts the character of justice, mercy and the nature of God by making it an essential and necessary feature of God's nature that he must exercise mercy to all and, in so doing, suspend his justice.

On the other hand, there are a number of ways in which effective atonement appears weak. We shall discuss below some biblical passages which appear to teach that Christ died for all. For now, there is the theological parameter of the free offer of the gospel. Often it is claimed that if Christ did not die with the intention of atoning for everybody then it is impossible for the gospel to be proclaimed indiscriminately, since it would be the case that Christ may not have died for many whom God invites to salvation. On the other hand, such an argument assumes that for an offer to be valid and sincere a co-extensive provision should exist. This can hardly be the case. The gospel tells us that whoever trusts Christ will be saved. For its offer to be sincere what is required is that it be true. This it is.

It is often contended, however, that effective atonement robs us of assurance. Since we cannot proclaim indiscriminately 'Christ died for you' for he did not die for everyone, we consequently will have the greatest difficulty in saying of ourselves, 'Christ died for me'. After all, how do we know? He may not have died for us at all!

This argument leaves out two vital factors. First of all, when we trust Christ in faith we cast ourselves, and all that we are, on him personally and on his promise to us. His covenant promise is 'I will be your God, you shall be my people'. We trust that promise. He is true and faithful. It is of the very essence of saving faith to rely for salvation on Christ and his word. Moreover, we are united personally to Jesus Christ in a bond so close that Paul describes it as a great mystery (Eph. 5:30–32), of which the marriage bond is a limited analogy. Secondly and directly related to this, faith is a gift of the Holy Spirit and grants us access to the reality of God as he has revealed himself. The Spirit is the 'circumambient atmosphere' (Geerhardus Vos[14]) in which we live, an earnest of heaven itself. He enables us to fasten on the things which we await with assurance (Heb. 11:1f.). The nature of saving faith, the work of the Spirit, union with Christ and the faithfulness of God's covenant promise in Christ all underwrite the effectiveness of the atonement in such a way as to buttress our assurance rather than undermine it. In fact, the opposing arguments are self-defeating. How can we have genuine Christian assurance if Christ on the cross did not die expressly on behalf of anyone? If his sufferings were merely provisional, contingent on appropriation on our part, the inevitable tendency is towards introspection. The decisive moment is with us. We must be doubly sure of our faith. The work of Christ at Calvary, being in principle unfinished, since provisional, must be effected in us. Our attention will then be diverted away from Christ to ourselves. It is no secret that the strong affirmation of effective atonement by the Synod of Dort went hand in hand with a defence of assurance, whereas the Arminian doctrine of atonement which it opposed raised question marks over certainty of ultimate salvation.

Exegetical factors

In the New Testament, a number of passages appear to counteract the theological strengths of effective atonement. John 3:16 immediately springs to mind:

> For God so loved the world that he gave his one and only Son, that whoever believes in him shall not perish but have eternal life.

The purpose clause directs us to the reason for God's sending his only Son: that he might save believers. That in itself does not lead us in any specific direction. But what of the reference to 'the world'? Is this not telling us that the coming of Christ was for each and every individual? Even if this is John's meaning, it does not alter the fact that God's purpose was to save believers. The focus is not on the quantity of God's love, however, but on its quality. The first clause 'For God so loved the world' does not mean that God loved the world *so much*. That would limit his love by placing it in a measurable context. Rather, the *houtōs* has the sense 'in such a manner'. God loved the world in such a manner, in this way, that he gave his only Son for the purpose that whoever believes in him might have eternal life. Moreover, the parallel *hina* purpose clause in verse 17 'that the world might be saved through him' does not refer to 'every single person'. It relates to the world which stands under judgment, the world in a qualitative sense, the world in enmity with God. We see the preference for evil that the world exhibits in verses 18–21. Therefore, the idea in verse 16 is not that the world is so big that it takes a great deal of love to love it but that it is so bad that it is a wonder that God loves it at all, let alone to the extent of giving his only Son. Neither the term 'world' (*kosmos*) nor the passage as a whole is reflecting on the question before us.

Secondly, Romans 8:32 is another place where Christ is said to have been 'delivered up for us all':

> He who did not spare his own Son, but gave him up for us all – how will he not also, along with him, graciously give us all things?

The context, however, is Christ's intercession for God's elect (verse 33f.) and God's own fore-ordination of his people (verses 28–30). The letter itself is written to the church. The reference of the pronoun 'us' in verse 32 is certainly not universal; the frame of reference of the context is to Christ's own people.

Thirdly, in 2 Corinthians 5:14–15 Paul says that Christ 'died for all':

> For Christ's love compels us, because we are convinced that one died for all, and therefore all died. And he died for all, that those who live should no longer live for themselves but for him who died for them, and was raised again.

In approaching this passage, we recall that Paul consistently sees Christ's death and resurrection as a unity. Here Christ is said to rise in union with those who live for him and not for themselves. In other words, he rises in union with his believing people. For his death to be other than in union with these would introduce a disruption into what everywhere else Paul maintains as a unity. The context is governed by the theme of Christ's union with his people and can hardly support a different reference.

241

Fourthly, in 1 John 2:1–2, Christ is presented as

> ... the atoning sacrifice [propitiation] for our sins, and not only for ours but also for the sins of the whole world.

Again, there can be no proof that John is speaking of each individual person in the world. His letter was written against a background of the teaching of an heretical group who apparently claimed that they had been liberated from sin. John's first chapter is a clear rebuttal of such teaching (see 1 Jn. 1:5–10). These people seem to have been élitist and to have claimed to possess special knowledge or insight necessary to advance in the Christian faith. In the face of this, John stresses that as Christians we have the true knowledge in Christ ('we know' occurs 55 times in the letter) and that we all sin. We cannot in this life claim to be free of sin. Far from being self-sufficient as a spiritual élite, we need forgiveness, for which the only source is the blood of Jesus Christ. In this context, it is natural for John to add that Christ is the one sufficient propitiation available for the whole world and not just for ourselves. Another possible thought is that now that Jesus Christ has come, salvation is no longer confined to the Jewish nation but is intended for the Gentiles. Thus, Christ is the propitiatory sacrifice for the sins not only of Israel but of the entire world. It is unlikely that John is commenting on the intent of the atonement at all. He is dealing with more basic issues than that.

Fifthly, a final text which, at first sight, appears to favour some form of universalism and therefore a provisional atonement is Paul's comment in 1 Timothy 2:4–6:

> [God our Saviour] wants all men to be saved and to come to a knowledge of the truth. For there is one God and one mediator between God and men, the man Christ Jesus, who gave himself as a ransom for all men – the testimony given in its proper time.

Is not Paul saying that Christ was 'a ransom for all' (*antilytron hyper pantōn*)? Does this not mean just what it says, that he died to redeem each and every individual in the human race? The context suggests that Paul's focus is not on individuals. He asks Timothy that public prayers be offered for all people. Apart from the sheer logistical impossibility of praying in the church for every single individual in the human race one by one, Paul makes evident that he is concerned with all kinds of people, especially with those in positions of power:

> I urge, then, first of all, that requests, prayers, intercession and thanksgiving be made for everyone – for kings and all those in authority, that we may live peaceful and quiet lives in all godliness and holiness (verses 1–2).

He wants conditions of civil order so that the church can get on with its task unimpeded by social strife. In verses 4–6 he gives his reasons: God wishes all people to be saved; Christ, the one mediator, gave himself a ransom for all; the church should pray for 'all sorts and conditions of men' since Christ is the redeemer of all kinds of human beings. His grace is not restricted to a certain social group but is diffused throughout humanity, crossing barriers of race, occupation and caste. Once again, we conclude that the passage in question does not address the concerns before us. It is talking in terms of generalities, of groups and not of individuals. Moreover, there is also a relation between the ransom Christ paid (verse 6) and God's will (verse 4). God wills all people to be saved, Paul says. Yet elsewhere he maintains God's sovereign choice in election. God's will here in verse 4 is most likely that will by which, in Peter's terms, he is not willing that any should perish but that all reach repentance (2 Pet. 3:8–9), and thus finds expression in the call of the gospel. This finds support in Paul's earlier request for prayers for kings and 'all sorts and conditions of men'. He is writing about conduct in church gatherings, in a pastoral manner. In that setting a reference to the universal sufficiency and total adequacy of Christ's atoning death is highly appropriate. We shall return to this theme shortly.

Other contexts point to Christ having died with the

intention of atoning for the sins of his people. John 10:11–15 is an example:

> I am the good shepherd. The good shepherd lays down his life for the sheep .... I am the good shepherd; I know my sheep and my sheep know me – just as the Father knows me and I know the Father – and I lay down my life for the sheep.

Jesus defines his role as a shepherd who cares for his sheep. He knows his sheep with the intimate knowledge which is a feature of his relationship with the Father (verses 14–15). Twice in this section he states that he lays down his life for the sheep (verses 11, 15). That these sheep are not coterminous with the whole world is evident from the wider context. His sheep hear his voice and follow him (verses 3–5, 14–16). In contrast, his opponents were not his sheep, since they did not believe (verses 26–29):

> ... but you do not believe because you are not my sheep. My sheep listen to my voice; I know them, and they follow me. I give them eternal life, and they shall never perish; no-one can snatch them out of my hand. My Father, who has given them to me, is greater than all; no-one can snatch them out of my Father's hand.

Here Jesus makes a sharp distinction between his own flock and that which is not his flock. In that context, he indicates that his forthcoming death was to be on behalf of his own flock ('I lay down my life on behalf of the sheep'): those who listen to his word, believe in him, follow him, receive eternal life and shall never perish. This purpose cannot fail, for it is the Father's will that not one of those he has given to Jesus be lost but that all should be raised from the dead at the last day (verse 18; 6:37–40).

This is in line with Paul in Ephesians 5:25–27:

> Husbands, love your wives, just as Christ loved the church and gave himself up for her ....

He points to an atonement that achieves its goal. Christ loved the church and gave himself for it. His self-giving has as its purpose the sanctification and glorification of the church. We are reminded of Paul's farewell discourse to the elders of the same Ephesian church in Acts 20:28, for there he again affirms that God 'purchased his church through the blood of his own' (*my translation*). By his death, therefore, Christ bought the church for God's own possession. Neither here nor in Ephesians is there any idea of something ineffectual or contingent. The real business of atonement took place at the cross and it was intended to redeem the church.

Jesus himself in prayer declares his intercession to be for his elect and not for all indiscriminately (John 17:9). Paul stresses that Christ died in covenant union with his people (Rom. 5:12–21) and that his death itself brings justification and life at least as surely as Adam's sin brought death and condemnation.

Before we conclude, we will assess some other dimensions of the atonement as they relate to the particularity of God's intent. As we mentioned above, there is clear indication in Scripture of God's desire that none should perish but that all should repent and believe the gospel (2 Pet. 3:9). How can a perspective like this be reconciled with what we have said? On one level, we must distinguish between our own capacity to reconcile such statements and their place in the mind of God. Evidently, God's distinguishing electing love is fully compatible with his expressed will that the gospel be preached to all and with his desire that none should perish, hard though it may be for us to work it out. On the one hand, God is sovereign, working all things together according to his own purpose (Eph. 1:11). On the other hand, he has made us and sincerely wants the best for us all, since he made us to be his representatives in this world. He did not, however, make us as puppets or automata. We are responsible agents. All who perish will do so both because they justly deserve it on account of their sinful rebellion against God and also because they freely prefer it, having spurned the merciful and loving offer of salvation through Christ, resisting the unmistakable evidence of God's goodness and deity seen all around them in the creation and in themselves as his image bearers. The same principles hold true in connection with the atonement, for at this point we are reflecting on the intention of God in election as it relates to the atoning death of Christ.

There are a number of ways in which the atonement relates to all without exception. First of all, since the death of Christ is the one, sufficient atonement for sin it is totally adequate for every single person insofar as there is no other way back to God and since it is completely sufficient to restore us to him. If the whole world was to be saved, Christ would not have needed to suffer one bit more. Secondly, the death of Christ is to be proclaimed to all without exception as the only and sufficient means of salvation. In the terms we are using here, the atonement is of infinite worth (since it is the Son of God who died), it is of the utmost sufficiency for all (since it is totally adequate in achieving its design of making full and effective atonement for sins) and is to be proclaimed to all (for there is no other means of salvation, no other atonement for human sin). There is no defect in Christ's atonement: it is effective atonement. Indeed, as we have seen, it has outworkings of a cosmos-wide nature. The renovation of the entire universe is to be grounded on the death of Christ as an atonement for the sin of human beings. The overthrow of Satan and the fallen angels is achieved by the death and resurrection of Christ. In human terms, the church will be a huge number beyond calculation (Rev. 7:9–17).

The relation between the particularity and universality of the atonement is somewhat akin to the wave and particle theories of light. We know that light behaves like discrete particles. Yet it also behaves like continuous waves. The two theories appear, on the surface, to be incompatible and so to cancel each other out. Nevertheless, both are true. In an analogous manner, Christ died with the intent of atoning for his elect, while the worth and scope of his atonement is sufficient for each and every person who ever lived. So too the Father chose us in Christ before the foundation of the world. His sovereign election of some, however, stands side by side with his expressed will that sinners should repent and be saved.

We should remember that, according to Gödel's theorem,

no single system can be both comprehensive and consistent. So we can expect loose ends to exist in any human belief system. As Polanyi and Kuhn have demonstrated in their different ways,[15] the presence of unreconciled information does not of itself disprove a theory. Only if such unreconciled (or unreconcilable) information reaches proportions such as to jeopardize the theory's capacity to explain should the theory be abandoned.

Notes

Chapter 1

[1]W. Pannenberg, *Jesus – God and Man* (London: SCM Press, 1968), p. 221.

[2]T. F. Torrance, *The Mediation of Christ* (Exeter: Paternoster Press, 1983), pp. 11–33.

[3]Pannenberg acknowledges that the origin of Jesus' priesthood is rooted in the New Testament (p. 221) but his assessment is that it has the value of 'a somewhat baroque picture'.

[4]See Lv. chs. 1–7 for details of the sacrificial ritual under the Mosaic system. The representative nature of the high priest is evident from his carrying twelve precious stones, standing for the twelve tribes of Israel, on his priestly robes (Ex. 39:8–21) and from his appointment to offer gifts and sacrifices for sin on behalf of the people (Heb. 5:1f.).

[5]W. Pannenberg, *op. cit.*, p. 218.

[6]See Colin E. Gunton, *Yesterday and Today: A Study of Continuities in Christology* (London: Darton, Longman & Todd, 1983).

[7]Some of the main spokesmen in the older Protestant dogmatics attempted to do justice to these dimensions. Thus Calvin (*Institutes*, II,13), in his discussion of the incarnation and Christ's role as mediator, and also (*Institutes*, II,16), where he follows the statements about Jesus Christ in the Apostles' Creed, lays great emphasis on the human life and experience of our Lord, quoting widely across the New Testament.

The Scots Confession (1560), written by John Knox, in Articles VI–XI also focuses on Christ's incarnate life. This is hardly surprising. At the time, catechisms were very popular, and the standard catechetical form included discussion of the Apostles' Creed, which focused on the life and ministry of Jesus Christ as recorded in the gospels. A statement on his session at God's right hand followed. The Second Helvetic Confession (1566), the most widely accepted of all Reformed confessions, has 18 references to the gospels and 27 to the rest of the New Testament, a balance in proportion to that of the New Testament itself. The great Reformed dogmatician of the late sixteenth and early seventeenth centuries, Amandus Polanus, wrote extensively in his *Partitiones theologiae* (*Divisions of Theology, 1590*) on the humiliation of Christ, mostly based on the synoptics (see pp. 119–159). See my article 'Amandus Polanus: a Neglected Theologian?', *SCJ*, 21, 1990, pp. 463–476. Recent research has also drawn attention to the christology of John Owen, with his impressive attention to the humanity of Christ and the Spirit (Colin Gunton, 'Two Dogmas Revisited: Edward Irving's Christology', *SJT*, 41, 1988, pp. 359–376).

[8]Gregory of Nazianzus, 'Epistolae 101' (*MPG*, 37, 181c). See also Aloys Grillmeier, *Christ in Christian Tradition*, 1 (London: Mowbrays, [2]1975), pp. 329–391; J. N. D. Kelly, *Early Christian Doctrines* (London: A. & C. Black, [4]1968), pp. 289–301.

[9]Karl Barth, *CD*, IV/1, p. 128.

[10]G. C. Berkouwer, *The Work of Christ* (Grand Rapids: Eerdmans, 1965), p. 19.

[11]W. Pannenberg, *op. cit.*, p. 48.

[12]See T. F. Torrance, *Theology in Reconciliation* (London: Chapman, 1975), pp. 215–266; Colin E. Gunton *op. cit.*, pp. 56–138.

[13]Oscar Cullmann, *The Christology of the New Testament* (London: SCM Press, 1959), pp. 326–327. For his later qualifications, see 'The Reply of Professor Cullmann to Roman Catholic Critics', *SJT*, 15, 1962, pp. 36–43.

[14]See James D. G. Dunn, *Christology in the Making* (London: SCM Press, [2]1989); Jon Sobrino, *Christology at the Crossroads* (London, SCM Press, 1978); Juan Luís Segundo, *The Historical Jesus and the Synoptics* (London: Sheed & Ward, 1985).

[15]Colin E. Gunton, *op. cit.*, pp. 10–32.

[16]See Timothy Ware, *The Orthodox Church* (Harmondsworth: Penguin, 1964); Jaroslav Pelikan, *The Christian Tradition*, 2 (Chicago: University of Chicago Press, 1974).

[17]John McLeod Campbell, *The Nature of the Atonement* (1856; London: James Clarke, [4]1959). See also James B. Torrance, 'The Contribution of McLeod Campbell to Scottish Theology', *SJT*, 26, 1973, pp. 295–311; M. Charles Bell, *Calvin and Scottish Theology* (Edinburgh: Handsel,

1985), pp. 185–197; Trevor A. Hart, 'Anselm of Canterbury and John McLeod Campbell: Where Opposites Meet?' *EQ*, 62, 1990, pp. 311–333. Hart's important qualifications should be noted. He makes some significant connections between Campbell and Anselm but, as he himself acknowledges, at the expense of omitting some profound differences.

[18]Irenaeus, *Against Heresies*, V,16,2–3; Jaroslav Pelikan, *op. cit.*, 1, pp. 142–148. See also Clement of Alexandria, *Protrepticus* 11,114:1–4, *GCS*, 12,80; Origen, *On First Principles* II,6,3, *GCS*, 22,141f.

[19]Gustav Aulén, *Christus Victor* (London: SPCK, 1931), pp. 1–60; Jaroslav Pelikan, *op. cit.*, 1, pp. 148–152.

[20]See Jürgen Moltmann, *Theology of Hope* (London: SCM Press, 1969); Eberhard Jüngel, 'Thesen zur Grundlegung der Christologie', in *Unterwegs zur Sache: Theologische Bemerkungen* (Munich: Kaiser, 1972), pp. 274–295; Sobrino, *op. cit.*, pp. 236–272.

[21]A. Ritschl, *The Christian Doctrine of Justification and Reconciliation*, 3 (Edinburgh:T. & T. Clark, 1900), pp. 449, 591–592.

[22]Adolf von Harnack, *What is Christianity?* (London: Williams & Norgate, [4]1923), pp. 144–164.

[23]Jürgen Moltmann, *The Crucified God* (London: SCM Press, 1974), pp. 235–249; see Richard Bauckham, 'Moltmann's Eschatology of the Cross', *SJT*, 30, 1977, pp. 301–311.

Chapter 2

[1]O. Palmer Robertson, *The Christ of the Covenants* (Grand Rapids: Baker, 1980), p. vii.

[2]John Murray, *The Covenant of Grace* (London: Tyndale, 1954); Robertson, *op. cit.*, pp. 3–15.

[3]Meredith G. Kline, *The Structure of Biblical Authority* (Grand Rapids: Eerdmans, 1972); G. E. Mendenhall, 'Ancient Orient and Biblical Law', *Biblical Archaeologist*, 17, 1954, pp. 26–46; 'Covenant Forms in Israelite Tradition', *Biblical Archaeologist*, 17, 1954, pp. 50–76; K. A. Kitchen, *Ancient Orient and Old Testament* (London: Tyndale, 1966), pp. 90–102; D. J. McCarthy, *Treaty and Covenant* (Rome: Pontifical Biblical Institute, 1963).

[4]James B. Torrance, 'Covenant or Contract? A Study of the Theological Background of Worship in Seventeenth Century Scotland', *SJT*, 23, 1970, pp. 51–76.

[5]J. Murray, *op. cit.*, pp. 30–31.

[6]Meredith G. Kline, *By Oath Consigned: A Reinterpretation of the Covenant Signs of Circumcision and Baptism* (Grand Rapids: Eerdmans, 1968), pp. 13–38. Note the statement on p. 33: 'Merciful he may be according to his sovereign will; but all his works are in righteousness and truth.'

[7]David Hill, *The Gospel of Matthew* (London: Marshall, Morgan & Scott, 1972), pp. 39, 120.

[8]H. W. Robinson, *Corporate Personality in Ancient Israel* (Philadelphia: Fortress Press, 1964), pp. 1–20; R. P. Shedd, *Man in Community* (Grand Rapids: Eerdmans, 1964); H. M. Ridderbos, *Paul: An Outline of his Theology* (Grand Rapids: Eerdmans, 1975); Richard B. Gaffin, Jr., *The Centrality of the Resurrection* (Grand Rapids: Baker, 1978), pp. 53–66; G. C. Berkouwer, *Sin* (Grand Rapids: Eerdmans, 1971), pp. 512ff.

[9]E. P. Sanders, *Paul and Palestinian Judaism: A Comparison of Patterns of Religion* (London: SCM Press, 1977).

[10]James D. G. Dunn, *Word Biblical Commentary, 38A: Romans 1–8* (Dallas: Word, 1988), p. lxxiv; p. lxv. See also his *Jesus, Paul and the Law* (London: SPCK, 1990), pp. 183–214, 242–264.

[11]Sanders' ideas have led to a huge debate on Paul and the law. While his claims have not met with uniform approval, there is a growing consensus that Paul's discussion of the law must be seen in terms of the realities of the day, rather than those of a much later era. Besides, he hardly seems to focus on the agonizing soul-searching of the individual as Augustine later introduced. See Douglas Moo, 'Paul and the Law in the Last Ten Years', *SJT*, 40, 1987, pp. 287–307, for a thorough survey of the literature provoked by Sanders up until 1986. Moo uses Robert Jewett's phrase 'paradigm shift' to describe this 'watershed in pauline (sic) studies'. Important recent articles, from a critical perspective, are by Robert B. Sloan, 'Paul and the Law: Why the Law Cannot Save', *NovT*, 33, 1991, pp. 35–60, and by Thomas R. Schreiner, '"Works of Law" in Paul', *NovT*, 33, 1991, pp. 217–244. One of the key issues is how reliable is Sanders' assessment of the Jewish sources (on which most New Testament scholars, let along dogmaticians, are not competent to pronounce). If Sanders is correct, that still begs the question as to whether Paul may have addressed a specific localized situation, evidence of which does not exist in writings other than his own.

[12]Philip Edgcumbe Hughes, *A Commentary on the Epistle to the Hebrews* (Grand Rapids: Eerdmans, 1977), p. 301.

[13]Philip Edgcumbe Hughes, *Paul's Second Epistle to the Corinthians* (London: Marshall, Morgan & Scott, 1962), p. 103. See also pp. 104–105.

[14]C. E. B. Cranfield, *A Critical and Exegetical Commentary on the Epistle of Paul to the Romans: International Critical Commentary*, 2 (Edinburgh: T. & T. Clark, 1979), pp. 853–857.

[15]See Peter R. Jones, 'The Apostle Paul: Second Moses to the New Covenant Community', in John Warwick Montgomery (ed.), *God's Inerrant Word: An International Symposium on the Trustworthiness of Scripture* (Minneapolis: Bethany Fellowship, 1974), pp. 219–241.

[16]C. E. B. Cranfield, *op. cit.*, 2, pp. 823–870; see 2, p. 861.

[17]There may be some theological justification for reading a subjective genitive in Rom. 3:22; Gal. 2:16, 20; 3:22. In Rom. 3:22 we would then read of the righteousness of God given through the faithfulness of Jesus Christ (*dia pisteōs Iēsou Christou*) rather than through the faith we ourselves exercise in Christ. See *TDNT*, 6, p. 182f.; T. F. Torrance, 'One Aspect of the Biblical Conception of Faith', *ExpT*, 48, 1957, pp. 111–114, and the interchanges with C. F. D. Moule in following issues. In Gal. 2:16 Paul would then be saying that justification was not grounded on works of the law but on the faithfulness of Jesus Christ, on the faith and obedience by which Jesus himself lived rather than on our own faith and obedience. Such a meaning is in harmony with Paul's message in Gal., where he insists that the source and foundation of righteousness lies exclusively in God's grace. He would hardly want to exalt our faith as virtually another work akin to circumcision. In fact, in 2:16 when he moves on to talk of our faith in Christ, it is the faithfulness of Christ that gives it value: 'no man is justified by works of the law but through faithfulness of Jesus Christ, and so we believed in Jesus Christ so that we might be justified by the faithfulness of Christ and not by works of the law'. Our faith therefore involves departing from reliance on works of the law (self-effort, ritual observance) and instead depending on the faithfulness of someone else (Jesus Christ).

[18]See George H. Williams, *The Radical Reformation* (Philadelphia: Westminster, 1962), pp. 300–311; Leonard Verduin, *The Reformers and their Stepchildren* (Exeter: Paternoster Press, 1966), pp. 189–220.

[19]George H. Williams, *op. cit.*, pp. 143–145, 224–226, 526f., 734–736, 747f.; Verduin (1966), pp. 63–94.

[20]H. Zwingli, *Opera* (Zürich, 1545), 2,32b–33, 108b, 318b; 3,34, 259b; 4,417.

[21]*Cf.* the title of Bullinger's major work on the covenant: *De Testamento seu foedere Dei unico & aeterno brevis expositio* (Zürich, 1534), ('On the one eternal covenant or testament of God').

[22]Johannes Oecolampadius, *In Jeremiam Prophetam Commentariorum* (Geneva, 1558), p. 149.

[23]Martin Bucer, *Praelectiones doctiss. in Epistolam D. P. ad Ephesios* (Basel, 1561), p. 796.

[24]Wolfgang Capito, *In Hoseam Prophetam Commentarius* (Strassburg, 1528), p. 27.

[25]See Jack W. Cottrell, 'Covenant and Baptism in the Theology of Huldreich Zwingli' (Princeton Theological Seminary: PhD diss., 1971), pp. 100–125, 194–214; W. P. Stephens, *The Theology of Huldrych Zwingli* (Oxford: Clarendon Press, 1986), pp. 194–217.

[26]H. Zwingli, *Opera*, 2,29a, 111a–112; 3,34; 4,131, 493.

[27]See Martin Bucer, *In Epistolam ad Romanos* (Basel, 1562), pp. 440d, 518e; *idem, Praelectiones doctiss in Epistolam D.P. ad Ephesias* (Basel, 1561),

pp. 75b, 78e–79a; Pietro Martire Vermigli, *Common Places* (London, 1583), 2:16:27; 3:3:50.

[28]H. Bullinger, *De testamento seu foedere Dei* (Zurich, 1534), p. 4; 12; 16; 42; See also J. Wayne Baker, *Heinrich Bullinger and the Covenant: The Other Reformed Tradition* (Athens, Ohio: Ohio University Press, 1980).

[29]*The Decades of Henry Bullinger*, 2 (Cambridge: Cambridge University Press for the Parker Society, 1849), pp. 169–170. (First published 1552; first English edition 1577.)

[30]David J. Keep, 'Henry Bullinger and the Elizabethan Church' (University of Sheffield: PhD thesis, 1970), pp. 1–2. Keep notes that there are 12,000 extant letters of Bullinger's compared with 9,500 for Luther, Zwingli and Calvin combined.

[31]See my 'Saving Faith and Assurance in Reformed Theology: Zwingli to the Synod of Dort', 2 vols. (University of Aberdeen: PhD thesis, 1979).

[32]The covenant of works typically involved a promise by God to Adam of eternal life on condition of perfect obedience, with a threat of death for disobedience. There was no covenant mediator since humanity was as yet without sin. In claiming that eternal life was to be given as a reward for human obedience it focused on a possibility inherent in human beings. It was directed to anthropological and soteriological concerns. There are grounds, however, for the view that its entrance on the theological scene was so as to preserve grace rather than to oppose it. Michael C. McGiffert argues that it provided an opportunity to place law aside from the covenant of grace and so preserve the purely gratuitous nature of the latter. See Michael C. McGiffert, 'From Moses to Adam: the Making of the Covenant of Works', *SCJ*, 19, 1988, pp. 131–155.

[33]Robert Letham, 'The *foedus operum*: some factors accounting for its development', *SCJ*, 14, 1983, pp. 457–467.

[34]Johannes Cocceius, *Summa doctrina de foedere et testamento Dei* (Amsterdam, 1648). See G. C. Berkouwer, *Divine Election* (Grand Rapids: Eerdmans, 1960), pp. 162f. Note that the Princeton theologian, A. A. Hodge, in his *Outlines of Theology* (1860; Grand Rapids: Zondervan, 1972), pp. 371–372, makes no reference to the Holy Spirit!

[35]Paul discusses election and predestination in Rom. 8:28 – 9:33; Eph. 1:4–5, 11; 2 Tim. 1:9; Peter in 1 Pet. 1:1–5; 2:4f.; 2 Pet. 1:5–10; John (citing Jesus) in Jn. 6:37–45, 59–71; 10:25–30; 17:1f; Matthew in Mt. 11:25–30.

[36]J. K. S. Reid, 'The office of Christ in Predestination', *SJT*, 1, 1948, pp. 1–12.

[37]K. Barth, *CD*, II/2, pp. 3–506.

[38]K. Barth, *CD*, II/2, pp. 417–419.

[39]G. C. Berkouwer, *op. cit.*, pp. 154–162.

[40]K. Barth, *CD*, II/2,105, where he acknowledges that the Father and the Holy Spirit share with Christ in election.

[41]J. Calvin, *Institutes*, III,24,5.

[42]In P. Schaff (ed.), *The Creeds of Christendom*, 3 (Grand Rapids: Baker, 1969), pp. 444–446.

[43]See P. Schaff, *op. cit.*, 3, p. 848; Hieronymous Zanchius, *Omnium operum theologicarum* (Complete Theological Works), 2 (Geneva, 1619), pp. 535–537; 6:1; pp. 11–13; Amandus Polanus, *Syntagma theologiae Christianae* (Compendium of Christian Theology), (Hanover, 1609), c. 1596; idem, *De aeterna Dei praedestinatione* ('On God's Eternal Predestination') (Basel, 1598), p. 62; see also Richard A. Muller, *Christ and the Decree: Christology and Predestination in Reformed Theology from Calvin to Perkins* (Durham, N.C.: Labyrinth, 1986).

[44]Jacobus Arminus, *Works*, 1 (London, 1825), pp. 589–591.

[45]John Hales, *Letters from the Synod of Dort to Sir Dudley Carlton the English Embassador at the Hague* (Glasgow, 1765), p. 138.

Chapter 3

[1]*TDNT*, 1, p. 582.

[2]G. R. Beasley-Murray, *Jesus and the Kingdom of God* (Exeter: Paternoster Press, 1986), pp. 3–35.

[3]Two works which develop these themes at length are G. R. Beasley-Murray, *op. cit.*, and H. M. Ridderbos, *The Coming of the Kingdom* (Philadelphia: Presbyterian & Reformed, 1962).

[4]G. R. Beasley-Murray, *op. cit.*, pp. 144–146.

[5]Joachim Jeremias, *New Testament Theology*, 1 (London: SCM Press, 1971), pp. 112–113.

[6]The context itself should be our guide in seeking the meaning intended by the gospel writers.

[7]G. Gutiérrez, *A Theology of Liberation* (London: SCM Press, 1973); Juan Luís Segundo, *The Historical Jesus and the Synoptics* (London: Sheed & Ward, 1985); Jon Sobrino, *Christology at the Crossroads* (London: SCM Press, 1978); idem, *The True Church and the Poor* (London: SCM Press, 1984).

[8]The plural can, of course, include the paralytic himself. We have no grounds for thinking that he had no faith himself! Jesus singles out the faith of the wider group, however, of which he was part.

[9]See David J. Graham, 'Jesus as Miracle Worker', *SBET*, 4, 1986, pp. 85–96.

[10]D. M. Baillie, *God was in Christ: An Essay in Incarnation and Atonement* (London: Faber, 1948), pp. 13–14.

[11]Adolf von Harnack, *What is Christianity?* (London: Williams & Norgate, [4]1923).

Chapter 4

[1]See John W. Nevin, *The Mystical Presence* (Philadelphia, 1846).

[2]J. Calvin, *Institutes*, III,1,1.

[3]See Philip Edgcumbe Hughes, *The True Image: The Origin and Destiny of Man in Christ* (Leicester: Inter-Varsity Press, 1989), pp. 281–286.

[4]Note that the verb *trōgein* in John 6:53f. has very crass physical connotations. See Raymond E. Brown, *The Gospel According to John (i–xii)* (London: Chapman, 1966), pp. 282–283, 291–292. Brown argues that the Eucharist is a secondary theme in this passage. Barnabas Lindars, *The Gospel of John* (London: Marshall, Morgan & Scott, 1972), p. 59, claims that the sacraments and church order are presupposed by John. Schnackenburg points out that recent work on the fourth gospel recognizes that the words of institution for the eucharistic bread lie behind the discourse; see Rudolf Schnackenburg, *The Gospel According to John*, 2 (London: Burns & Oates, 1980), 2, p. 55. See also Ernst Haenchen, *John*, 1 (Philadelphia: Fortress Press, 1984), p. 294f. On the other hand Beasley-Murray doubts that the words of institution underlie the section. He still concedes, however, that neither the evangelist nor his readers could have written or read the saying without referring consciously to the Eucharist; George R. Beasley-Murray, *Word Biblical Commentary*, 36, *John* (Waco, Texas: Word, 1987), pp. 94–95. D. A. Carson is more reticent. He distinguishes between metaphorical and non-metaphorical elements in John's language. The reference is to Christ, he argues, who is the reality behind the Eucharist. It does not refer directly to the Eucharist at all. Yet, even so, Carson acknowledges that no passage in Scripture unfolds the true meaning of the Eucharist as clearly as this. See D. A. Carson, *The Gospel According to John* (Leicester: Inter-Varsity Press, 1991), pp. 288–298.

[5]J. Calvin, *Institutes*, IV,17,1–50; comments on Eph. 5:30 in David W. Torrance and Thomas F. Torrance (eds.), *Calvin's Commentaries: The Epistles of Paul to the Galatians, Ephesians, Philippians and Colossians* (Edinburgh: Oliver & Boyd, 1965), pp. 208–210; 'The Thirty-Nine Articles of Religion of the Church of England, Art. XXVIII', in P. Schaff (ed.), *The Creeds of Christendom*, 3 (Grand Rapids: Baker, 1969), pp. 505–506; 'The Westminster Confession of Faith', 29:1, 7 in *ibid.*, 3, pp. 663–666.

[6]Nowhere does the New Testament imply that Christ was a sinner. He was without sin (*cf.* 2 Cor. 5:21). He lived in a fallen world, however, and shared the experience of frustration and disorder brought about by human sinfulness. He himself was tempted; he suffered and was, as Isaiah portrayed, 'a man of sorrows and acquainted with grief' (Is. 53:3, AV).

[7]John Murray, 'Definitive Sanctification', *CTJ*, 2, 1967, pp. 5–21; see also H. M. Ridderbos, *Paul: An Outline of his Theology* (Grand Rapids:

Eerdmans, 1975), pp. 406–410; Richard B. Gaffin, Jr., *The Centrality of the Resurrection: A Study in Paul's Soteriology* (Grand Rapids: Baker, 1978), pp. 53–58.

[8]Charles Hodge, *Systematic Theology*, 3 vols. (Grand Rapids: Eerdmans, 1977), Louis Berkhof, *Systematic Theology* (Edinburgh: Banner of Truth, 1958), p. 114.

Chapter 5

[1]David Hill, *The Gospel of Matthew* (London: Oliphants, 1972), pp. 119ff.

[2]The overall purpose of Hebrews appears to be to establish the supremacy of Jesus Christ, in the face of a threat from some form of idealistic Judaism.

[3]*TDNT*, 1, pp. 414–420.

[4]Peter R. Jones, 'The Apostle Paul: Second Moses to the New Covenant Community', in J. W. Montgomery (ed.), *God's Inerrant Word: An International Symposium on the Trustworthiness of Scripture* (Minneapolis: Bethany Fellowship, 1974), pp. 219–241.

[5]There is a wider meaning of the term *apostolos* in the New Testament, in which it is applied to the bearers of the Christian message or to representatives of churches. Thus, Barnabas is called an apostle, as are a variety of other persons, about whom we know little. As in all questions of meaning, the various contexts determine for us what the writer is saying. By the strict and precise qualifications laid down for the twelve, we can tell that their activity and authority could not be shared. The persons described in these other passages functioned in a quite different and more limited manner. Simply because they are termed *apostoloi* they do not thereby share the role that elsewhere is said to be peculiar to the select group chosen personally by Jesus. It is linguistically illegitimate to take all possible meanings that a word can bear and import them into any one occurrence of its use.

[6]C. E. B. Cranfield, *A Critical and Exegetical Commentary on the Epistle of Paul to the Romans*, 2 (Edinburgh: T. & T. Clark, 1979), p. 532. See the discussion in the literature on the question of whether the genitive should be objective or subjective.

[7]The Westminster Confession of Faith, 14.2.

Chapter 6

[1]'Urim' from *'ārar* 'to curse'; 'thumim', from *tāmîm* 'to be perfect'. For their use see 1 Sa. 14:3, 41; 23:6f. Possibly there was a similarity to the drawing of lots.

[2]Salem was most probably a name for what eventually became

Jerusalem (*cf.* Ps. 76:2), the bread and wine intended for refreshment rather than a typical reference to the Eucharist, as some of the Fathers supposed.

[3]The interesting theory of B. F. Westcott and Abraham Kuyper that Melchizedek represented the last vestige of an original priesthood of human beings, stemming from creation, should be rejected. This priesthood was a universal one, they claimed, unrestricted by racial or geographical boundaries. The Aaronic priesthood was to supplant it for a time but only as a preparation for the perfect Melchizedek priesthood that was to appear later. Unfortunately, there is not a shred of biblical evidence for this intriguing idea. Moreover, such a priesthood could have had no vicarious significance, since before the fall man did not need salvation.

[4]For details of the bizarre range of speculations on the identity of Melchizedek, from a christophany through pneumatophany to angelophany, see Philip Edgcumbe Hughes, *A Commentary on the Epistle to the Hebrews* (Grand Rapids: Eerdmans, 1977), pp. 237–245.

[5]T. W. Manson, *The Teaching of Jesus* (Cambridge: Cambridge University Press, 1939).

[6]Oscar Cullmann, *The Christology of the New Testament* (London: SCM Press, 1959), pp. 88–89.

[7]*ta pros ton thēon* can best be taken as an accusative of respect. See P. E. Hughes, *op. cit.*, p. 120.

[8]While this passage was almost certainly not part of the original text of the fourth gospel it probably reflects an early tradition concerning Jesus' conflict with the Pharisees.

[9]Raymond E. Brown, *The Gospel According to John: i–xii* (London: Chapman, 1966), p. 358.

[10]Thomas F. Torrance, *Theology in Reconstruction* (London: SCM Press, 1976), pp. 267–293; *idem, Transformation and Convergence in the Frame of Knowledge: Explorations in the Interrelations of Scientific and Theological Enterprise* (Belfast: Christian Journals, 1984), pp. 1–60, 215–283.

Chapter 7

[1]See Leonard Hodgson, *The Doctrine of the Atonement* (London: Nisbet, 1951), pp. 52–67, who cites F. H. Bradley in support. See also Leon Morris, *The Cross in the New Testament* (Exeter: Paternoster Press, 1967), pp. 382–388.

[2]*Turretin on the Atonement of Christ* (Eng. tr. 1859, reprinted Grand Rapids: Baker, 1978), pp. 14–30.

[3]*The Collected Writings of James Henley Thornwell*, 2 (Edinburgh: Banner of Truth, 1974), pp. 205–261.

[4]L. Hodgson, *op. cit.*, pp. 52–67; L. Morris, *op. cit.*, pp. 382–388.

[5]See Leon Morris, *The Apostolic Preaching of the Cross* (London: Tyndale Press, [3]1965), pp. 147–154, 158f., 174–184, 208–213; R. V. G. Tasker, *The Biblical Doctrine of the Wrath of God* (London: Tyndale, 1951).

[6]See P. E. Hughes, *A Commentary on the Epistle to the Hebrews* (Grand Rapids: Eerdmans, 1977), introduction.

[7]The meaning of the phrase 'through [the] eternal spirit' has been a matter of long discussion. Many commentators prefer a reference to 'eternal spirit', to the nature of Christ as divine and therefore eternal. The absence of the article is seen as supporting their case. Westcott, Vos, Spicq and Hughes all favour this reading. While these authors do not all accept its influence, such an understanding of the phrase suggests the influence of Platonism. The idea that Philo had an impact on the author has been decisively rejected by, *e.g.*, Ronald Williamson, *Philo and the Epistle to the Hebrews* (Leiden: E. J. Brill, 1970). Since this is the likeliest possible source for a mediation of Platonism, the probability is that the passage here does not show such features.

[8]See A. M. Stibbs, *The Meaning of the Word 'Blood' in Scripture* (London: Tyndale, 1948); L. Morris, *The Apostolic Preaching of the Cross* (London: Tyndale, [3]1965), pp. 112–128; Wilfrid Stott, 'The Conception of "Offering" in the Epistle to the Hebrews', *NTS*, 9, 1962, pp. 65–67.

[9]See also Rom. 5:9; 1 Cor. 10:16; Eph. 1:7; 2:13; Col. 1:14, 20; Heb. 9:12, 14; 10:19, 29; 12:24; 13:12, 20; 1 Jn. 1:7; 5:6, 8; Rev. 1:5; 5:9; 7:14; 12:11.

[10]See J. Calvin, *Institutes*, II,16,5; Heidelberg Catechism, Q. 37, '"What do you understand by the word suffered?" Answer: "That all the time he lived on earth, but especially at the end of his life, he bore, in body and soul, the wrath of God against the sin of the whole human race . . ."', Philip Schaff (ed.), *The Creeds of Christendom*, 3 (Grand Rapids: Baker, 1966), p. 319 (spelling modernized).

[11]L. Morris, *The Apostolic Preaching of the Cross* (London: Tyndale, [3]1965), pp. 62ff.

[12]P. E. Hughes, *Paul's Second Epistle to the Corinthians* (London: Marshall, Morgan & Scott, 1962), p. 211.

[13]For a discussion on the respective merits of the readings *epathen* and *apethanen* see Bruce M. Metzger, *A Textual Commentary on the Greek New Testament* (London: UBS, 1971), pp. 692–693.

[14]Martin Hengel, *The Atonement: A Study of the Origins of the Doctrine in the New Testament* (London: SCM Press, 1981), pp. 1–32.

[15]Colin Gunton, 'Two Dogmas Revisited: Edward Irving's Christology', *SJT*, 41, 1988, p. 367.

[16]C. H. Dodd, '*Hilaskesthai*, its Cognates, Derivatives and Synonyms in the Septuagint', *JTS*, 32, 1931, pp. 352–360.

[17]Roger Nicole, ' C. H. Dodd and the Doctrine of Propitiation', *WTJ*, 17, 1955, pp. 117–157; Morris, *op. cit.*, pp. 144–213.

[18]C. E. B. Cranfield, *A Critical and Exegetical Commentary on the Epistle to the Romans*, 1 (Edinburgh: T. & T. Clark, 1975), pp. 214–218.

[19]See note 5 above.

[20]K. Schilder, *Christ on Trial* (Grand Rapids: Eerdmans, 1950), pp. 277–288, 415–549. See also the first chapter of the same author's subsequent book, the third in a trilogy on the crucifixion, *Christ Crucified*.

[21]See J. Moltmann, *The Crucified God* (London: SCM Press, 1974), pp. 200–290; J. Sobrino, *Christology at the Crossroads* (London: SCM Press, 1978), pp. 179–235.

[22]L. Morris, *The Apostle Preaching of the Cross* (London: Tyndale, [3]1965), pp. 214–250.

[23]*Ibid.*, pp. 11–64.

[24]See W. J. Dalton, *Christ's Proclamation to the Spirits: A Study of 1 Peter 3:18 – 4:6* (Rome: Pontifical Biblical Institute, 1965); Bo Reicke, *The Disobedient Spirits and Christian Baptism* (Copenhagen: Acta Seminarii Neotestamentici Upsaliensis, 1946); J. N. D. Kelly, *A Commentary on the Epistles of Peter and of Jude* (London: A. & C. Black, 1969), pp. 150–164; W. Grudem, *The First Epistle of Peter: An Introduction and Commentary* (Leicester: Inter-Varsity Press, 1988), pp. 203–239.

[25]See Leon Morris, *The Cross of Jesus* (Exeter: Paternoster Press, 1988), for a helpful discussion of how the atonement bears upon questions of frustration, ignorance, loneliness, sickness, death and selfishness.

[26]John Murray, 'Definitive Sanctification', *CTJ*, 2, 1967, pp. 5–21; see also H. M. Ridderbos, *Paul: An Outline of his Theology* (Grand Rapids: Eerdmans, 1975), pp. 406–410; Richard B. Gaffin, Jr., *The Centrality of the Resurrection: A Study in Paul's Soteriology* (Grand Rapids: Baker, 1978), pp. 53–58.

[27]D-Day, 6 June 1944, was the day in the Second World War when Allied troops invaded Normandy. It was the decisive turning-point of the war. VE-Day, in May 1945, was the day Nazi Germany finally capitulated. Between these two dates there were many fierce battles and much loss of life, but the overwhelming fire-power of the Allies made final victory certain.

[28]The idea that the blood of Christ was his life offered up to God, preserved and active beyond death, was popularized by B. F. Westcott, *The Epistles of St John* (London: Macmillan, 1886), pp. 34–37. This argument was refuted by A. M. Stibbs, *The Meaning of the Word 'Blood' in Scripture* (London: Tyndale, 1948), and again by Wilfrid Stott, 'The Conception of "Offering" in the Epistle to the Hebrews', *NTS*, 9, 1962, pp. 65–67.

Chapter 8

[1]Athanasius, *Discourses against the Arians*, I,43–44, *MPG*, 26,100–104; II,61–68, *MPG*, 26,276–293; Cyril of Alexandria, *Passover Homilies* XVII, *MPG*, 77,785–787; *Against the Nestorians* I, *MPG*, 76,17; *Commentary on the Gospel of John*, *MPG*, 73,161; 74,432.

[2]See J. Zizioulas, 'Human capacity and human incapacity: a theological exploration of personhood', *SJT*, 28, 1975, pp. 401–447.

[3]See G. Aulén, *Christus Victor* (London: SPCK, 1931), p. 19.

[4]Origen, *Matthew*, Tom. XIII,8–9 *GCS*, 40.203–204.

[5]Origen, *Matthew*, Tom. XIII,8–9, *GCS*, 40:203–204.

[6]Origen, *Against Celsus* VII,17, *GCS*, 3,169; *On First Principles* I,6,2, *GCS*, 22,79–80.

[7]Origen, *Commentary on John*, VI,57, *GCS*, 10,166.

[8]Gregory of Nyssa, *Catechetical Discourses magna*, 22–26, *MPG*, 45,60–69.

[9]Ambrose, *Letters* 41,7f.; 72,8, *MPL*, 16,1115, 1245–1246.

[10]Gregory of Nazianzen, *Discourses* 45:22, *MPG*, 36,654.

[11]Peter Damian, *Sermon* 46, *MPL*, 144,751.

[12]G. Aulén, *op. cit.*, pp. 53f.

[13]*Ibid.*, pp. 101–122.

[14]J. N. D. Kelly, *Early Christian Doctrines* (London: A. & C. Black, [4]1968), p. 388.

[15]*Ibid.*, pp. 375–377.

[16]R. E. Weingart, *The Logic of Divine Love: A Critical Analysis of the Soteriology of Peter Abailard* (Oxford: Clarendon, 1970), pp. 78–96, 125–126; R. O. P. Taylor, 'Was Abelard an Exemplarist?', *Theology* 31, 1935, pp. 207–213; Alister McGrath, 'The Moral Theory of the Atonement: An Historical and Theological Critique', *SJT*, 38, 1985, pp. 205–220.

[17]B. B. Warfield, *The Person and Work of Christ* (Philadelphia: Presbyterian & Reformed, 1970), pp. 363–366, 373–387; John Stott, *The Cross of Christ* (Leicester: Inter-Varsity Press, 1986), p. 122.

[18]John McLeod Campbell, *The Nature of the Atonement* (1856; London: James Clarke, [4]1959).

[19]Trevor Hart points out that Campbell did not remove the wrath of God from his consideration of the atonement. Christ indeed bore the divine wrath but not in terms of punishment, See Trevor A. Hart, 'Anselm of Canterbury and John McLeod Campbell: Where Opposites Meet?' *EQ*, 62, 1990, pp. 311–333.

[20]J. Moltmann, *The Crucified God* (London: SCM Press, 1974), pp. 235–249.

[21]J. Sobrino, *Christology at the Crossroads* (London: SCM Press, 1978), pp. 179–235.

[22]*Ibid.*, pp. 118f.; *passim*.

[23]G. Gutiérrez, *A Theology of Liberation* (London: SCM Press, 1973), pp. 186–202.

[24]José Porfirio Miranda, *Being and the Messiah: The Message of St. John* (Maryknoll, New York: Orbis, 1977), *passim*.

[25]J. L. Segundo, *The Historical Jesus and the Synoptics* (London: Sheed & Ward, 1985), pp. 87–132.

Chapter 9

[1]E. P. Sanders, *Paul and Palestinian Judaism* (London: SCM Press, 1977), pp. 543–556; J. D. G. Dunn, *Word Biblical Commentary*, 38A, *Romans 1–8* (Texas: Word, 1988), pp. lxiii–lxxii; *idem, Jesus, Paul and the Law* (London: SPCK, 1990), pp. 183–214, 242–264. See chapter 2, note 10 above, for some qualifications and further references.

[2]Sanctification is essentially a spatial concept, referring to our being God's possession and so separated from the rule of sin and Satan. In this sense, it consists of a definitive breach with the power of sin effected by Christ, a change which has already taken place when, in baptism, we died to sin (*cf.* Rom. 6:1f). See also *The Collected Writings of John Murray*, 2 (Edinburgh: Banner of Truth, 1977), pp. 277–284. It also has a present and ongoing significance, in which it is a lifelong process, incomplete and partial, by which we are conformed to the image of Christ. In terms of the future, it takes the form of glorification, when we shall be entirely conformed to Christ after his parousia.

[3]That justification is not merely a legal fiction (just-as-if) is clear from the following considerations: (1) Union with Christ takes legal forms (he is our representative, acting on our behalf and in our place) but it is not exhausted by such categories. It is also dynamic and personal. Paul prays that the Ephesians might know the power of God in them which was exerted in raising Christ from the dead (Eph. 1:18f.). As such, we are united to Christ in a real, personal, organic manner. His humanity is communicated to us in the Eucharist by the Holy Spirit in a real, spiritual sense. Thus, Christ's righteousness is ours, actually and really, not only legally, since he is one with us and we are one with him. Reformed theology of the sixteenth century (Calvin, for instance) held to this, while later exponents such as Jonathan Edwards and Charles Hodge conceived of such union in purely legal, contractual terms. See John W. Nevin, *The Mystical Presence* (Philadelphia, 1846). (2) Passages such as 2 Cor. 5:21 and Rom. 5:19 convey the idea that not only is righteousness imputed to us but that we are also constituted righteous. We do not become personally righteous any more than Christ became personally a sinner. In other words, we are still sinners and, while the Holy Spirit is transforming us, we are still liable to sin. Christ, on the other hand, is completely righteous. Just as the sinless Christ took our

sins and our guilt, however, becoming legally liable to receive God's wrath in our place, really and actually suffering such wrath, so we are accounted righteous and become legally just, and consequently we are also actually just *in Christ*, due to the reality of this exchange. (3) This constituting of us as righteous is still thoroughly objective and gracious. This is no inherent or imparted righteousness. Justification is still distinct from sanctification. As Murray points out, however, 'Justification is a constitutive act, not barely declarative. And this constitutive act consists in our being placed in the category of righteous persons by reason of our relation to Christ . . . we must not tone down the formula "constituted righteous" to any lower terms than the gracious judgment on God's part whereby the obedience of Christ is reckoned to our account and therefore reckoned as ours with all the entail of consequence which righteousness carries with it.' John Murray, *The Epistle to the Romans: The English Text with Introduction, Exposition and Notes* (London: Marshall, Morgan & Scott, 1967), pp. 205–206. See also Calvin, *Institutes*, III,11,10.

[4]Alister E. McGrath, *Iustitia Dei: A History of the Christian Doctrine of Justification*, 1 (Cambridge: Cambridge University Press, 1986), pp. 23–36.

[5]Augustine, *On the Holy Trinity*, XV,18,32, in *NPNF*, 3, p. 217; *Homilies on the Gospel of John*, 25,12; 29,6, in *NPNF*, 7, pp. 164–165, 184–185; *Expositions on the Book of Psalms*, 32,1–8, in *NPNF*, 8, pp. 70–7; *Homilies on the First Epistle of John*, 5,7, in *NPNF*, 7, pp. 490–491; *The Spirit and the Letter*, 56: xxxii, in John Burnaby (ed.), *Augustine: Later Works*, Library of Christian Classics, 8 (London: SCM Press, 1955), pp. 239–241.

[6]See Heiko Augustinus Oberman, *The Harvest of Medieval Theology: Gabriel Biel and Late Medieval Nominalism* (Grand Rapids: Eerdmans, 1967); Alister E. McGrath, 'Mira et Nova Diffinitio Iustitiae: Luther and Scholastic Doctrines of Justification', *ARG*, 73, 1982, pp. 37–60.

[7]A. E. McGrath, *op. cit.*, 2, pp. 17–18.

[8]*Ibid.*, pp. 10–20, 54–86.

[9]The Formula of Concord, art. 3.

[10]W. R. Stephens, *The Holy Spirit in the Theology of Martin Bucer* (Cambridge, Cambridge University Press, 1970), pp. 155–167; McGrath, 2, pp. 32–33.

[11]Martin Bucer, *Metaphrasis et Enarratio in Epist. D. Pauli ad Romanos* (Basel, 1562), pp. 11–14; 231a-b; 232d-e.

[12]Calvin, *Institutes*, III,11,6; III,16,1–4.

[13]A. E. McGrath, *op. cit.*, 2, pp. 184–191.

[14]*Cf.* The Westminster Shorter Catechism, Q.1.

[15]A. E. McGrath, *op. cit.*, 2, p. 85.

[16]*Ibid.*, 2, pp. 55–68.

[17]Hans Küng, *Justification: The Doctrine of Karl Barth and a Catholic Reflection* (London: Burns & Oates, 1964).

[18]Karl Barth, *CD*, II/2, pp. 757ff.; IV/1, pp. 516ff.

[19]H. George Anderson, T. Austin Murphy and Joseph Burgess (eds.), *Justification by Faith: Lutherans and Catholics in Dialogue VII* (Minneapolis: Augsburg, 1985).

[20]Alister McGrath, *ARCIC II and Justification: an Evangelical Anglican Assessment of 'Salvation and the Church'* (Oxford: Latimer House, 1987), pp. 39–43.

[21]The Second Anglican–Roman Catholic International Commission (ARCIC II), *Salvation and the Church: An Agreed Statement* (London: Church House, 1987), section 15 p. 17.

Chapter 10

[1]The question of whether this is a pre-Pauline hymn or an original composition by Paul himself does not materially affect the argument, for even if Paul was not the original author he gives it his sanction by citing it in support of what he is saying.

[2]Karl Barth, *CD*, III/1,54ff.; Marcellus of Ancyra, cited in J. B. Lightfoot, *Saint Paul's Epistles to the Colossians and Philemon* (London: Macmillan, 1879), p. 147.

[3]James D. G. Dunn, *Christology in the Making* (London: SCM Press, 1980), pp. 187–196; reviewed by C. F. D. Moule in *JTS*, 33, 1982, pp. 258–263.

[4]Seyoon Kim, *The Origin of Paul's Gospel* (Grand Rapids: Eerdmans, 1982), pp. 151ff., 196ff.

[5]*Enhypostasia* was accorded the status of dogma by the second council of Constantinople in AD 553. See H. M. Relton, *A Study in Christology* (London: SPCK, 1917).

[6]St Athanasius, *On the Incarnation: the Treatise 'De incarnatione Verbi Dei'*; trans. Sister Penelope Lawson (New York: Macmillan, 1946), p. 4=section 1. See also p. 11=section 6, where Athanasius talks of humanity as 'beings which once had shared the nature of the Word'.

[7]Chul Won Suh, *The Creation Mediatorship of Jesus Christ* (Amsterdam: Rodopi, 1982). See my review of the above in *WTJ*, 46, 1984, pp. 213–216.

[8]Supralapsarianism and infralapsarianism are theories which arose in the context of discussions on the relation of God's predestination to the fall of the human race into sin. Supralapsarians held that God's decree of election *logically* preceeded his decree to permit Adam to sin. Infralapsarians maintained that God's decree of election *logically* followed his decree to permit Adam to sin. Thus, supralapsarianism placed a stress on predestination, while infralapsarianism attempted to

follow the biblical and historical order. Although the debate was speculative, relating to matters beyond our knowledge, it nevertheless reflected significant and pervasive differences of emphasis that impinged on other areas.

[9]Suh, pp. 304–305, being dependent to a great extent on suggestions made by Abraham Kuyper.

[10]Colin E. Gunton, *The Actuality of Atonement* (Edinburgh: T. & T. Clark, 1988), pp. 145–155, 168–169.

[11]Caroline M. Noel, 'At the Name of Jesus'.

Chapter 11

[1]Geerhardus Vos, *The Pauline Eschatology* (Grand Rapids: Eerdmans, 1972), p. 163.

[2]Those who reject infant baptism tend to restrict membership of the visible church to professing believers, while those who practise infant baptism would include the children of believers as church members.

[3]Cyprian, *On the Unity of the Catholic Church, CSEL*, 3,1,214.

[4]Calvin, *Institutes*, IV,1,1.

[5]Calvin, *Institutes*, IV,1,4, reflecting the teaching of Augustine.

[6]See the Dogmatic Decrees of Vatican, I, chapter 2, in Philip Schaff (ed.), *The Creeds of Christendom*, 2 (Grand Rapids: Baker, 1983), p. 242.

[7]*The Documents of Vatican II* (New York: Guild, 1966), pp. 111ff.

Appendix

[1]Augustine, *Homilies on John*, 48,4; 55,6; 92,1; 109,5; 123,5. However, Augustine is only implicit in his discussion of the matter and has in fact been claimed by both sides.

[2]Prosper of Aquitaine, *Prosper of Aquitaine: Defence of St Augustine*, Ancient Christian Writers (London: Longmans, 1963), cited by W. Robert Godfrey, 'Reformed Thought on the Extent of the Atonement to 1618', *WTJ*, 37 (1975), p 135.

[3]See Geoffrey W. Bromiley, *Historical Theology: an Introduction* (Edinburgh: T. & T. Clark, 1978), pp. 165–170; Jaroslav Pelikan, *The Christian Tradition*, 3 (Chicago: University of Chicago Press, 1978), pp. 81–95.

[4]Peter Lombard, *Libri Quatuor Sententiarum*, 3:20, in *MPL*, 192,799. Note that this distinction was to be used by advocates both of effective and also provisional atonement; see Curt D. Daniel, 'HyperCalvinism and John Gill' (University of Edinburgh: PhD thesis, 1983), pp. 504–529; 777ff.

[5]*'Multorum dixit, & non omnium, quia multi vocari, pauci vero electi.'* ('He says many, and not all, because many are called but few chosen.')

Ioannes Oecolampadius, *In Epistolam ad Hebraeos* (Strassburg, 1534), p. 104. See also his *In Daniel Prophetarum* (Geneva, 1567 [1558], p. 107; Wilhelm Pauck (ed.), *Martin Bucer: De Regno Christi*, Library of Christian Classics, 19 (London: SCM Press, 1969), p. 201; see also the citation in W. P. Stephens, *The Holy Spirit in the Theology of Martin Bucer* (Cambridge: Cambridge University Press, 1970), p. 106; Pietro Martire Vermigli, *Common Places* (London, 1583), III,1,44; III,1,21; *In Epistolam ad Romanos* (Basel, 1560), pp. 985–986. The position of Calvin has been hotly disputed. The following have advocated that he adopted a form of provisional atonement: R. T. Kendall, *Calvin and English Calvinism to 1649* (Oxford: Oxford University Press, 1979), pp. 13–28; James B. Torrance, 'The Incarnation and Limited Atonement', *EQ*, 55, 1983, pp. 82–94; M. Charles Bell, *Calvin and Scottish Theology: the Doctrine of Assurance* (Edinburgh: Handsel, 1985), pp. 13–40; Daniel, *op. cit.*, pp. 777–829. The following argue that Calvin explicitly taught effective atonement or else his theology demanded it: Paul Helm, *Calvin and the Calvinists* (Edinburgh: Banner of Truth, 1982); 'Calvin and the Covenant: Unity and Continuity', *EQ*, 55, 1983, pp. 65–81; W. Robert Godfrey, 'Reformed Thought on the Extent of the Atonement to 1618', *WTJ*, 37, 1975, pp. 137–138; Roger Nicole, 'John Calvin's View of the Extent of the Atonement', *WTJ*, 47, 1985, pp. 197–225. My position is that Calvin was ambiguous or contradictory on the question but that he maintained the intrinsic efficacy of the atonement; see R. Letham, 'Saving Faith and Assurance in Reformed Theology: Zwingli to the Synod of Dort', 1 (University of Aberdeen: PhD thesis, (1979), pp. 122–126; 2, pp. 65–67. See also Tony Lane, 'In search of the historical Calvin', *EQ*, 55, 1983, pp. 95–113.

[6]'A spillover from Calvinism into Arminianism has occurred in recent decades. Thus many Arminians whose theology is not very precise say that Christ paid the penalty for our sins. Yet such a view is foreign to Arminianism, which teaches instead that Christ suffered for us.' J. K. Grider, 'Arminianism', in Walter A. Elwell (ed.), *Evangelical Dictionary of Theology* (Basingstoke: Marshall Pickering, 1985), pp. 79–81. See also R. Letham, 'Arminianism', in S. B. Ferguson, D. F. Wright and J. I. Packer (eds.), *New Dictionary of Theology* (Leicester: Inter-Varsity Press, 1988), pp. 45–46.

[7]William H. Goold (ed.), *The Works of John Owen*, 10 (London: Banner of Truth, 1967), pp. 173–174.

[8]John Murray, *Redemption Accomplished and Applied* (London: Banner of Truth, 1961), p. 64.

[9]C. E. B. Cranfield, *A Critical and Exegetical Commentary on the Epistle to the Romans* (Edinburgh: T. & T. Clark, 1975), 1:431. See also Ernst Käsemann, *Commentary on Romans* (London: SCM Press, 1980), p. 244, who also refers *proegnō* to eternal election. Bultmann argues too that in

the New Testament *proginōskō* is the foreordination by God of his people; *TDNT*, 1, p. 715.

[10]Arguing the case that for Paul union with Christ in his death and resurrection is at the heart of the biblical message is H. M. Ridderbos, *Paul: An Outline of his Theology* (Grand Rapids: Eerdmans, 1975).

[11]Simon Episcopius, *Opera Theologica* (Amsterdam, 1660–65), 1:332–334, where he states that the Son and Holy Spirit have divinity and divine perfections not as equals but as subordinates (*non collateraliter aut coordinate sed subordinate*). See also Richard A. Muller, 'The Christological Problem in the Thought of Jacobus Arminius', *NAK*, 68, 1988, pp. 145–163.

[12]See J. McLeod Campbell, *The Nature of the Atonement* (1856; London: James Clark, [4]1959); James B. Torrance, 'Covenant or Contract? A Study of the Theological Background of Worship in Seventeenth Century Scotland', *SJT*, 23, 1970, pp. 51–76; *idem*, 'The Contribution of Mcleod Campbell to Scottish Theology', *SJT*, 26, 1973, pp. 295–311; *idem*, 'The Incarnation and Limited Atonement', *EQ*, 55, 1983, pp. 82–94.

[13]Paul Helm, 'The Logic of Limited Atonement', *SBET*, 3, 1985, p. 50.

[14]Geerhardus Vos, *The Pauline Eschatology* (Grand Rapids: Eerdmans, 1972), p. 163.

[15]Michael Polanyi, *Personal Knowledge* (Chicago: University of Chicago Press, 1958); Thomas S. Kuhn, *The Structure of Scientific Revolutions* (Chicago: University of Chicago Press, 1962).

For Further Reading

For background on the historical controversies that led to the church's conciliar decisions on the person of Christ, see Frances M. Young, *From Nicea to Chalcedon: A Guide to the Literature and its Background* (London: SCM Press, 1983), a readable survey; or for a more exhaustive treatment, Aloys Grillmeier, *Christ in Christian Tradition*, 1 (London: Mowbrays, ²1975).

For general coverage of the work of Christ, see John Calvin, *Institutes of the Christian Religion*, edited by John T. McNeill and translated by Ford Lewis Battles, vols. 20–21 in *The Library of Christian Classics* (London: SCM Press, 1960).

In addition to the notes found throughout the book, the following are particularly worth exploring:

Covenant and election
O. Palmer Robertson, *The Christ of the Covenants* (Grand Rapids: Baker, 1980), and Paul K. Jewett, *Election and Predestination* (Grand Rapids: Eerdmans, 1986).

The kingdom of God
G. R. Beasley-Murray, *Jesus and the Kingdom of God* (Exeter: Paternoster Press, 1986). The Christological themes of liberation theology can be investigated by means of Jon Sobrino, *Christology at the Crossroads* (London: SCM Press, 1978) and Juan Luís Segundo, *The Historical Jesus and the Synoptics* (London: Sheed & Ward, 1985).

Union with Christ
Richard B. Gaffin, Jr., *The Centrality of the Resurrection* (Grand Rapids: Baker, 1978), and Herman N. Ridderbos, *Paul: An Outline of his Theology* (Grand Rapids: Eerdmans, 1975). For the persistent, the long-out-of-print work of John W. Nevin, *The Mystical Presence* (Philadelphia, 1846) is well worth reading. It is available at some theological libraries, and the British Library.

Christ's human priesthood
Thomas F. Torrance, 'The Mind of Christ in Worship: Problem of Apollinarianism in the Liturgy', in *Theology in Reconciliation: Essays Towards Evangelical and Catholic Unity in East and West* (London: Chapman, 1975), pp. 139–214; *idem, The Trinitarian Faith: The Evangelical Theology of the Ancient Catholic Church* (Edinburgh: T. & T. Clark, 1988), pp. 62ff., 135f., 158ff., 168f., 176ff.

The nature of the atonement
Leon Morris, *The Apostolic Preaching of the Cross* (London: Tyndale Press, [3]1965) – an example of New Testament scholarship at its best.

Theories of the atonement
The best follow-up is to examine the primary sources. Irenaeus and Origen can be consulted in translation via the *Nicene and Post-Nicene Fathers* series, edited by Philip Schaff (see Abbreviations above, p. 14). Both works by Abelard and Anselm are available in English in *The Library of Christian Classics*, volume 10, entitled *A Scholastic Miscellany* (London: SCM Press, 1970). Of the other works cited, Grotius, Bushnell and McLeod Campbell are not, to my knowledge, in print but should be accessible at most major theological libraries.

The history of discussion on justification
Alister E. McGrath, *Iustitia Dei: A History of the Christian Doctrine of Justification*, 2 vols. (Cambridge: Cambridge University Press, 1986).

Christ's resurrection and the cosmos
Thomas F. Torrance, *Space, Time and Resurrection* (Grand Rapids: Eerdmans, 1976).

Christ's Kingship and the future
B. B. Warfield, 'The Prophecies of St Paul', in *Biblical and Theological Studies* (Philadelphia: Presbyterian & Reformed, 1952), pp. 463–502.

Index of Biblical References

Genesis

1:1–3	198
2:17	125
12	109
12:2	46
12:3	47
12:6	46
13:14–17	46
13:16	46
14	109
14:18–20	108
15:1–21	48
15:6	48, 185
15:18	42, 43
15:18–21	46
17:1	48
17:4–6	46
17:7–8	42, 43
17:8	46
17:9–14	48
18:1f.	40
22:1f.	48, 185
22:9–15	48
22:15–18	46
22:18	47

Exodus

19:6	121
20:2	183
20:5–6	43
23:31	42
24:8–11	40
28:17–21	106
28:29	106
28:30	106
29	106
30:31–33	106
32:1–6	109
32:13–14	42
39:8–21	249

Leviticus

1 – 7	249

1:4	133
4:20	133
4:26	133
4:31	133
5:1f.	47
6:7	133
8	106
10:1–7	109
10:9–11	106
16	107
16:20–22	139
16:26–28	142
18:8	106
21:16–23	106

Numbers

3:10	106
6:22–27	106
6:24–27	156

Deuteronomy

5:2–3	43

Index of Names

Index of Subjects